Introduction to
POLICE STUDIES

Introduction to
POLICE STUDIES

Mike Winacott
Georgian College

Simon Bradford
Georgian College

Phil DeBruyne
Ontario Police College (Retired)

NELSON EDUCATION

NELSON / **EDUCATION**

Introduction to Police Studies

by Mike Winacott, Simon Bradford, Phil DeBruyne

Vice President, Editorial Higher Education:
Anne Williams

Executive Editor:
Lenore Taylor-Atkins

Marketing Manager:
Terry Fedorkiw

Developmental Editors:
Caroline Winter/MyEditor Inc.

Photo Researcher:
Julie Pratt

Permissions Coordinator:
Julie Pratt

Content Production Manager:
Christine Gilbert

Production Service:
MPS Limited

Copy Editor:
Marcia Gallego

Proofreader:
MPS Limited

Indexer:
Edwin Durbin

Manufacturing Manager–Higher Education:
Joanne McNeil

Design Director:
Ken Phipps

Managing Designer:
Franca Amore

Interior Design:
Peter Papayanakis

Interior Image:
Police badge illustration (Policing in Practice box): shutswis/Shutterstock

Cover Design:
Peter Papayanakis

Cover Image:
Tetra Images/Alamy Images

Compositor:
MPS Limited

Printer:
RR Donnelley

Library and Archives Canada Cataloguing in Publication

Winacott, Mike, 1970-

    Introduction to police studies / Mike Winacott, Simon Bradford, Phil DeBruyne.

Includes bibliographical references and index.
ISBN 978-0-17-652753-2

    1. Police--Canada. 2. Law enforcement--Canada.
I. Bradford, Simon, 1957-
II. DeBruyne, Phil, 1954-
III. Title.

HV8157.W52 2012   363.20971
C2012-906512-9

ISBN-13: 978-0-17-652753-2
ISBN-10: 0-17-652753-2

The views and opinions in this book are those of the authors and do not necessarily reflect the views of Georgian College, the Ontario Police College, or the Ministry of Community Safety and Correctional Services.

This book is dedicated to my wife, Sheri, our wonderful children, Kaiden and Taylin for their unconditional support and patience throughout the process of writing this book. I would also like to thank the many people who have supported me throughout my policing career, for their words of wisdom and support that pointed me in the right direction at the beginning of my career.
Mike Winacott

I would like to dedicate my chapters of this book to my wife, Charlene, whose patience and understanding allowed me to write this book for days on end. I'd also like to thank the Ontario Provincial Police for enabling me to enjoy many opportunities and experiences, which I attempted to draw upon and convey throughout this book.
Simon Bradford

I dedicate this book to my wife, Susan Robillard, whose patience and guidance encouraged me to pursue higher education and believe in myself. To Rob Warman, former Law and Security Administration Coordinator at Georgian College; H. R. (Bud) Knight, former Criminal Investigation Coordinator, Ontario Police College; and the late Ronald K. James, Chief of Police, Ingersoll Police Service. They were my inspiration to teach. Constable Chuck Byham, York Regional Police, for his insightfulness into performance management and unsatisfactory work performance. To Dr. Carole Roy, Department Chair, Master of Adult Education program, St. Francis Xavier University, for her continued words of encouragement and support throughout my master's program.
Phil DeBruyne

About the Authors

MIKE WINACOTT

Mike began his policing career in 1998 as a police constable with the Elliot Lake Police Service. Mike was also the vice president of the Elliot Lake Police Association. Mike then went on to work with the Durham Regional Police Service, where he performed the duties of uniform patrol, coach officer, snowmobile operator and worked several years as a recruiting and diversity officer.

In 2006, Mike became a part-time faculty member at Georgian College, where he taught in the Police Foundations program and coordinated the work placements for students in the Bachelor of Human Services Police Studies degree. In 2008, Mike was offered a full-time faculty position at Georgian College in the School of Public Safety and Emergency Services teaching in the Bachelor of Human Services Police Studies degree program. Since that time Mike has been teaching and developing curriculum in various justice programs and has coordinated the Police Studies degree program, the Protection, Security, and Investigation Program, and the Community and Justice Services program.

Mike holds a Master of Arts degree from Griffith University in criminology and criminal justice and a Bachelor of Arts degree in law from Carleton University. He is also a graduate of Sault College with a certificate from the Enforcement Services Preparation program.

SIMON BRADFORD

In 1980, Simon began his policing career with the Toronto Police Service at 11 Division, followed by a posting to the Central Traffic Unit. In 1990, Simon was hired by the OPP and was initially posted at the Burlington Detachment; from there, he took advantage of many opportunities within the OPP, including a secondment to the Ontario Police College followed by positions at the Provincial Police Academy, the Business Planning Unit, Audit Services, OPP Central Region HQ, Office of the Deputy Commissioner—Field Operations, and finally G8/G20 as the lead manager for OPP logistics.

During his career, Simon graduated with a Bachelor of Arts in crime and deviance (University of Toronto), a diploma in adult education (St. Francis Xavier University), and a master's degree in education (Athabasca University). In addition to his police duties, Simon taught at Georgian College and Dalhousie University.

In 2010, Simon retired from the OPP and was offered a full-time faculty position in the School of Public Safety and Emergency Services at Georgian College teaching in the Police Foundations program and the Bachelor of Human Services—Police Studies degree program.

Phil DeBruyne

PHIL DEBRUYNE

Phil's policing career spans over 35 years from 1974 to his retirement in 2010. He started his policing career in 1974 in Tillsonburg, Ontario, and subsequently joined the Ingersoll Police Service in 1977. In 1983, he was seconded to the Ontario Police College. During his secondment, Phil became a full-time instructor. He has taught in both the Recruit Training program and the Criminal Investigation program. From 1997 to 2002, Phil was seconded to the Campbell Report Implementation Project, which was responsible for implementing the recommendations from the late Justice Archie Campbell's review of the Paul Bernardo investigation. Phil was the Major Case Management training coordinator and the Major Case Management manual coordinator. Phil finished the last year of his career with a secondment at the Centre of Forensic Sciences in Toronto.

He is a graduate of the Bachelor of Human Services—Police Studies degree program at Georgian College and the Master of Adult Education program at St. Francis Xavier University, Nova Scotia. Phil is a member of the part-time faculty of the School of Public Safety and Emergency Services at Georgian College and teaches in the Police Studies degree program.

Contents

Detailed Contents

Preface

This first edition of *Introduction to Police Studies* examines the practical aspects of policing. Police work is often portrayed in movies and TV shows as a glamorous and fascinating career with thrilling car chases, glorious shootouts, and endings where the "bad guy" is always caught. The reality is that police work is very demanding at times, and every crucial decision that police officers make is scrutinized and examined in depth, with officers being held accountable, sometimes with major consequences, for their actions. Canadian police services enjoy the support of the public they serve. This support is accompanied by a high degree of accountability—all police officers are accountable and must clearly articulate their actions, as seen during the G20 summit in Toronto in 2010.

A career in policing is primarily about one thing: working with people to ensure public safety through crime prevention and law enforcement. Police officers must be able to build relationships in the community by showing sensitivity to and concern for the needs of people from all races, cultures, and backgrounds. Police work is also demanding on a personal level, as officers are required to work shifts, including evenings, nights, and weekends, at all times of the year. This is not a job that will appeal to everyone.

For those who are truly interested in serving the needs of the community, police work is a rewarding career. The job challenges you each day in complex ways. Whether you are dealing with the security concerns of a store merchant, talking with a senior citizen, or interacting with a group of local kids, you will find that as a police officer you have a great deal of responsibility to the public. Fulfilling this responsibility will give you a sense of accomplishment and the confidence that you are making a contribution.

THE GOAL OF THIS BOOK

A major objective of this book is to provide the reader with a comprehensive understanding of policing in Canada and an appreciation of the importance of the developing role of the police in society today. *Introduction to Police Studies* is intended to be used as a main text for undergraduate students, both in community colleges and in degree-level studies.

We collaborated and wrote *Introduction to Police Studies* because we saw the need for such a book

and because of the specific program requirements in the Police Foundations Program in Ontario. The information is presented in a reader-friendly manner that includes case studies and exercises to assist readers in truly understanding policing both academically and practically. We have developed this book based on our years of policing experience, education, teaching of police courses, and research in the police field, along with information gained from attending conferences and meetings at local, provincial, national, and international levels.

ORGANIZATION

The book is logically organized into twelve chapters and four parts.

PART 1: Career Opportunities in Policing. This part of the text includes a review of the policing profession, a review of the hiring process, and a review of the role of the police in today's society. Part One includes the following chapters: Chapter 1: Police History and Organization; Chapter 2: Becoming a Police Officer; and Chapter 3: The Police Role and Police Discretion.

PART 2: Skills Required for Providing Police Service Excellence. This part of the text includes a review of communication skills required to be successful in the policing profession; customer service and police service excellence practices; and the culture, personality, and stress related to the policing profession. Part Two includes the following chapters: Chapter 4: Communication Skills; Chapter 5: Customer Service; and Chapter 6: Police Culture, Personality, and Stress.

PART 3: Legislation Affecting Policing Conduct. This part of the text includes a review of the policing professional standards, the police code of conduct, and the role of the public complaints system. Part Three includes the following chapters: Chapter 7: Professionalism and Ethics; Chapter 8: The Police Disciplinary Process and Code of Conduct; and Chapter 9: The Public Complaints System.

PART 4: Policing Governance and Oversight. This part of the text includes a review of the civilian authorities with administrative and oversight power over the actions of police officers. This part also reviews the policies and procedures affecting policing today. Part Four includes the following chapters: Chapter 10: Civilian Governance; Chapter 11: Policing Policies and Procedures; and Chapter 12: Civilian Oversight.

The major features of this book include the following. At the beginning of each chapter, Learning Outcomes assist the student in understanding the major points within each chapter. In addition, glossary terms are defined in the margins to assist the students in understanding the basic concepts in policing. Boxes with case studies are used throughout the book to demonstrate the practical aspects of police work and the material discussed in the chapters. Policing Online boxes have been added to give students a tool for further research on policing topics discussed in the chapters. Policing in Practice boxes throughout the book allow students to apply their knowledge and bring the context of the chapter "to life" for them. Decoding Police Terms boxes provide detailed explanations of some common terms used in policing. Finally, at the end of each chapter, the Summary reviews the material and the Learning Outcomes.

ANCILLARIES

About NETA ◯neTa

The **Nelson Education Teaching Advantage (NETA)** program delivers research-based instructor resources that promote student engagement and higher-order thinking to enable the success of Canadian students and educators.

Instructors today face many challenges. Resources are limited, time is scarce, and a new kind of student has emerged: one who is juggling school with work, has gaps in his or her basic knowledge, and is immersed in technology in a way that has led to a completely new style of learning. In response, Nelson Education has gathered a group of dedicated instructors to advise us on the creation of richer and more flexible ancillaries that respond to the needs of today's teaching environments.

The members of our editorial advisory board have experience across a variety of disciplines and are recognized for their commitment to teaching. In consultation with the editorial advisory board, Nelson Education has completely rethought the structure, approaches, and formats of our key textbook ancillaries. We've also increased our investment in editorial support for our ancillary authors. The result is the Nelson Education Teaching Advantage and its key components: *NETA Assessment* and *NETA Presentation*. Each component includes one or more ancillaries prepared according to our best practices, and a document explaining the theory behind the practices.

NETA Assessment relates to testing materials: not only Nelson's Test Banks and Computerized Test Banks but also in-text self-tests, Study Guides and web quizzes, and homework programs like CNOW. Under *NETA Assessment*, Nelson's authors create multiple-choice questions that reflect research-based best practices for constructing effective questions and testing not only recall but also higher-order thinking. Our guidelines were developed by David DiBattista, a 3M National Teaching Fellow whose recent research as a professor of psychology at Brock University has focused on multiple-choice testing. All Test Bank authors receive training at workshops conducted by Prof. DiBattista, as do the copyeditors assigned to each Test Bank. A copy of *Multiple Choice Tests: Getting Beyond Remembering,* Prof. DiBattista's guide to writing effective tests, is included with every Nelson Test Bank/Computerized Test Bank package.

NETA Presentation has been developed to help instructors make the best use of PowerPoint® in their classrooms. With a clean and uncluttered design developed by Maureen Stone of StoneSoup Consulting, *NETA Presentation* features slides with improved readability, more multi-media and graphic materials, activities to use in class, and tips for instructors on the Notes page. A copy of *NETA Guidelines for Classroom Presentations* by Maureen Stone is included with each set of PowerPoint slides.

Instructor Resources

Instructor Resource Website: Key instructor ancillaries are provided on the *Instructor Resource Website* (www.introtopolicestudies.nelson.com).

- **NETA Assessment:** The Test Bank was written by Cindy Gervais, Sir Sandford Fleming College. It includes over approximately 360 multiple-choice questions written according to NETA guidelines for effective construction and development of higher-order questions. Also included are approximately 100 short-answer questions. Test Bank files are provided in Word format for easy editing and in PDF format for convenient printing whatever your system.

- **NETA Presentation:** Microsoft® PowerPoint® lecture slides for every chapter have been created by Catharine Schiller, University of Northern British Columbia. There is an average of 10 to 15 slides per chapter, many featuring key figures, tables, and photographs from the text. NETA principles of clear design and engaging content have been incorporated throughout.

ACKNOWLEDGMENTS

We would like to acknowledge and thank the many people who have contributed information and ideas that have shaped this book. We would also like to acknowledge the guidance and direction the editors at Nelson Education provided throughout this project, including acquisitions editor Lenore Taylor-Atkins; developmental editors Katherine Goodes and Caroline Winter; content production manager Christine Gilbert; permissions manager Debbie Yea; permissions and photo researcher Julie Pratt; and copy editor Marcia Gallego. Thanks also to Naman Mahisauria, senior project manager at MPS Limited. We would especially like to acknowledge our families for their continued support and patience throughout the research and development of this book.

Many thanks to Mr. Paul Ceyssens, author of *Legal Aspects in Policing*, Salt Spring Island, B.C.; retired Supt. Joe Wolfe, Police Services Act Adjudicator, Toronto Police Service; Inspector Tessa Youngson-Larochelle, Ottawa Police Service; and Mr. Greg Smith, Associate Director, Institute for Law Enforcement Administration, Plano, Texas.

Mike Winacott
Simon Bradford
Phil DeBruyne

PART 1

Career Opportunities in Policing

Police History and Organization

LEARNING OUTCOMES

After reading this chapter, you will be able to:

LO1 Explain the English roots of policing in Canada.

LO2 Describe Sir Robert Peel's nine principles of policing.

LO3 Define the duties of a police officer.

LO4 Summarize the history of Canadian police forces, including federal, provincial, regional, municipal, and First Nations policing.

LO5 Describe the command structures of police services.

> *Police, at all times, should maintain a relationship with the public that gives reality to the historic tradition that the police are the public and the public are the police; the police being only members of the public who are paid to give full-time attention to duties which are incumbent on every citizen in the interests of community welfare and existence.* *

—*Sir Robert Peel*

LO¹ THE ENGLISH ROOTS OF CANADIAN POLICING

Policing in Canada has evolved considerably over the years, especially since advances in technology have made modern-day policing a complex occupation. In order to understand contemporary policing, it is useful to reflect on the history of policing and the trends that have led us to where we are today. Canadian policing is greatly influenced by the traditions of the English and French societies from which many early Canadians first emigrated.

Policing in England emerged with the advent of the **Industrial Revolution**. The country evolved from a society based on agriculture and small villages to one based on industry and urban areas. Along with this transition came changes in society, which required changes in approaches to social order. Previously, law and order in small villages had been the responsibility of community members, with males between the ages of fifteen and sixty being required to take turns volunteering to be in charge of local village security (Sutton, 2005).

As people migrated from rural villages to cities in the early 1800s, the need for a full-time, centralized, state-operated police force became apparent. In 1829, the *Metropolitan Police Act* was enacted, allowing Sir Robert Peel to form the first metropolitan police force in London, England (see Figure 1.1). Sir Robert Peel's police force consisted of a thousand unarmed police officers, often referred to as **"bobbies"** or "peelers" (see Figure 1.2). At first the public was resistant to the notion of a centralized police force, as previous law enforcement personnel had become corrupt and failed to serve the public's best interests. In response to this public perception, Sir Robert Peel drafted nine principles of policing, which were as much a marketing strategy as they were a code of conduct (see Box 1.1).

These principles are as relevant today as they were in 1829 when Peel created them. The underlying messages are related to preventing crime, keeping the peace and working "with the community" to solve crimes and maintain order. If you compare the duties of a police officer today, like those outlined in Box 1.2, with Sir Robert Peel's nine principles, you will see many similarities.

Peel's ninth principle still affects the way police services are measured today—if calls for service

Industrial Revolution: A period of significant change from 1750 to the late 1800s, when the economy of England and Europe transitioned from agriculture to urban factories. Changes took place in agriculture, manufacturing, mining, transportation, and technology and had a major impact on society.

Bobbie: A term used to describe a British police officer. It is based on the founder of British policing, Sir Robert Peel, whose officers were referred to as "Peel's bobbies."

FIGURE 1.1
Sir Robert Peel, the father of policing.

*Sir Robert Peel

BOX 1.1

LO² SIR ROBERT PEEL'S NINE PRINCIPLES OF POLICING

1. The basic mission for which the police exist is to prevent crime and disorder.

2. The ability of the police to perform their duties is dependent upon public approval of police actions.

3. Police must secure the willing co-operation of the public in voluntary observance of the law to be able to secure and maintain the respect of the public.

4. The degree of co-operation of the public that can be secured diminishes proportionately to the necessity of the use of physical force.

5. Police seek and preserve public favour not by catering to public opinion but by constantly demonstrating absolute impartial service to the law.

6. Police use physical force to the extent necessary to secure observance of the law or to restore order

only when the exercise of persuasion, advice and warning is found to be insufficient.

7. Police, at all times, should maintain a relationship with the public that gives reality to the historic tradition that the police are the public and the public are the police; the police being only members of the public who are paid to give full-time attention to duties which are incumbent on every citizen in the interests of community welfare and existence.

8. Police should always direct their action strictly towards their functions and never appear to usurp the powers of the judiciary.

9. The test of police efficiency is the absence of crime and disorder, not the visible evidence of police action in dealing with it.

Source: Reprinted from New Westminster Police Service. (2011). Sir Robert Peel's nine principles. Retrieved from http://www.nwpolice.org/peel.html

and crime rates decrease, this is a measure of police efficiency. A reduction in calls for service and crime rates may be caused by other issues, such as weather, good economic times, or the public's lack of confidence in the police. That is why these data are measured and compared with three- to five-year averages rather than just the previous year.

LO⁴ THE HISTORY OF CANADIAN POLICE FORCES

Canada has a variety of police and enforcement agencies serving local, national, and international communities.

BOX 1.2

LO³ DUTIES OF A POLICE OFFICER

The *Police Services Act* describes key areas of responsibility for police constables:

- preserving the peace;

- preventing crimes and providing assistance to others in the prevention of crime;

- assisting victims of crime;

- apprehending and charging offenders; and

- executing warrants.

In addition, police officers are responsible for:

- referring individuals to community services and agencies;

- educating the public.

Source: Ministry of Community Safety and Correctional Services, "Police Services: Constable Selection System: Constable Selection Information Package" (2008) http://www.mcscs .jus.gov.on.ca/english/police_serv/const_select_sys/const_select_info/info_package/info_package.html. © Queen's Printer for Ontario, 2008. Reproduced with permission.

FIGURE 1.2

Police officers have long been tasked with walking the beat. This is one of the best ways for police officers to connect with the public.

FEDERAL POLICING

The Royal Canadian Mounted Police (RCMP) serves Canada by enforcing federal, provincial, and municipal communities, depending on the agreements in place in each community. The Dominion Police, created in 1868, were one of the first police forces.

This police service consisted of a grand total of two officers. Over the next few years the number of officers grew, with their focus being on Ontario and Quebec. "The Dominion Police established a national fingerprint bureau and a branch that maintained the records of paroled and reporting prisoners" (Whitelaw & Parent, 2010, p. 10).

In the late 1800s, Sir John A. Macdonald, Canada's first prime minister, formed the North-West Mounted Police (NWMP) to help prevent conflicts with Native tribes during settlement of the Northwest Territory. The NWMP's headquarters were in Regina. In 1920, Parliament voted to establish a national force by merging the 150-member Dominion Police with the NWMP (Whitelaw & Parent, 2010). The new force was renamed the Royal Canadian Mounted Police, and the headquarters were moved to Ottawa (RCMP, 2007a).

The current RCMP is a modern police service providing cutting-edge services across the country and internationally. The RCMP is a well-respected police service and, with its distinctive red uniform, is world renowned as a symbol of Canada (see Figure 1.3).

The RCMP is **a paramilitary organization**, meaning that its members are ranked hierarchically (see Figure 1.4). Table 1.1 provides the number of

> **Paramilitary organization:** An organization that structures its personnel, policies, and procedures along the lines of a military organization. A chain of command is followed as information is passed from the top to the bottom of the organization. Every member must report to a superior rank.

BOX 1.3

RCMP QUICK FACTS

- Prime Minister Sir John A. Macdonald used the Royal Irish Constabulary as the model for the force.
- In 1903, the first mounted police post north of the Arctic Circle was established at Fort McPherson.
- In 1904, King Edward VII granted the Force the prefix "Royal" in recognition of its many services to Canada and the Empire.
- The image of the scarlet-coated Mountie has been used to promote Canada abroad since the 1800s.
- The NWMP provided support for the successful construction of the Canada Pacific Railway and subsequent settlement of western Canada.
- In the 1990s, the RCMP's role in peacekeeping expanded significantly in countries such as Haiti, Namibia, Kosovo and East Timor.

Source: Reprinted from Royal Canadian Mounted Police. (2007, July 9). Quick facts. The RCMP's history. Retrieved from http://www.rcmp-grc.gc.ca/hist/index-eng.htm.
© 2007 HER MAJESTY THE QUEEN IN RIGHT OF CANADA as represented by the Royal Canadian Mounted Police (RCMP). Reproduced with the permission of the RCMP.

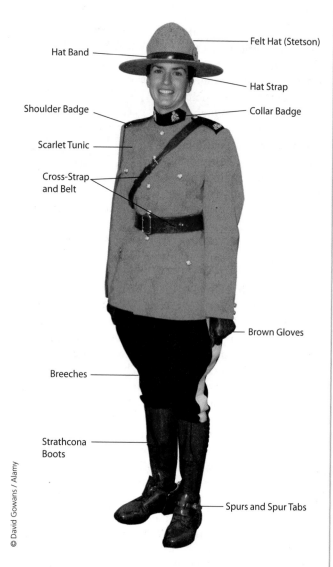

Felt Hat (Stetson)

Hat Band

Hat Strap

Shoulder Badge

Collar Badge

Scarlet Tunic

Cross-Strap and Belt

Brown Gloves

Breeches

Strathcona Boots

Spurs and Spur Tabs

© David Gowans / Alamy

FIGURE 1.3

Police officers' uniforms are unique to each police service. Among police uniforms, the RCMP dress uniform of red serge, breeches, and Stetson stands out.

TABLE 1.1
RCMP Actual Strength,* 2011

Commissioner	1
Deputy Commissioner	9
Assistant Commissioner	25
Chief Superintendent	51
Superintendent	186
Inspector	440
Corps Sergeant Major	1
Sergeants Major	3
Staff Sergeants Major	16
Staff Sergeants	942
Sergeants	2,140
Corporals	3,672
Constables	11,717
Special Constables	78
Civilian Members	3,760
Public Servants	6,194
Total	**29,235**

* "Authorized strength" refers to the number of positions authorized by the police budget, whereas "actual strength" refers to the number of positions occupied in a given year (Statistics Canada, 2010).

Source: Royal Canadian Mounted Police. (2012). Organizational structure. Retrieved from http://www.rcmp-grc.gc.ca/about-ausujet/organi-eng.htm. © 2012 HER MAJESTY THE QUEEN IN RIGHT OF CANADA as represented by the Royal Canadian Mounted Police (RCMP). Reproduced with the permission of the RCMP.

© Universal Images Group / DeAgostini/Alamy

FIGURE 1.4

Policing is paramilitary in nature; this is best observed during ceremonial events such as memorials, funerals, and recruit graduations.

Regular members: RCMP officers responsible for keeping the peace, preventing crime, assisting victims, upholding the law, and working with the communities they serve.

members as of 2011, ordered by rank. As you can see from this list, there are over 29,000 full-time positions in the RCMP, which are posted not only across Canada but around the world. This is an impressive organization with a vast amount of responsibilities and opportunities for each of its three categories of employees: **regular members** (police officers), **civilian members**, and **public service employees** (RCMP, 2012d).

PROVINCIAL POLICING

In all provinces and territories other than Ontario and Quebec, the RCMP provides provincial policing duties. Newfoundland contracts with the RCMP, and the Royal Newfoundland Constabulary provides partial provincial policing. Ontario has the Ontario Provincial Police (OPP), and Quebec has the Sûreté du Québec (SQ).

Provincial policing has affected the structure of the RCMP over the years, "From 1932–38, the size of the RCMP nearly doubled, to 2,350 employees, as it took over provincial policing in Alberta, Manitoba, New Brunswick, Nova Scotia and Prince Edward Island. . . . In 1950, it assumed responsibility for provincial policing in Newfoundland and absorbed the British Columbia provincial police"* (RCMP, 2007a, para. 10).

Today, policing in each province requires the delivery of many complex services. The RCMP, the OPP, and the SQ provide provincial policing services. These services include, but are not limited to, the functions described in Table 1.2. One important function, emergency response, is shown in Figure 1.5.

The OPP has a paramilitary organizational structure, which is typical for a police service, with reporting relationships going up a hierarchy (see Table 1.3). The OPP is a **deployed organization**, providing provincial and municipal services over a large area, and the number of personnel reflects these responsibilities. Box 1.4 details some key events in OPP history.

After reviewing the services in Table 1.2, think

Civilian members: RCMP members who work in non-policing roles such as human resources, forensics, computer programming, and project management, providing support to frontline policing operations.

Public service employees: RCMP members who work in non-policing roles such as administration, communications, and information technology, providing business management support.

Deployed organization: An organization that spans a vast geographical area, with members being posted in areas far from the general headquarters. Examples include the RCMP and the OPP.

TABLE 1.2
OPP Programs and Services

24-Hour Proactive and Reactive Policing	Crisis Negotiations	Ontario Sex Offender Registry
Aboriginal Policing	Differential Response	Organized Crime Investigation
Auxiliary Policing	Drug Enforcement	Protective Services
Aviation	E-Crime (Electronic crime)	RIDE (Reduce Impaired Driving Everywhere)
Behavioural Sciences and Analysis	Emergency Planning and Response	Search and Rescue
Canine	Forensic Identification	Surveillance—Electronic and Physical
Chemical, Biological, Radiological, Nuclear and Explosive Response	Hate Crimes/Extremism Investigation	Tactics and Rescue
Child Exploitation Investigation	Illegal Gaming Investigation	Technical Traffic Collision Investigation
Communications	Incident Command	Traffic Safety
Community Policing	Intelligence	Training
Complaint Investigation	Major Case Management	Underwater Search and Recovery
Court Case Management	Marine/Motorized Snow Vehicle/All-terrain Vehicle	Urban Search and Rescue
Crime Prevention	Media Relations	ViCLAS (Violent Crime Linkage Analysis System)
Crime Stoppers	Offender Transportation	Victim Assistance

Source: Reprinted from Ontario Provincial Police. (2011). *2010 Annual Report*, p. 5. Retrieved from http://www.opp.ca/ecms/files/250258838.6.pdf. © Queen's Printer for Ontario, 2011. Reproduced with permission.

*Source: http://www.rcmp-grc.gc.ca/hist/index-eng.htm. © 2007 HER MAJESTY THE QUEEN IN RIGHT OF CANADA as represented by the Royal Canadian Mounted Police (RCMP). Reproduced with the permission of the RCMP.

FIGURE 1.5

OPP emergency response equipment is needed to perform major event operations, such as policing of the G8 and G20 summits; search and rescue operations; and response to disaster situations, such as plane crashes, multi-vehicle collisions on major highways, and homicides.

> **Regional policing:** The amalgamation of small-town Ontario police services in the 1970s to form policing services within each region. Ontario has regional policing in York Region, Niagara Region, Durham Region, Halton Region, Peel Region, and Waterloo Region.

about which ones you would be interested in and consider the notion of being able to work in various specialty areas while working for the same employer—the opportunities are endless! As shown in Figure 1.6, even the way you conduct your daily patrols can vary—from foot to car, bicycle, horse, or motorcycle. There are not many other professions that can offer you so many opportunities over the span of your career.

REGIONAL POLICING

In Ontario, several areas of the province opted to create regional levels of government; these include York Region, Niagara Region, Durham Region, Halton Region, Peel Region, and Waterloo Region (Association of Municipalities Ontario, 2011). Each region is made up of several cities and towns. At one time each city and town had its own police service; however, **regional policing** evolved along with regional governments. Each region in Ontario now has a regional police service, which is made up of former town and city police services. When the regional police services were first formed, a major task was to break down

BOX 1.4

OPP HISTORY HIGHLIGHTS

- OPP motorcycles were introduced in 1930 and the first patrol car in 1944. Today the fleet consists of 2,290 vehicles, 114 marine vessels, 286 snow and all-terrain vehicles, 2 helicopters and aircraft.

- World War II gave rise to the "Veterans Guard," a body of volunteers (primarily World War I veterans), who under the supervision of regular police members, protected vulnerable hydro-electric plants and the Welland ship canal. This was the forerunner of today's OPP Auxiliary, which boasts 830 volunteers and is the largest police auxiliary unit in Canada.

- Women joined the uniform ranks in 1974 as constables and their numbers now exceed the national average for women in policing across the country.

- In 1985, the OPP uniform was made more distinctive with the introduction of a blue trouser stripe to match a blue peak cap band.

- In 1995, General Headquarters moved into its new facility in Orillia and for the first time in the history of the organization, all Bureaus were in one building.

- Today's emphasis is on our values: accountability; respectful relationships; fairness, courage and caring; continuous learning and diversity.

Source: Reprinted from Ontario Provincial Police. (2009). A brief history. Retrieved from http://www.opp.ca/ecms/index.php?id=129. © Queen's Printer for Ontario, 2009. Reproduced with permission.

TABLE 1.3
OPP Authorized Strength, 2010

OPP Uniform	
Commissioner	1
Deputy Commissioner	3
Chief Superintendent	13
Superintendent	36
Inspector	142
Sergeants Major	6
Staff Sergeant	217
Sergeant	999
Constable	4735
Uniform Total	**6152**
Civilian	
Provincial Commander	1
Classified Civilians	1861
Total Civilian	**1862**
OPP-Administered First Nations	
Civilian	55
Uniform	68
Total	123
2010 Total OPP	**8137**

Source: Ontario Provincial Police. (2011). *2010 Annual Report*, p. 72. Retrieved from http://www.opp.ca/ecms/files/250258838.6.pdf.
© Queen's Printer for Ontario, 2011. Reproduced with permission.

barriers and build relationships. Regional police members were aligned by their former town police forces, causing conflict in these organizations for many years. "Attrition has reduced the parochialism that at first caused members

FIGURE 1.6
Uniform officers patrol their areas using different modes of transportation. This OPP sergeant is riding a Harley Davidson motorcycle while performing her duties.

of the old municipal forces to withhold loyalty to the larger amalgamated Force. Over the years, many of the problems mentioned have been eliminated or at least diminished" (Colter, 1993, p. 203).

Table 1.4 details the staffing strength of the Niagara Regional Police Service in 2010. This organization has over 1000 employees, both uniform and civilian. When compared to provincial and federal police strengths, the number of positions may appear to be low; however, the number of officers is set as a ratio to the population of each area. This is done to reflect the cost of providing policing to each community. "International comparisons show how Canada's police strength compares to other countries. In 2010, Canada's police strength (203 per 100,000 population) was 8% lower than Australia (222), 11% lower than England and Wales (229), and 17% lower than the United States (244)" (Statistics Canada, 2010, p. 5).

> **Municipal policing:**
> Policing organizations that report directly to a municipal police services board (PSB), which reports to a municipal council. These types of police services focus on providing policing to one municipality.

MUNICIPAL POLICING

Municipal policing should be the simplest example of policing: each city has its own police service, run by the municipal government. However, it's not that straightforward. In fact, municipal policing in Canada can be seen as one of the most complex forms of policing, due to the many options that municipalities can select for their police service.

Newfoundland and Labrador, Yukon, the Northwest Territories, and Nunavut are the only areas in Canada without municipal police services. In Newfoundland and Labrador, the Royal Newfoundland Constabulary, provides policing to the following municipalities: St. John's, Corner Brook, Labrador City, and Churchill Falls. Newfoundland and Labrador contracts the RCMP to provide policing to the remaining municipalities and the rural areas (Statistics Canada, 2010).

The Toronto Police Service is an example of the least complicated structure of municipal policing. The City of Toronto has a police service, a municipal council, and a police services board. The chief of police reports to the police services board, and the citizens of Toronto pay for the police services out of the municipal budget—it is a straightforward relationship between employer and employee. There are many examples of this structure throughout Canada.

The next option for municipalities is contract policing. In this type of structure, the RCMP or OPP (depending on the province) provides policing

TABLE 1.4
Niagara Regional Police 2012 Authorized Staffing Levels

Sworn		Civilian	
Rank	**Strength**	**SOA Members (Senior Officers)**	**No. of Personnel (Actual and Percent)**
Chief of Police	1	Director	2 (0.6%)
Deputy Chief of Police	1	Manager	9 (2.8%)
Superintendent	5	Executive Assistant	6 (1.9%)
Inspector	13	NRPA Members	
Staff Sergeant	27	Civilian	302 (94.7%)
Sergeant	109		
Constable	548		
Total Uniform	704	Total Civilian	319
Total Authorized Strength: 1023			

Source: Niagara Regional Police. (2012). Authorized Staffing Levels. Reproduced with permission from the Niagara Regional Police Service, Corporate Communications and Community Engagement.

Rank structure: An organizational hierarchy designed to provide a clear chain of command related to communication and discipline.

services to municipalities based on a negotiated contract between the federal or provincial government and the municipality—the police agency is the service provider.* These contracts require the local detachment commanders to report to a police services board made up of municipal and provincially appointed members. Often the mayor of a town or city sits on the board.

The last option for municipalities is a non-contract situation, where the RCMP or the OPP provides the service to a municipality and at the end of the fiscal year the municipality is billed for the services rendered. This situation often meets the needs of many small communities. Municipalities also have the option of being partners with neighbouring municipalities; this gives them a shared resource capable of providing policing services to each municipality. "The number of municipalities contracting services from the OPP continues to increase and now stands at 141; while a further 172 municipalities receive OPP non-contract policing services (total 313)" (OPP, 2009b, para. 1).

FIRST NATIONS POLICING

Policing agreements have been put in place to serve First Nations communities across Canada. "The First Nations Policing Policy (FNPP) announced in June 1991 by the federal government, was introduced in order to provide First Nations across Canada (with the exception of Northwest Territories and Nunavut) with access to police services that are professional, effective, culturally appropriate, and accountable to the communities they serve" (Statistics Canada, 2010, p. 9).

First Nations policing has been implemented across Canada through tripartite agreements between the federal government, provincial or territorial governments, and First Nations. "The agreements are cost-shared 52% by the Government of Canada and 48% by the province involved" (Statistics Canada, 2010, p. 9). First Nations communities face many challenges requiring unique policing approaches. In Ontario, the remote locations of these communities sometimes necessitate support from the OPP in the form of personnel and equipment; however, there is a conscious effort to have First Nations people provide the required policing services to First Nations communities.

LO5 COMMAND STRUCTURES FOR POLICE SERVICES IN CANADA

Police services are considered paramilitary in organizational design, as is demonstrated by the **rank structure** of

*Source: OPP Home — What We Do — Municipal Policing. Retrieved from http://www.opp.ca/ecms/index.php?id=13. © Queen's Printer for Ontario, 2009. Reproduced with permission.

TABLE 1.5

Canadian Rank Structures

Municipal	RCMP/OPP
Chief of Police	Commissioner
Deputy Chief	Deputy Commissioner
	Assistant Commissioner (RCMP)
Staff Superintendent	Chief Superintendent
Superintendent	Superintendent
Staff Inspector	
Inspector	Inspector
	Sergeant Major
Staff Sergeant	Staff Sergeant
Sergeant	Sergeant
	Corporal (RCMP)
Constable	Constable
Cadet	Cadet
(Detective ranks are prefaced by the word *Detective*)	

Chain of command: A structure whereby instructions and orders are driven down from the top of an organization through each position with authority. Information is provided from a superior to a subordinate.

Coach officer: A person who mentors and supervises a new recruit during the probationary period. This person provides direction and evaluates the performance of the recruit.

every police service. Table 1.5 provides the rank structure that is reflective of most police services. Each rank has to follow a **chain of command** up to and including the chief of police and the commissioner. The head of each policing organization reports to a governing body and is accountable for the actions of each member of the organization.

As a newly hired constable, you will report to a corporal or a sergeant. Your first encounter with this rank will take place during basic training, when you will be required to successfully complete every task assigned to you by the corporal or sergeant. Once you finish your initial training, you will be assigned to a **coach officer**. This is the person you must report to and take instruction from. Upon completing your probationary period, you will report directly to your shift supervisor. As previously mentioned, you have entered a profession with a chain of command and this chain has to be respected at all times.

The chain of command for an organization establishes the responsible person next in line with whom you can address issues or concerns. You must deal with your immediate supervisor to resolve items of concern—you cannot go up to the next level of command without the permission of your supervisor. This chain of command does not work in reverse—a deputy chief can call you up at any time and discuss any concerns he or she has with you or your work! In addition to this direction, whenever you address someone who is of a higher rank you should refer to that individual by his or her rank. This shows respect for the position the person has in the organization and it shows that you recognize the hierarchy of the paramilitary organization.

MODERN-DAY POLICING AND FUTURE TRENDS

Now is a great time to enter the policing profession, as the number of police officers is currently at its highest point since 1981. As illustrated in Figure 1.7, police hiring has increased significantly over the last six years. Often as economies progress or regress, so do the hiring practices of police services. But because there is a constant need for police officers to be hired due to attrition, there will always be vacancies to fill. In difficult economic times, police services implement hiring freezes, where they stop hiring for a short period of time; however, every policing hiring freeze in Canada has been followed by a hiring frenzy. "There were 69,299 active police officers in Canada on May 15, 2010, an increase of almost 2,000 officers from 2009. The national-level increase was primarily driven by growth in Ontario (803 additional officers, or +2% in the rate) and Alberta (403 additional officers, or +5% in the rate)" (Statistics Canada, 2010, p. 5).

Today's candidates interested in a policing career should be aware that the competition is intense but the rewarding career is worth the effort, and there is no better time to work toward a policing career. In Chapter 2 you will learn what is required to be successful in achieving your goal of becoming a police officer.

CHANGES IN POLICING

A research project was conducted in British Columbia in 2004 to examine the changes in policing and the capacity of police services to respond to crime over the past 30 years. The report concludes "that the demand for police services in British Columbia has increased at a substantially disproportionate rate to the increases

FIGURE 1.7
Police Resources in Canada, 1964–2010

Policing strength grows as the population grows; this fact, combined with the retirement of the baby boomers, makes policing an occupation with many opportunities for new employees.

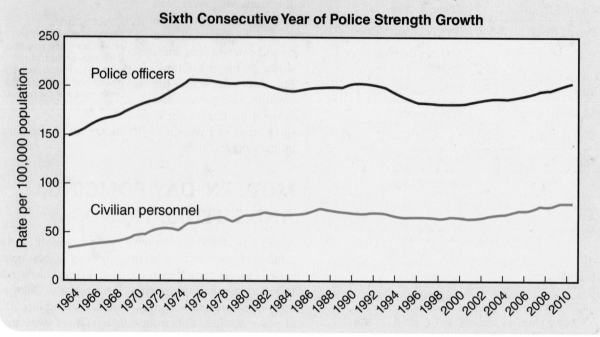

Sixth Consecutive Year of Police Strength Growth

Source: Statistics Canada. (2010). *Police Resources in Canada*. Catalogue no. 85-225-X. Ottawa, ON: Minister of Industry, p. 6. Retrieved from http://publications .gc.ca/collection_2010/statcan/85-225-X/85-225-x2010000-eng.pdf. Reproduced and distributed on an "as is" basis with the permission of Statistics Canada.

in population and that the amount of police time and resources spent responding, processing, and clearing criminal events has increased disproportionately to police budgets and staffing" (Malm et al., 2005, p. 2). There is a consensus among police managers that while this study focused on British Columbia, its findings are reflective of the situation right across Canada.

The report concluded that there has been a significant increase in reported crimes and that the mandatory procedures and administrative duties associated with investigating these crimes have increased dramatically as well. There is also a demand on police personnel to obtain more technical education and training to be effective in their jobs. "Evolving case law, statutory law, and individual criminal justice agencies' policies . . . have added enormous procedural complexity to police work" (Malm et al., 2005, p. 2). An investigation that took perhaps one hour in 1980 can now take up to twelve hours. As a result of procedural changes, all notes and paperwork must be duplicated and disclosed to defence lawyers, and in major cases this takes a considerable amount of time and money. Major fraud cases can fill a room with

bankers' boxes, the contents of which have to be scanned or photocopied and sent to the defence, along with all officers' notes, warrants, photos, et cetera. These are tasks that were not required of police officers in the past.

Along with these changes, many exciting new trends are influencing policing in Canada. Technology is assisting in investigations as well as in day-to-day policing duties. Everything is computerized, digitized, and captured in ways that would have been seen as science fiction not so long ago. From the beginning to end of your career, you will be impressed with the changes that will occur to the policing profession. Flash forward 30 years to when you retire and you will be amazed!

INTERNATIONAL POLICING

Over the last 10 to 15 years, policing in Canada has evolved to include international policing opportunities. In 2010, Canadian police officers were deployed to Afghanistan, Kosovo, Haiti, and the Sudan (see Figure 1.8). "Civilian police missions require officers to work closely with domestic and international partners to rebuild and

Source: Photo: Canadian Forces Combat Camera, IS2010-4047-17. URL: http://www.combatcamera.forces.gc.ca/netpub/server.np?find&catalog=photos&template=detail_eng.np&field=itemid&op=matches&value=23220&site=combatcamera, Department of National Defence, 2010. Reproduced with the permission of the Minister of Public Works and Government Services Canada, 2012.

FIGURE 1.8

Canadian police officers have many opportunities to serve around the world. These Toronto police officers are serving in Afghanistan for the Canadian civilian police (CIVPOL). Most tours are nine to twelve months long.

strengthen local police services in countries that, most often as a result of conflict or upheaval, do not have the capacity to maintain law and order"* (OPP, 2010, p. 29). Canadian police officers perform many duties to assist these local police services in strengthening their knowledge, skills, and abilities to police their own countries.

POLICING MAJOR EVENTS

In 2010, Ontario hosted both the G8 and G20 Summits. These events required over two years of planning of security personnel and resources. Numerous government, military, international, national, provincial, and municipal partners were involved in these events, resulting in the largest policing operation to date in Canada. Many officers and civilians who attended echoed the sentiment that they were extremely glad to have been a part of Canadian policing history.

Providing security for major events is an important part of police services. Events such as the Vancouver Winter Olympics, the Summit of the Americas, the

© Queen's Printer for Ontario, 2011. Reproduced with permission.

FIGURE 1.9

Police officers in Canada are expected to perform crowd control duties. These police officers are wearing hard tactical gear, but some officers wear normal uniforms and perform regular duties until situations escalate. The goal is always to de-escalate situations so they remain peaceful.

Francophonie Summit, royal visits, and the Pan Am games have required police to provide security for those attending. These events cost millions of dollars for the policing and security costs alone, as large numbers of police officers are needed to police these events. "Providing security for Internationally Protected Persons, and ensuring public safety and security required the unprecedented mobilization of nearly 21,000 police and security personnel from across Canada"† (OPP, 2010, p. 22). Some officers refer to a syndrome called "event fatigue." They can develop and implement only so many operational and logistical plans before they become burned out. This is an issue for both those who attend the events and the officers who continue to work at the home detachments, which are understaffed to accommodate the events.

All major events involve the preparation of crowd control, and this is the part of the job that makes it to the news every time! Figure 1.9 illustrates a fully functioning crowd control team in action. This is a difficult and demanding job, but it's all part of the diversity of policing.

POLICING ONLINE

For further information on Canadian police services, review the following website:
http://www.canadianpoliceservices.com/

---

*Ontario Provincial Police *2010 Annual report*, p. 29. http://www.opp.ca/ecms/files/250258838.6.pdf. © Queen's Printer for Ontario, 2011. Reproduced with permission.
†Ontario Provincial Police *2010 Annual report*, p. 22. http://www.opp.ca/ecms/files/250258838.6.pdf. © Queen's Printer for Ontario, 2011. Reproduced with permission.

CHAPTER SUMMARY

In this chapter we have reviewed the history of policing in Canada, the English roots affecting policing in Canada, Sir Robert Peel's nine principles of policing, the duties of a police officer, and the history of Canadian police forces, including federal, provincial, regional, municipal, and First Nations. We reviewed the various command structures of police services and the trends affecting modern-day policing. You are embarking on what could be an exciting journey into the profession of policing, and this chapter was intended to give you insight into what lies ahead.

LO1 Explain the English roots of policing in Canada.

This chapter discussed the development of policing in England and the relationship to the Industrial Revolution, with the evolution from rural to urban industrial societies. Law and order evolved from a volunteer basis to a structured policing organization.

LO2 Describe Sir Robert Peel's nine principles of policing.

These principles are as relevant today as they were in 1829, when the author created them. The underlying messages are related to preventing crime, keeping the peace, and working *with* the community to solve crimes and maintain order.

LO3 Define the duties of a police officer.

In this chapter we reviewed the duties of a police officer as defined in the *Police Services Act* of Ontario. These duties are all-encompassing, with duties clearly defined and discussed at all levels.

LO4 Summarize the history of Canadian police forces, including federal, provincial, regional, municipal, and First Nations policing.

While the duties of Canadian police officers are similar, the responsibilities vary depending on the type of policing being carried out. Canadian police services have a rich history and are seen as some of the best police services in the world.

LO5 Describe the command structures of police services.

Command structures vary from organization to organization. Federal, provincial, municipal, and First Nations police services have a variety of rank structures; however, they are similar in approach as they are all paramilitary with a respected chain of command.

Becoming a Police Officer

LEARNING OUTCOMES

After reading this chapter, you will be able to:

LO¹ List and discuss the minimum requirements to become a police constable.

LO² Define essential competencies and development competencies.

LO³ Explain the police recruitment and selection process in Ontario.

LO⁴ Briefly describe commonalities in the police recruitment process across Canada.

FIGURE 2.1
What does it take to put on this uniform?

Policing in Canada has a long and rich history with deep roots, as outlined in Chapter 1, and since the inception of modern-day policing, society has relied on police officers for the public's safety and security. It is imperative that the police preserve the peace to sustain balance and justice in society and maintain social order. It takes a unique individual to fill such an essential role in society (see Figure 2.1).

LO1 SO YOU WANT TO BE A POLICE OFFICER

Why do people want to become police officers? Some people have noble intentions and want to give back to their community by making a difference and playing an integral part in society, while others see a career in policing as a stable position with a good salary and benefits.

Regardless of the reasons why people want to be police officers, they need to meet **minimum requirements** outlined in Ontario by the Ministry of Community Safety and Correctional Services (MCSCS). This chapter will elaborate on the

minimum requirements in policing: The fundamental requirements set forth by the government as the basic qualifications required to be a police officer.

medical requirements: The established vision, hearing, and health standards that a candidate must meet in order to be a police officer.

requirements for police officers in Ontario and for the Royal Canadian Mounted Police (RCMP). In addition, a brief outline of the minimum requirements and selection process to become a police constable in other provinces in Canada will be discussed for anyone who wishes to explore these career options.

BECOMING A POLICE OFFICER IN ONTARIO

MINIMUM REQUIREMENTS*

In Ontario, the Ministry of Community Safety and Correctional Services has developed and implemented the following minimum requirements for applicants for the position of police constable, as outlined in the *Police Services Act*.

No person shall be appointed as a police officer unless he or she
(a) is a Canadian citizen or a permanent resident of Canada;
(b) is at least eighteen years of age;
(c) is physically and mentally able to perform the duties of the position, having regard to his or her own safety and the safety of members of the public;
(d) is of good moral character and habits; and
(e) has successfully completed at least four years of secondary school education or its equivalent.
(*Police Services Act*, 1990, s. 43(1))

Additionally, the applicant must

- possess a valid Class G driver's licence with no more than six demerit points;
- possess a standard first aid certificate and CPR certificate (Basic Rescuer Level C);
- hold a current Ontario Association of Chiefs of Police (OACP) Certificate of Results;
- not have a criminal conviction for which a pardon has not been granted; and
- have vision and hearing within acceptable standards.

For further information on the particulars regarding vision, speech, and hearing standards, refer to Box 2.1, which provides the MCSCS **medical requirements** for candidates. Once the candidate has met the minimum requirements, he or she may apply to each individual police service within the province of Ontario.

*Source: "Constable Selection System: Constable Selection Information Package" Minimum Requirements and Competencies" (2008) http://www.mcscs.jus.gov.on.ca/english/police_serv/const_select_sys/const_select_info/info_what_it_takes.html. © Queen's Printer for Ontario, 2008. Reproduced with permission.

BOX 2.1

VISION AND HEARING REQUIREMENTS

Vision Requirements

- Uncorrected Visual Acuity—At least 20/40 (6/12) with both eyes open

- Corrected Visual Acuity—At least 20/20 (6/6) with both eyes open …

- Colour Vision—Pass Farnsworth D-15 without any colour corrective (e.g., X-Chrom, Chromagen) lenses …

- Corneal Refractive Surgery—Allowed; however, the candidate must meet additional requirements and must provide specific documentation on vision stability and night vision

Hearing Requirements

For each ear, pure-tone thresholds measured under audiometric earphones shall not exceed a four-frequency average (500, 1000, 2000, 3000 Hz) of 25 dB HL, thresholds at none of these single frequencies shall exceed 35 dB HL and thresholds at 4000 Hz shall not exceed 45 dB HL. …

    Only complete-in-canal (CIC) hearing aids may be used to meet the above standards. However, the applicant's unaided hearing loss must not exceed 40 dB in each ear at the following frequencies: 500, 1000, 2000 and 3000, and shall not exceed 55 dB at 4000 Hz."

Source: Reprinted from Ministry of Community Safety and Correctional Services "Constable Selection System: Self-Assess -- Medical Requirements for Candidates" (2011). Retrieved from http://www.mcscs.jus.gov.on.ca/english/police_serv/const_select_sys/Self-Assess-MedicalRequirementsforCandidates/Self_Assess.html. © Queen's Printer for Ontario, 2011. Reproduced with permission.

LO² COMPETENCIES

The role of a police constable has shifted from traditional enforcement and authoritative policing to community policing. In addition to the minimum requirements, candidates must possess certain competencies. A **competency** is defined as any skill, knowledge, ability, motive, behaviour, or attitude essential to successful performance on the job. Two sets of competencies have been identified by the Ministry of Community Safety and Correctional Services for the job of policing: **essential competencies** and **developmental competencies**.

Essential Competencies

A candidate for police officer should possess the following knowledge, skills, and abilities:

1. *analytical thinking*: ability to analyze situations and events in a logical way, and to organize the parts of a problem in a systematic way.*
2. *self-confidence*: belief abilities and judgment and a recognition of personal limitations and developmental needs.
3. *communication*: ability to demonstrate effective listening, verbal and written communication skills.

competency: Any skill, knowledge, ability, motive, behaviour, or attitude essential to successful performance on the job.

essential competencies: The knowledge, skills, and abilities a candidate must exhibit before becoming a police officer.

developmental competencies: Specific skills and abilities that can be acquired through training that are preferred by some police services.

POLICING ONLINE

To find out the medical requirements to be a police officer in Ontario, visit http://www.mcscs.jus.gov.on.ca/stellent/groups/public/@mcscs/@www/@com/documents/webasset/ec075034.pdf

*Source: "Constable Selection System: Constable Selection Information Package" Minimum Requirements and Competencies" (2008). Retrieved from http://www.mcscs.jus.gov.on.ca/english/police_serv/const_select_sys/const_select_info/info_what_it_takes.html. © Queen's Printer for Ontario, 2008. Reproduced with permission.

4. *flexibility/valuing diversity:* ability to adapt to a variety of situations, and to work effectively with a wide cross-section of the community representing diverse backgrounds, cultures, and socio-economic circumstances.

5. *self-control:* ability to keep emotions under control and to restrain negative actions when provoked or when working under stressful conditions.

6. *relationship building:* ability to develop and maintain a network of contacts, both inside and outside the police service.

7. *achievement orientation:* desire for continuous improvement in service or accomplishments.

8. *medical/physical skills and abilities:* job-related medical/physical skills and abilities, including vision, hearing, motor skills, cardiovascular endurance and upper-body strength (MCSCS, 2011a, "Essential Competencies").

Developmental Competencies

Other competencies that some police services choose to include in the hiring process and in training are as follows:

9. *information seeking:* ability to seek out information from various sources before making decisions.

10. *concern for safety:* ability to exercise caution in hazardous situations in order to ensure safety of self and others.

11. *assertiveness:* ability to use authority confidently and to set and enforce rules appropriately.

12. *initiative:* demonstrated ability to be self-motivated and self-directed in identifying and addressing important issues.

13. *co-operation:* ability to collaborate with others by seeking their input, encouraging their participation, and sharing information.

14. *negotiation/facilitation:* ability to influence or persuade others by anticipating and addressing their interests and perspectives.

15. *work organization:* ability to develop and maintain systems for organizing information and activities.

16. *community-service orientation:* proven commitment to helping or serving others.

17. *commitment to learning:* demonstrated pattern of activities which contribute to personal and professional growth.

18. *organizational awareness:* understanding the dynamics of organizations, including formal and informal cultures and decision making processes.

19. *developing others:* commitment to helping others improve their skills* (MCSCS, 2011a, "Developmental Competencies").

LO³ DO YOU HAVE WHAT IT TAKES TO BE A POLICE OFFICER?

The steps in the application (hiring) process are in place to provide candidates the opportunity to demonstrate that they meet and/or exceed the required and preferred developmental competencies to become a police officer—in other words, as noted in Figure 2.2, to prove that they "have what it takes." The purpose of the hiring process is to provide police services with a tool not only to test candidates for their suitability for police work but also to screen out inappropriate candidates. Each step in the hiring process will challenge the candidate and, in the process, filter out unqualified candidates. It should be noted that no hiring process is perfect, and from time to time inappropriate candidates may slip through the hiring process and become police officers, which may cause a great deal of problems later for the public and the police service that has hired them. These problematic issues are a dilemma for police services and will be discussed in further detail in Chapters 7, 8, and 9.

THE APPLICATION PROCESS

All candidates applying for the position of police constable go through various multi-stage selection processes, depending on the particular police service they are applying to. For the purposes of this chapter, a summary of the hiring process in Ontario will be discussed in detail. Applicants must successfully complete each stage of the hiring process before going on to the next stage. The hiring process is very competitive, and the successful

FIGURE 2.2
Do you have what it takes to fill this uniform?

---

* Source: "Constable Selection System: Constable Selection Information Package" Minimum Requirements and Competencies" (2008). Retrieved from http://www.mcscs.jus.gov.on.ca/english/police_serv/const_select_sys/const_select_info/info_what_it_takes.html. © Queen's Printer for Ontario, 2008. Reproduced with permission.

completion of these stages does not guarantee an offer of employment. The Ministry of Community Safety and Correctional Services, in partnership with the Ontario Association of Chiefs of Police (OACP), developed the Constable Selection System (CSS) to provide a standardized selection system for Ontario police services to use in selecting police recruits in Ontario. The CSS began in February 1998 when the ministry granted permission to the OACP to sub-license the system to individual police services and the private sector as a tool for assessing police constable applicants. "To date, there are 42 police services, including 10 of Ontario's largest police services using the CSS. Approximately 80 per cent of police applicants in the province are assessed using CSS criteria"* (MCSCS, 2011d, para. 3).

The CSS improves the selection process for both applicants and police services by preventing problems such as the following:

- multiple applications by candidates to police services across the province requiring costly and time-consuming multiple assessment of the same candidates;
- inconsistent assessment of candidates by police services with differing selection criteria;
- potential application of arbitrary selection practices not grounded on actual job requirements. (MCSCS, 2011d, para. 5)

The following is an example of the hiring stages candidates may go through when they meet the minimum requirements and apply to a police service in Ontario:

- Stage 1: Pre-interview assessment
- Stage 2: Application and résumé submission
- Stage 3: Pre-interview paperwork, including the Pre-Background Questionnaire (PBQ)
- Stage 4: Local focus interview
- Stage 5: Essential competencies interview
- Stage 6: Psychological testing
- Stage 7: Background investigation
- Stage 8: Final selection

Stage 1: Pre-interview Assessment

Before a candidate can even apply to be a police constable, he or she must first successfully complete the pre-interview assessment stages of the OACP's Constable Selection System (see Figure 2.3). The pre-interview assessment evaluates the candidate's suitability based on the essential competencies set forth by the Ministry of Community Safety and Correctional Services. This stage of the hiring process focuses on a candidate's analytical

FIGURE 2.3
The aptitude test is the first step in the selection process.

thinking, communication, physical skills, and abilities or competencies. After successful completion of the pre-screening tests, the candidate is issued a Certificate of Results (COR) by the OACP.

The pre-interview assessment stages include the following evaluations:

- Police Analytical Thinking Inventory (PATI);
- Written Communication Test (WCT);
- Physical Readiness Evaluation for Police (PREP);
- Vision and hearing tests; and
- Behavioural Personnel Assessment Device (BPAD).

Police Analytical Thinking Inventory (PATI) The PATI tests three key areas required of police constables when performing their jobs. These areas are

- Deductive Reasoning: The ability to draw appropriate conclusions from information provided. Police are often required to make sense of evidence by drawing conclusions about its relevance and meaning. This is tested through the Syllogism and Travel Time tasks.
- Inductive Reasoning: The ability to identify trends or common characteristics in a series of objects or information presented. Police officers often need to sift through seemingly disconnected facts and make judgments about how they fit together. This is tested through the Classification and Series Completion tasks.
- Quantitative Reasoning: The ability to apply basic arithmetic operations like addition, subtraction, multiplication, division, and fractions to solve problems. Police are required to apply arithmetic processes to determine rates of speed, stopping distance, etc. and this ability is tested on the word problems and arithmetic tasks. (MCSCS, 2011c, "Stage 1—Pre-Interview Assessment," para. 2)†

*Source: Ministry of Community Safety and Correctional Services, "Policing Services: Constable Selection System: Becoming a Police Constable" (2011). Retrieved from http://www.mcscs.jus.gov.on.ca/english/police_serv/const_select_sys/become_police_const/become_police_const.html. © Queen's Printer for Ontario, 2011. Reproduced with permission.

†Source: Ministry of Community Safety and Correctional Services, "Police Services: Constable Selection System: Stage 1 -- Pre-Interview Assessment" (2010). Retrieved from http://www.mcscs.jus.gov.on.ca/english/police_serv/const_select_sys/const_select_info/info_selection/info_selection/info_selection.html. © Queen's Printer for Ontario, 2010. Reproduced with permission.

POLICING IN PRACTICE

SAMPLE PATI TEST QUESTIONS

The following questions and Figures 2.4–2.6 are samples of similar questions in the six sections of the PATI test. Once you have completed the practice questions, check your answers in the end-of-chapter answer key (p. 37).

Section 1: Mapping

Below you will see a picture, an arrow pointing north, and some directions on how to use the picture. Read the directions and use this information to answer all of the Travel Time questions. Circle the correct letter to indicate your answer.

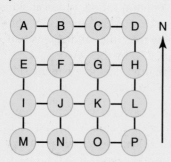

Figure 2.4 Mapping

Each line represents one block of a two-lane road. You may only travel on the roads. Unless you are specifically told you must travel by a particular method, you may travel by any method or combination of methods. Unless you are specifically told otherwise, the travel times are as follows: The time required to drive one block is 2 minutes. Riding a bike takes 3 minutes per block. Pursuits on foot take 5 minutes per block.

1. Using any method or combination of methods, what is the shortest amount of time it would take to get from B to C?
   a. 2 minutes
   b. 3 minutes
   c. 5 minutes
   d. 6 minutes

Section 2: Arithmetic

The next set of questions includes different kinds of arithmetic questions. There are four possible answers listed below the question. You should not use a calculator to answer these questions; however, you are permitted to do the calculations on a scrap piece of paper. Circle the correct letter to indicate your answer.

1. Solve for m:
   $4 - 3 (m + 1) = (-38)$
   a. 13
   b. −32
   c. −38
   d. none of the above

Section 3: Classification

In the next section, each question consists of four figures. Some figures have characteristics that are the same and some have characteristics that are different. Three of the figures go together, and one does not. Your task is to figure out why three of the figures go together and then select the figure that does not go with the others. Circle the correct letter to indicate your answer.

1. Select the figure that does not belong:

Figure 2.5 Classification

Section 4: Word Problems

In the next section, you will be asked a series of arithmetic word problems. You should not use a calculator to answer these questions; however, you are permitted to do the calculations on a scrap piece of paper. Circle the correct letter to indicate your answer.

1. There are two police officers and six firearms. What is the average number of firearms per officer?
   a. 2
   b. 3
   c. 5
   d. 6

2. The month has 31 days. On even numbered days, section A of the city is patrolled. On odd numbered days, section B of the city is patrolled. How many days of the month is section B patrolled?
   a. 14
   b. 15
   c. 16
   d. none of the above

(continued)

Section 5: Syllogisms

In the next section, each question begins with two statements. You must assume that the information in each of the first two statements is correct. Given these two true statements, only one of the conclusions is completely and absolutely correct. Your task is to determine which of the four possible answers is the correct one. Only one of the answers is correct.

1. All boys are people. All people are alive.
   a. All boys are alive
   b. Some boys are not alive
   c. Some boys are not people
   d. None of the above conclusions are valid

Section 6: Figure Series

In the next section, each question consists of three figures and a blank circle, followed by four more figures. The first three figures are shown in a specific order, or series. Your task is to figure out what the

order is, and then to complete it by selecting one of the last four figures to put in the empty circle. Remember, the figure in the circle should logically follow the other three.

1. Select the figure that completes the series:

Figure 2.6 Figure Series

Source: Reprinted from Ministry of Community Safety and Correctional Services. (2011). Constable selection information package: Testing tips and practice exercise. Retrieved from http://www.mcscs.jus.gov.on.ca/english/police_serv/const_select_sys /const_select_info/testing_tips_practice/practice_exercise/practice_exercise.html. © Queen's Printer for Ontario, 2009. Reproduced with permission.

The PATI test is a pencil-and-paper, multiple-choice aptitude test that evaluates the candidate's analytical thinking skills. This is a 90-question, 90-minute test consisting of six different sections. The six sections each contain 15 questions involving mapping, arithmetic, problem solving, classification, figure series, and syllogisms.

Most candidates will finish the PATI test in the time allotted. Read the questions carefully and be sure you understand what is being asked before responding. It may help to try to answer the question in your head before looking at the options. Do not spend too much time on questions you find difficult, as there may be other questions that you can answer more easily. The candidate is

not penalized for wrong answers so it is to your advantage to mark an answer for every question, even if you are guessing.

For additional practice test questions and for preparation material on the PATI, refer to the following Policing Online box and to Box 2.2.

Written Communications Test (WCT) Candidates are tested on their ability to organize information in a clear, coherent, and comprehensive manner. The WCT involves reading a short scenario and then summarizing the events in a logical manner before making a conclusion by organizing pertinent facts and reconstructing what happened in writing. Candidates are asked to put themselves in the role of a police constable at the scene

POLICING ONLINE

For private sector resources on the PATI test, go to
http://www.policeprep.com/
http://www.policeready.com/
http://testreadypro.com/

BOX 2.2

POLICE PREP

Police Prep is a leader in Canadian police exam preparation (Figure 2.7). This private sector corporation assists people in practicing and studying to successfully complete police entrance testing in Canada. The motto of this company is "Take control, realize your lifelong dreams." Candidates who are prepared and practice testing styles and questions similar to those on the exam have a greater chance of passing. Police Prep offers programs with practice tests and tips for police testing across Canada, the United States, Australia, and the United Kingdom. For sample questions and an in-depth analysis and explanation of each of the six sections on the PATI and other police tests in Canada, refer to the Police Prep website at http://www.policeprep.com or refer to the Police Prep textbook *Comprehensive Guide to Canadian Police Officer Exams*.

Figure 2.7 Police Exam and Preparation

Source: www.policeprep.com

of a motor vehicle accident as described in the test. Read the scenario very carefully as the information has been jumbled to test your ability to decipher the facts and issues and prepare an incident report based on your observations and comments from witnesses in the scenario. See Box 2.3 for some tips on completing the WCT. This test takes approximately one hour to complete.

BOX 2.3

WCT "CHEAT" SHEET

Hints for the WCT stage of the testing: In point form, on a scrap piece of paper, list all the facts you think are important, including the time, location, and evidence at the scene. This is all the pertinent information from the incident, sometimes referred to as the "tombstone" information. Next, reconstruct what you think happened in essay form, drawing on the information you have listed. The facts you have listed should support your view of the incident. Proper spelling and grammar are very important at this point. For additional practice WCT questions and for preparation material on the WCT, refer to the following Policing Online box.

Source: Ministry of Community Safety and Correctional Services, http://www.mcscs.jus.gov.on.ca/english/police_serv/const_select_sys/const_select_info/testing_tips_practice/written_exercise/written_exercise.html

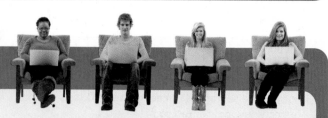

POLICING ONLINE

For private sector resources on the WCT test, go to
http://www.policeprep.com/
http://www.policeready.com/
http://testreadypro.com/

Physical Readiness Evaluation for Police (PREP) The candidate is required to successfully pass both components of the PREP: the Pursuit/Restraint Circuit and the Aerobic Shuttle Run.

"The Pursuit/Restraint Circuit … simulates a police foot chase that includes obstacles, control of a person who resists arrest and the dragging of an incapacitated person. Throughout this test, you must wear a 9 lb. soft weight belt to simulate the weight of standard police equipment"* (MCSCS, 2011b, para. 1; see Figure 2.8). The candidate completes as quickly as possible a Pursuit Restraint Circuit that includes running four rotations for a total distance of 100 metres. During each rotation, the participant climbs a set of stairs, and on the second and third rotation, scales a 1.2-metre fence. Following the circuit, the participant completes pushing and pulling on the "body control" simulator, performs two "arm restraint" simulations, then drags a 68-kilogram rescue mannequin a distance of 15 metres. This component must be completed in 162 seconds (2 minutes, 42 seconds) or less for the candidate to be successful (MCSCS, 2011b).

In the Aerobic Shuttle Run, the candidate runs back and forth over a 20-metre course in time with a recorded signal; the participant must reach the warning line before the signal sounds (see Figure 2.9). The time to cover

FIGURE 2.8
The Pursuit/Restraint Circuit for the PREP

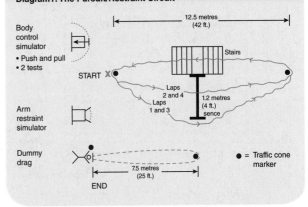

Source: Ministry of Community Safety and Correctional Services, "Policing Services: Constable Selection System: PREP Performance Components" (2007). Retrieved from http://www.mcscs.jus.gov.on.ca/english/police_serv /const_select_sys/const_select_info/prep/performance/PREP_performance. html. © Queen's Printer for Ontario, 2007. Reproduced with permission.

POLICING IN PRACTICE

WCT SAMPLE SCENARIO

The following is a sample WCT question that would be similar to the question on the WCT. To check your answer, refer to the answer key at the end of this chapter (p. 39).

Scenario

"A blue Jeep was on the other side of the street from the Mazda. It is June 13. Ms. Helen Elogar parked her car facing west at 10:20 a.m. When she returned to her car, Ms. Elogar found the paint on her driver's door had been scratched. The owner of a grey Chevette had parked his car at 10:30 a.m. A blue Jeep was parked, facing east. Most of the parking spaces were blocked by craft displays. There was a shopping cart overturned in the street, beside a grey Chevette. There was a large community sale being conducted in front of the stores. A red Mazda was parked in front of the Coarville Pharmacy. The police were notified of the damage at 10:52 a.m. A Chevette was parked in front of the Mazda. Traffic was detouring around a shopping cart which was blocking the westbound lane. The pharmacy is at 342 Elm Street. It was a very windy day. There were a lot of people on the sidewalk. All of Ms. Elogar's purchases were in her car. There were only three vehicles parked along the street. There was red paint evident on the front right corner of the shopping cart. The owner of the grey Chevette said he had parked in front of the red Mazda, and that he had taken the last available parking spot. He stated that the shopping cart was not there when he pulled in.

Summarize the above information to describe what may have taken place. Draw any interpretations and conclusions you can about the incident."

Source: Reprinted from Ministry of Community Safety and Correctional Services, "Policing Services: Constable Selection System: Constable Selection Information Package: Practice Written Test" (2007). Retrieved from http://www.mcscs.jus.gov.on.ca/english/police_serv/const_select_sys/ const_select_info/testing_tips_practice/written_exercise/ written_exercise.html. © Queen's Printer for Ontario, 2007. Reproduced with permission.

*Source: Ministry of Community Safety and Correctional Services, "Policing Services: Constable Selection System: PREP Performance Components" (2007). Retrieved from http://www.mcscs.jus.gov.on.ca/english/police_serv/const_select_sys/const_select_info/prep/performance/PREP_performance.html. © Queen's Printer for Ontario, 2007. Reproduced with permission.

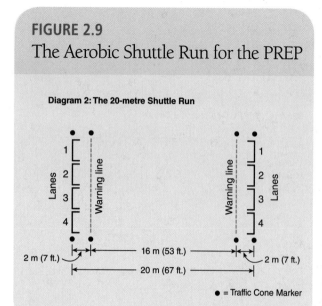

FIGURE 2.9

The Aerobic Shuttle Run for the PREP

Diagram 2: The 20-metre Shuttle Run

Source: Ministry of Community Safety and Correctional Services, "Policing Services: Constable Selection System: PREP Performance Components" (2007). Retrieved from http://www.mcscs.jus.gov.on.ca/english/police_serv /const_select_sys/const_select_info/prep/performance/PREP_performance. html. © Queen's Printer for Ontario, 2007. Reproduced with permission.

the course is shortened progressively, so in each stage participants must run at a faster pace. Candidates must complete stage 6.5 to be successful on this component.

Behavioural Personnel Assessment Device (BPAD)
When the PATI, WCT, and PREP tests have been successfully completed, the candidate will then be invited to participate in the Behavioural Personnel Assessment Device (BPAD) scenarios. The scenarios, displayed on a TV screen, represent what police constables may experience on the job. Candidates respond as if they are speaking to the people in the scenario and the responses are recorded. Knowledge of police procedures is not required, as candidates will be evaluated on the judgment and common sense they demonstrate in responding. The video simulation test takes approximately 20 minutes to complete. For additional practice test questions and further preparation material on the BPAD, refer to http://www.policeprep.com shown in Box 2.2.

The vision and hearing standards for this component of the testing are outlined at the beginning of this chapter in Box 2.1. Candidates who have unacceptable performance on any of the vision or hearing assessments will be referred for further examination by an appropriate specialist.

For candidates who do not meet the standards on their first attempt at the PATI or WCT for the OACP Certificate of Results, the waiting period to retest is three months from their test date and six months for each

attempt after that. Candidates who did not meet the standard with the PREP on their first attempt are eligible to retest within two months of their test date. Successful candidates are awarded the Ontario Association of Chiefs of Police Certificate of Results (MCSCS, 2011c).

Figure 2.10 outlines the steps in the constable selection process.

Stage 2: Application and Résumé Submission

For most police services in Ontario, candidates must possess a valid OACP Certificate of Results before they can even apply to the police service. At this stage the candidate will submit a completed police application form and provide the following supporting documents, demonstrating that the candidate meets the minimum and/or preferred qualifications:

- cover letter;
- résumé or curriculum vitae;
- high school diploma and transcripts;
- postsecondary school diploma or degree and transcripts (if applicable);
- Ontario driver's licence;
- proof of citizenship (birth certificate or passport); and
- standard first aid and Basic Rescuer Level C CPR certificates.

The candidate's documents will be reviewed, and if selected the candidate will be invited to attend a pre-interview paperwork session (stage 3) or in some instances a local focus interview (stage 4).

Stage 3: Pre-Interview Paperwork Session

Candidates invited to this stage of the process will be required to complete the following documents at the police service they have applied to:

- Police Waiver Form;
- Pre-Background Questionnaire;
- Ontario Constable Selection System Consent and Release of Liability Form;
- Personal History Form;
- Personal History Form—Friends;
- Supplementary Personal History Form;
- Applicant Survey Form; and
- Police Constable Application Form (if applicable).

The information disclosed in the above documents will provide the police service with a complete and detailed history of the candidate's life; any further supplementary information will be uncovered in the background stage of the hiring process. In addition, the candidate will have to provide three personal references, three school

FIGURE 2.10
The Constable Selection System

This flow chart outlines the steps required to become a police constable in Ontario. The process starts with self-assessment, proceeds to the pre-interview testing with a private sector firm, and concludes with the fine screening process of the Constable Selection System.

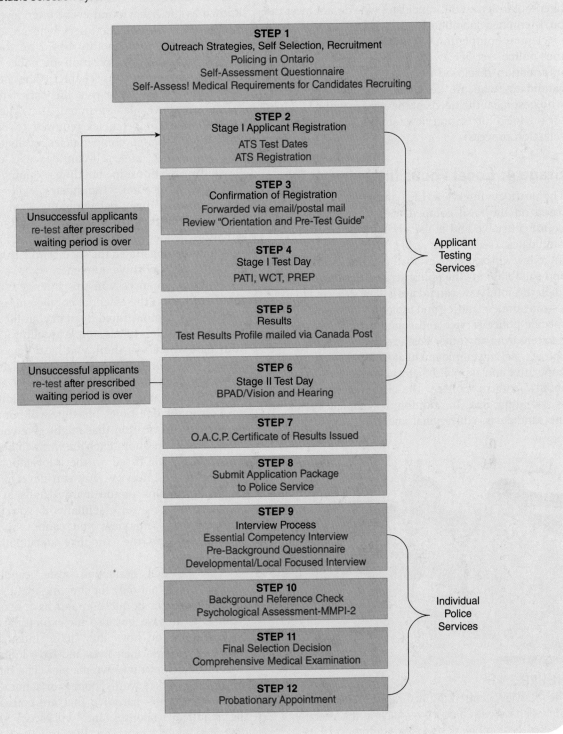

STEP 1
Outreach Strategies, Self Selection, Recruitment
Policing in Ontario
Self-Assessment Questionnaire
Self-Assess! Medical Requirements for Candidates Recruiting

STEP 2
Stage I Applicant Registration
ATS Test Dates
ATS Registration

STEP 3
Confirmation of Registration
Forwarded via email/postal mail
Review "Orientation and Pre-Test Guide"

Unsuccessful applicants re-test after prescribed waiting period is over

STEP 4
Stage I Test Day
PATI, WCT, PREP

STEP 5
Results
Test Results Profile mailed via Canada Post

Applicant Testing Services

Unsuccessful applicants re-test after prescribed waiting period is over

STEP 6
Stage II Test Day
BPAD/Vision and Hearing

STEP 7
O.A.C.P. Certificate of Results Issued

STEP 8
Submit Application Package
to Police Service

STEP 9
Interview Process
Essential Competency Interview
Pre-Background Questionnaire
Developmental/Local Focused Interview

STEP 10
Background Reference Check
Psychological Assessment-MMPI-2

Individual Police Services

STEP 11
Final Selection Decision
Comprehensive Medical Examination

STEP 12
Probationary Appointment

Source: ATS Inc., http://www.applicanttesting.com/career-paths/police-constable.html

references, and three employment references; the references will be interviewed as part of the background investigation. The Pre-Background Questionnaire (PBQ) is an in-depth document that addresses various questions about the candidate's life history and personal traits. Specific responses to certain questions on the PBQ are considered red flags when assessing a candidate in the hiring process. Police services use the PBQ as a filter tool to screen out candidates who do not meet the predetermined conditions.

Upon completion of the paperwork session, the police service will review and evaluate all information disclosed by the applicant. Only those candidates who are deemed most competitive and who best meet the needs of the service will be invited for the local focus interview (stage 4 of the constable selection process).

Stage 4: Local Focus Interview (LFI)

The local focus interview (LFI) is a one-on-one interview based on the local competencies for the position of police constable and is usually the first interview for candidates (see Figure 2.11). This comprehensive interview will be used to evaluate candidates' knowledge and suitability for the police service they have applied to. In this interview, candidates will be expected to have a strong understanding and profound knowledge of the specific police service and community. Policing is no different from any other business that you apply to—if you are seeking employment at Georgian College, it is imperative and expected that you will know something about Georgian College, the city of Barrie, and the surrounding area. In addition, a complete review of the candidates' educational and employment history

FIGURE 2.11
The interview is often the first face-to-face contact you will have with a police recruiter in the selection process. First impressions make a difference!

will be undertaken, and candidates will be evaluated on their commitment to community service/volunteer work.

Stage 5: Essential Competencies Interview (ECI)

The essential competencies interview (ECI), also known as the behavioural event interview, is usually administered by two recruiters who are certified to assess candidates' suitability based on the essential competencies for the position of police constable, outlined earlier in this chapter. The interview is designed to draw upon past life experiences where candidates have demonstrated that they possess the essential competencies required to be a police constable. The six competencies evaluated in the ECI interview are self-confidence, self-control, flexibility, relationship building, valuing diversity, and communication. Candidates will be asked approximately five behavioural event interview questions; in their answers, they must describe a situation, incident, or true story from their past where they have demonstrated the six essential competencies and have had a positive outcome.

The key to success in this interview is to show that you possess the essential competencies and have successfully demonstrated them in your life within the past two years. It is not as simple as telling a story from your past where you think you have demonstrated a certain competency. The interviewers will ask probing questions about dates and people involved in your story to verify and follow up on the validity of your answers to the questions, but they will not probe you for further information that might give you a higher score on that question. Each answer will be evaluated on a points scale based on the information that you provide in the interview. You can never provide too much information or too many details in this style of interview because essentially if you don't "say it" during the interview, you cannot be evaluated appropriately on the complete story, situation, or incident.

On the ECI evaluation scale, candidates are awarded points not only for showing that they possess the competencies in question and have demonstrated them in their past, but also for exhibiting what they have learned or how they have integrated these competencies into their lives and have influenced the lives of others in a positive manner. The interviewers are looking for key words, points, or actions described in the candidate's narrative that are consistent with the required responses and will score the candidate maximum points on the evaluation scale for each interview question. The evaluation scale for each question is established on an integer number system based on the candidate's response, from a rating scale of –2 to +5. The target score for a candidate to be successful is a score of 2 or higher on the flexibility, relationship building, and dealing with diversity questions and 3 or higher on the questions on self-control, self-confidence, and communication. The candidate must meet the target score for each question in order to be successful; however, since the hiring process is very competitive, the higher the candidate's overall score is on all five questions, the more likely the candidate will be to move on to the next stage of the hiring process.

Below is a comprehensive explanation of the essential competencies and example questions that the candidate may be asked at the ECI interview stage:

- *Self-confidence:* The candidate must demonstrate belief in his or her abilities and judgment and recognize personal limitations and development needs.
- *Question:* "Tell us about a time when someone pointed out a mistake that you made."
- *Self-control:* The candidate must demonstrate the ability to keep emotions under control and to restrain negative actions when provoked or when working under stressful conditions.
- *Question:* "Describe a situation where you were confronted by an irate or out-of-control person and explain how you dealt with that person or situation."
- *Flexibility:* The candidate must demonstrate the ability to adapt to a variety of situations.
- *Question:* "Tell us about a time when you

were presented with a new idea on how to do something."
- *Relationship building:* The candidate must demonstrate the ability to develop and maintain a network of contacts, both inside and outside the police service.
- *Question:* "Tell us about a time when you developed a relationship with someone."
- *Valuing diversity:* The candidate must demonstrate the ability to work effectively in a community with diverse backgrounds, cultures, and socio-economic circumstances.
- *Question:* "Tell us about a time when you have had a prejudiced thought or demonstrated a prejudiced belief or action toward a person from a diverse background or culture as described by the Ontario *Human Rights Code* (refer to Box 2.4)."
- *Communication:* The candidate must demonstrate effective listening, verbal, and written communication skills.

The communication competency is normally evaluated right through the interview and will be scored based on the candidate's ability to communicate effectively throughout the interview questions.

Stage 6: Psychological Testing

Candidates are required to complete a psychological assessment, which may include a clinical interview with a psychologist or psychiatrist. The assessment is not to measure a person's sanity but to determine if the candidate is suitable to cope with the situations that police officers may encounter both on and off the job (see

BOX 2.4

THE ONTARIO HUMAN RIGHTS CODE

The Ontario *Human Rights Code* is a provincial law that gives everybody equal rights and opportunities without discrimination in specific areas such as jobs, housing and services. The *Code*'s goal is to prevent discrimination and harassment because of the following sixteen grounds of discrimination under the Ontario *Human Rights Code*:

- race
- ancestry
- place of origin
- colour
- ethnic origin
- citizenship
- creed (religion)
- sex (including pregnancy)
- sexual orientation

- handicap
- age (18 to 65 in employment, and 16 and over in occupancy of accommodation)
- marital status
- family status
- same-sex partnership status
- receipt of public assistance (in accommodation only)
- record of offences (in employment only)

Source: Reprinted from Ontario *Human Rights Code*, R.S.O. 1990, Chapter H.19. Last amendment 2009, c. 33, Sched. 2, s. 35. Retrieved from http://www.ohrc.on.ca/en/resources/Guides/GuideHRcode2/pdf.

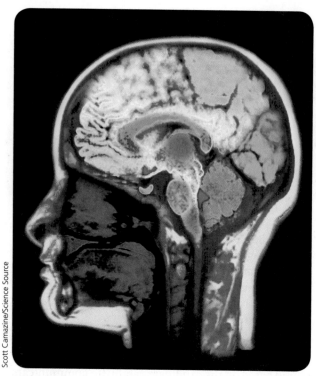

Scott Camazine/Science Source

FIGURE 2.12
Psychological testing will measure your suitability to perform the duties of a police officer.

Figure 2.12). If a police service does not have a qualified psychologist or psychiatrist on staff, they will contract out this portion of the hiring process. The psychologist or psychiatrist will use several psychological tests to assist in assessing candidates. The two most common tests used for this purpose are the Minnesota Multiphasic Personality Inventory-2 (MMPI-2) test and the Sixteen Personality Factor Questionnaire (16PF).

The MMPI-2 is a personality test that is used to identify personality structure and psychopathology in a person. The test contains between 500 and 1000 questions and takes approximately 60 to 90 minutes to complete. The test incorporates validity scales to determine if candidates are trying to lie or answer the question the way they believe it should be answered in order to present themselves as suitable candidates for policing. The psychological assessment is about you as a person, so you cannot study or prepare for the test. Just be genuine and answer the questions truthfully and honestly.

The 16PF is a multiple-choice personality questionnaire. This test contains 185 questions and takes approximately 35 to 50 minutes to complete. The 16PF test is normally used for personnel selection and career development in policing. Again, this assessment is about who you are as a person, so you cannot study for the test.

Often the MMPI-2 and the 16PF will be used in conjunction with a clinical interview with a psychologist

or psychiatrist to assess the candidate's suitability to be a police officer, be promoted, and/or be selected to be part of a specialty unit. For example, police officers interested in applying to become a member of a Tactical Response Unit maybe required to participate in a psychological assessment even if they were successful on the test when they were hired by the police service.

Stage 7: Background Investigation

The background investigation may include, but is not limited to, reference checks, verification of educational documents, verification of employment history, and credit checks. The Personal History Forms and PBQ completed in Step 3 will provide the background investigator with all the required information to conduct a thorough and complete investigation of the candidate and his or her family and close friends. That's right, your association and connection with your family and friends may have an impact on your background investigation. As a police officer, you are required to have good moral character and judgment. You will be allocated immense power and authority, and you could be influenced to use this power in a negative manner. Therefore, it is imperative that you associate yourself with friends and family who have a positive influence on you and abide by the law. Harper Lee's statement that "you can choose your friends, but not your family" is true, but you can choose your career and the path you are willing to take to get there.

The background investigator will interview the nine references (three employment, three educational, and three personal) that the candidate was required to provide in addition to any supplementary references. Obviously, the candidate will provide only references that will be favourable and complimentary, so the supplementary references could be from people that the candidate may not know are being interviewed in hopes that they will provide constructive, impartial insight into the candidate's history and personal traits. The references will be asked questions that relate to their specific connection to the candidate with regards to personal habits and traits, as well as performance at work and/or school where applicable.

The background investigation is normally conducted by a serving or retired police officer and could take up to a week or two to complete. Included in the background investigation is a home visit with the candidate. The background investigator will schedule a home visit to the candidate's current residence at the time of the investigation and may request an additional home visit to the candidate's permanent residence, if applicable. The home visit is a valuable part of the background investigation and will divulge a great deal about the candidate's daily life habits.

Stage 8: Final Selection

In the final review, all the information collected in the previous stages of the selection process is reviewed and compared to the selection criteria and other candidates. The selection process is very competitive, and each police service will have excellent candidates to select from the hiring pool.

With some services, a final selection interview is scheduled with a panel of senior officers from that particular police service. The senior officers will review the candidate's completed file and ask relevant questions that will coincide with the police service's selection criteria.

Successful candidates will be given a conditional offer of employment. The offer is conditional upon the successful completion of a comprehensive medical examination and appointment by the police services board. A physician appointed by the service will conduct the medical examination.

Applicants must provide proof of valid standard first aid and CPR Basic Rescuer (Level C) certification prior to confirmation of employment.

Unsuccessful Applicants Applicants who are unsuccessful in the selection process at steps 2, 3, 4, 6, or 7 may reapply for a police constable position with the police service they applied to after a period of one year from the date they were removed from the selection process. If applicants are unsuccessful at step 8 of the selection process, the waiting period to reapply is at the discretion of the police service.

At step 5 of the selection process, in accordance with the OACP Constable Selection System, applicants who are unsuccessful in their first essential competencies interview may be considered by other OACP-licensed services after a period of three months. If an applicant is unsuccessful a second time at the essential competency interview stage, there is a six-month waiting period prior to any further consideration.

ONTARIO PROVINCIAL POLICE (OPP)

The information below relates specifically to the OPP constable hiring process (Figure 2.13). The OPP recruitment process is similar to that of most police services in Ontario, and the OPP participates in the Constable Selection System. The steps in the OPP recruitment process are as follows:

1. Obtain Certificate of Results
   - Register for Certificate of Results

Source: OPP Home -- Organization -- OPP Vision, Mandate and Purpose (http://www.opp.ca/ecms/index.php?id=20). © Queen's Printer for Ontario, 2009. Reproduced with permission.

FIGURE 2.13

In its hiring process, the OPP looks for "people who want to make a difference in the lives of others" (OPP, 2009a, para. 2).

   - Pre-interview Assessment Testing
   - Police Analytical Thinking Inventory (P.A.T.I.)
   - Written Communication Test (W.C.T.)
   - Physical Readiness Evaluation For Police (P.R.E.P.)
   - Vision/Hearing
   - Behavioural Personnel Assessment Device for Police (B.P.A.D.)
   - Certificate of Results (C.O.R.) Achieved
2. Application Package
3. Pre-screening
4. Pre-background Questionnaire & Local Focused Interview
5. Background Investigation
6. Medical Assessment
7. Psychological Assessment
8. Final Review
9. Eligible for Hire (OPP, 2009a, para. 4)*

ROYAL CANADIAN MOUNTED POLICE (RCMP)

Because the RCMP is Canada's national police service, this organization offers unmatched mobility for its members (Figure 2.14). "With hundreds of detachments across Canada, RCMP members have the chance to experience life in many parts of Canada, and work at different levels of policing—municipal, provincial, and federal" (RCMP, 2011a, para. 11). For the most part, cadets are not posted to Quebec or Ontario because the RCMP is limited to federal enforcement duties in these provinces and new members would not get

---

*Source: Ontario Provincial Police website, OPP Home -- Careers -- Uniform Recruiting -- Application Process. Retrieved from http://www.opp.ca/ecms/index.php?id=95. © Queen's Printer for Ontario, 2009. Reproduced with permission.

FIGURE 2.14
RCMP officers must be willing to relocate within Canada.

the exposure to all facets of policing required to gain valuable policing experience (RCMP, 2011a).

BASIC REQUIREMENTS

As outlined in the *Royal Canadian Mounted Police Act*, to be considered for the position of police constable with the RCMP, a candidate must

- be a Canadian citizen;
- be at least 19 years of age;
- be physically and mentally able to perform the duties of the position;
- be of good moral character and habits;
- have a Canadian high school diploma or equivalent;
- be proficient in English or French;
- possess an unrestricted Canadian driver's licence; and
- be willing to relocate anywhere in Canada (RCMP, 2011a).

Once candidates meet the basic requirements and apply to be a police constable with the RCMP, they go through the cadet selection process:

Step 1: Career Presentation

Step 2: RCMP Police Aptitude Battery (RPAB)

Step 3: Initial Rank List (IRL)

Step 4: Selection Package

Step 5: Regular Member Applicant Questionnaire

Step 6: Physical Abilities Requirement Evaluation (PARE)

Step 7: Regular Member Selection Interview (RMSI)

Step 8: Post Interview Ranked List (PIRL)

Step 9: Pre-Employment Polygraph (PEP) Interview and Examination

Step 10: Field Investigation

Step 11: Health Assessment

Step 12: Prerequisites and Enrollment (RCMP, 2012a)*

STEP 1: CAREER PRESENTATION

The career presentation is an information session that is delivered by an RCMP uniform recruiting officer to answer any question candidates may have about the RCMP and the hiring process.

STEP 2: APPLICATION AND RCMP POLICE APTITUDE BATTERY (RPAB)

After candidates have completed and submitted a uniform member application, they will be required to complete the RCMP Police Aptitude Battery test. The RPAB is made up of two tests, the first of which is the RCMP Police Aptitude Test (RPAT). The RPAT is a multiple-choice test of 114 questions that evaluates the applicant's aptitude to be a police officer. The RPAT measures the following seven skills: "composition (spelling, grammar, and vocabulary); comprehension; memory; judgment; observation; logic; and computation"† (RCMP, 2011d, para. 3).

The selection process is very competitive and the RCMP takes only the top applicants; therefore, applicants who pass the RPAT will be placed on an eligibility list ranked by score. Applicants with the highest scores will be selected to advance to the next step of the selection process. If the applicant is unsuccessful on the RPAT, there is a mandatory wait period of one year from the date of the test before the applicant may reapply (RCMP, 2011d).

The second component of the RPAB measures a concept not captured by the RPAT. The Six Factor

---

*Source: Retrieved from http://www.rcmp-grc.gc.ca/recruiting-recrutement/rec/process-processus-eng.htm. © 2012 HER MAJESTY THE QUEEN IN RIGHT OF CANADA as represented by the Royal Canadian Mounted Police (RCMP). Reproduced with the permission of the RCMP.

†Source: Retrieved from http://www.rcmp-grc.gc.ca/recruiting-recrutement/rec/rpab-btatpg-eng.htm. © 2012 HER MAJESTY THE QUEEN IN RIGHT OF CANADA as represented by the Royal Canadian Mounted Police (RCMP). Reproduced with the permission of the RCMP.

Personality Questionnaire (SFPQ) consists of statements that the candidate is asked to agree or disagree with. There is no right or wrong answer on this test and there is no way to study for it (RCMP, 2011d).

STEP 3: INITIAL RANK LIST (IRL)

Again, the selection process is very competitive; therefore, applicants who pass the RPAB will be placed on the Initial Rank List (IRL). Applicants will be selected from the IRL to proceed to the next stage of the selection process. "The IRL is a **dynamic list** meaning that an applicant's position on the list will fluctuate as additional exams are scored and as applications are selected from the list for further processing. As a result, an applicant's position on the list is not fixed and may move up or down throughout the year"* (RCMP, 2011b, para. 3).

STEP 4: SELECTION PACKAGE

At this point applicants who have been selected to continue in the process must complete various documents and forms, such as personal information forms, the Police Officer Applicant Questionnaire, PARE medical waiver forms, and a vision examination form.

STEP 5: POLICE OFFICER APPLICANT QUESTIONNAIRE

This questionnaire is an in-depth document that is used to analyze the suitability and reliability of the applicant, and assist in the security clearance assessment. The forms and documents in this section will explore the applicant's personal and family history, including personal traits and habits that the applicant has demonstrated in the past. Any answers given on this questionnaire will be verified at stage 9 of the selection process by way of the Pre-Employment Polygraph (PEP) (RCMP, 2012a).

STEP 6: PHYSICAL ABILITIES REQUIREMENT EVALUATION (PARE)

The PARE is a job-related physical ability test that simulates a critical incident of chasing, controlling, and apprehending a suspect. Applicants must complete the obstacle course and push/pull sections in 4:45 minutes for a passing score. The weight carry section is not timed. The PARE is divided into the following three sections.

Obstacle Course Section

The obstacle course simulates the physical demands that an officer may encounter on a daily basis. The course involves running six laps, with direction changes; jumping across a 1.5-metre distance; going up and down stairs; jumping over 45-centimetre hurdles; jumping over a 0.9-metre barrier, followed by performing a controlled fall (forward and backwards) and getting back up before starting the next lap. At the end of the last lap, the participant proceeds to the push/pull section of the test.

Push/Pull Section

The push/pull section of this test simulates having to take physical control of a person. The participant first has to pull a 32-kilogram weight through six 180-degree arcs and then has to push the same weight through six more 180-degree arcs. Between the push and pull tasks, the participant performs four controlled falls.

Weight Carry

The weight carry section of this test simulates having to carry a person to safety. A 36-kilogram bag must be carried for a distance of 15 metres without dropping or putting the weight down. The participant will be given three attempts to complete this test within two minutes after completing the push/pull section.

STEP 7: REGULAR MEMBER SELECTION INTERVIEW (RMSI)

The Regular Member Selection Interview (RMSI) contains behavioural and situational questions and is a one-on-one interview. The purpose of the interview is to determine if the applicant meets the identified competencies to become a police officer with the RCMP: developing self, flexibility, problem solving, conscientiousness and reliability, meeting client needs, communication, teamwork, self-control, and composure (RCMP, 2012a).

STEP 8: POST INTERVIEW RANKED LIST (PIRL)

Applicants who are successful at the interview stage are again ranked and placed on the RCMP Post Interview Ranked List (PIRL). The PIRL ranks applicants from

---

highest to lowest score by way of a **weighted combination** of the RPAB and the RMSI. Applicants **scoring at the highest end of this ranking** will proceed to the next stages of the selection process (RCMP, 2012a).

STEP 9: SUITABILITY/RELIABILITY INTERVIEW: POLYGRAPH EXAMINATION

The Pre-Employment Polygraph (PEP) interview and examination is designed to help verify suitability and reliability (see Box 2.5). The PEP examination is not a lie detector test, and it doesn't have surprise or trick questions. There is no pass or fail on this test, and applicants know the questions they will be asked before the examination starts. "PEP is just one of many tools used to help the RCMP verify that an applicant is the person they have claimed to be in their employment application forms, questionnaires, and prior interviews in the recruiting process" (RCMP, 2011e, "RCMP Pre-Employment Polygraph," para. 2)*.

STEP 10: FIELD INVESTIGATION AND SECURITY CLEARANCE

The field investigation and security clearance is a thorough background investigation of applicants to assist in assessing their character. During the background investigation, the focus is on applicants'

previous employment and educational history, personal finances, drug and alcohol use, criminal activities, and character references (RCMP, 2012a).

STEP 11: HEALTH ASSESSMENT

The health assessment determines whether the applicant will be able to perform the job requirements of a police officer, both mentally and physically. A designated physician will screen the applicant by completing a full medical, dental, and psychological exam.

STEP 12: PREREQUISITES AND ENROLLMENT

Once an applicant has successfully completed the selection process, he or she is deemed a suitable applicant and is hired as a police cadet to start training at Depot, the RCMP training academy in Regina, Saskatchewan (RCMP, 2012a).

CANADIAN MILITARY POLICE

The Canadian Forces (CF) is a community of over 200,000 people in Canada and abroad. To address policing and law-related issues for CF members residing and working on military bases in Canada and internationally, the Department of National Defence (DND) established the Canadian Forces Military

BOX 2.5

RCMP PRE-EMPLOYMENT POLYGRAPH (PEP) INTERVIEW AND EXAMINATION

As outlined in the sections of the Applicant Questionnaire, the RCMP is interested in:

- Past work and education;
- Driving history;
- Alcohol and drug use;
- Use of force;
- Use of computers and technology;
- Dealings with law enforcement, the courts;
- Unlawful or unsuitable activities/associations; and
- Any past military and/or peace officer experience.

Source: Retrieved from http://www.rcmp-grc.gc.ca/recruiting-recrutement/rec/poly-eng.htm. © 2011 HER MAJESTY THE QUEEN IN RIGHT OF CANADA as represented by the Royal Canadian Mounted Police (RCMP). Reproduced with the permission of the RCMP.

*Source: Retrieved from http://www.rcmp-grc.gc.ca/recruiting-recrutement/rec/poly-eng.htm. © 2011 HER MAJESTY THE QUEEN IN RIGHT OF CANADA as represented by the Royal Canadian Mounted Police (RCMP). Reproduced with the permission of the RCMP.

FIGURE 2.15
The military police are responsible for Canada's military personnel around the world.

Police (CFMP). The CFMP is one of the largest police services in Canada, with over 1200 full-time police officers around the world (see Figure 2.15). The function of the military police is to deal with incidents that involve the criminal and military justice system; military police officers have the same authority as peace officers under the *Criminal Code of Canada.*

In order to become a military police officer, you must first join the Canadian Forces. The application process is similar to the process of applying to a police service. The candidate has to submit an application and attend a series of tests and interviews, including a physical fitness test. Applicants who are successful in the recruitment process and have qualified for a position with the military police are then sent for basic military qualification (BMQ). All candidates who join the Canadian Forces must attend and pass basic military training. The BMQ is a 13-week course that focuses on the core skills required to be a member of the Canadian military. The minimum academic achievement needed to join the military police is a community college diploma. After successfully completing BMQ training, candidates attend the Military Police Assessment Centre (MPAC), where they undergo an aptitude assessment to ensure they will succeed as a military police officer.

Once candidates have been successfully assessed by the MPAC, they are sent for basic military police training at CFB Borden, Ontario. CFB Borden is the national training facility for all military police officers in Canada. Over the six-month Basic Military Police course, candidates will train and acquire the skills and knowledge required to perform the duties of a military police officer.

LO⁴ OTHER POLICE SERVICES IN CANADA

As mentioned earlier in this chapter, police testing and recruitment in Canada is divided into provincially specific tests and requirements. Although this book is primarily focused on policing in Ontario and touches briefly on policing at the national level with the RCMP and the Canadian military police, the following sections will explore a few other recruitment processes in other provinces. In reviewing the selection process in other parts of the country, you will notice that similar steps and requirements have been adopted and implemented from province to province (see Figure 2.16). The minimum requirements to be a police officer (excluding RCMP officers) in each province are outlined in provincial legislation.

The RCMP provides policing services in every community in Nunavut, the Northwest Territories, and Yukon. Newfoundland and Labrador, Yukon, the

POLICING ONLINE

For Canadian Forces recruiting, see

http://www.forces.ca/en/page/howtoapply-106

For military police officer recruiting, see

http://www.forces.ca/en/job/militarypoliceofficer-144

FIGURE 2.16

Policing in Canada is similar from coast to coast; therefore, so are the recruiting requirements.

Northwest Territories, and Nunavut are the only areas in Canada without municipal police services. Although there are no municipal police services in Newfoundland and Labrador, the province has established a provincial police service called the Royal Newfoundland Constabulary.

MINIMUM REQUIREMENTS

In most provinces across Canada, the minimum requirements to be a police officer are that the individual

- is a Canadian citizen or permanent resident of Canada;
- is at least 18 or 19 years of age;
- is physically and mentally able to perform the duties of the position;
- is of good moral character and habits;
- has successfully completed a Grade 12 diploma or equivalent (certain provinces require a postsecondary education or specific police training at an approved postsecondary institution);

POLICING ONLINE

For provincial legislation that mandates the minimum requirements to be a police officer in each province, see the following websites:

- *British Columbia Police Act:* **http://www.qp.gov.bc.ca/police/**

- *Alberta Police Act:* **http://www.qp.alberta.ca/documents/Acts/P17.pdf**

- *Saskatchewan Police Act:* **http://www.qp.gov.sk.ca/documents/English/Statutes/Statutes/P15-01.pdf**

- *Manitoba Police Services Act:* **http://web2.gov.mb.ca/bills/39-3/b016e.php**

- *Ontario Police Services Act:* **http://www.e-laws.gov.on.ca/html/statutes/english/elaws_statutes_90p15_e.htm**

- *Quebec Police Act:* **http://www.canlii.org/en/qc/laws/stat/rsq-c-p-13/latest/rsq-c-p-13.html**

- *Nova Scotia Police Act:* **http://nslegislature.ca/legc/statutes/police.htm**

- *New Brunswick Police Act:* **http://laws.gnb.ca/en/ShowTdm/cs/P-9.2//**

- *Prince Edward Island Police Act:* **http://www.gov.pe.ca/law/statutes/pdf/p-11_1.pdf**

- *Royal Newfoundland Constabulary Act:* **http://assembly.nl.ca/Legislation/sr/statutes/r17.htm**

- has a valid driver's licence with a good driving record;
- has no unpardoned criminal convictions and no criminal charges pending (certain provinces are specific in the requirement that the candidate must not have any criminal convictions);
- has no history of improper conduct, poor employment, or a military, educational, or driving record that would affect his or her suitability for policing duties;
- has a working knowledge of English; and
- has a functional knowledge of French (Quebec only).

POLICE RECRUITMENT PROCESS

Police recruitment across Canada is specific to each police service. Although the police services must adhere to the minimum requirements set forth in provincial legislation, they have the freedom to establish their own recruitment processes in order to meet the needs of the communities they serve and to satisfy their own requirements. As discussed earlier in this chapter with the recruitment process in Ontario, each police service can require additional qualifications above and beyond the minimum requirements set out for that particular province, often referred to as "preferred" qualifications.

Although the selection process for police officers is unique to each police service in Canada, again, there are some commonalities across the country. These similarities exist because for the most part, police officers perform the same policing duties in every community in Canada. Therefore, each police service across Canada has established a recruitment and selection process similar to the following:

Step 1: Application package (résumé, police application, etc.)

Step 2: Aptitude tests (written examinations)

Step 3: Physical fitness testing (police specific)

Step 4: Interview(s) (local focus, intake, behavioural, descriptive, etc.)

Step 5: Psychological evaluation and medical examination

Step 6: Polygraph interview/examination (the majority of police services outside of Ontario have this requirement)

POLICING ONLINE

For further information on the particulars of the recruitment and selection process for a variety of police services in Canada outside of Ontario, refer to the following websites.

- *Royal Canadian Mounted Police:* **http://www.rcmp-grc.gc.ca**
- *Calgary Police Service:* **http://www.calgarypolice.ca**
- *Charlottetown Police Service:* **http://www.charlottetownpolice.com**
- *École nationale de police Québec:* **http://www.enpq.qc.ca**
- *Edmonton Police Service:* **http://www.edmontonpolice.ca/**
- *Halifax Regional Police:* **http://www.halifax.ca/police/**
- *Regina Police Service:* **http://www.reginapolice.ca**
- *Royal Newfoundland Constabulary:* **http://www.rnc.gov.nl.ca**
- *Vancouver Police Department:* **http://vancouver.ca/police**
- *Winnipeg Police Service:* **http://www.winnipeg.ca/police**

Step 7: Background investigation

Step 8: Final review committee (selection panel, final approval, job offer)

FIRST NATIONS POLICING

In order to improve policing services for First Nations communities in Canada, the federal government established the on-reserve First Nations Policing Policy (FNPP). The Aboriginal Policing Directorate (APD) was created from the FNPP and was given responsibility for developing, implementing, and maintaining the First Nations Policing Program within the framework of the FNPP. The program was successfully implemented across Canada through tripartite agreements between the federal government, provincial or territorial governments, and First Nations to provide police services that are effective, professional, and tailored to meet the needs of each community. As a result, First Nation communities are policed by either a self-administered police service (Figure 2.17) or under agreement by the provincial, territorial, or other existing police service.

First Nations communities that have established self-administered policing agreements across Canada have various requirements to become a police officer. Here, we will briefly examine the selection process for the Nishnawbe-Aski Police Service (NAPS; Figure 2.18) in Northern Ontario, which has established a self-administered policing tripartite agreement.

NISHNAWBE-ASKI POLICE SERVICE (NAPS)

The Nishnawbe-Aski Police Service serves 35 First Nations communities in the Nishnawbe-Aski Nation Territory of

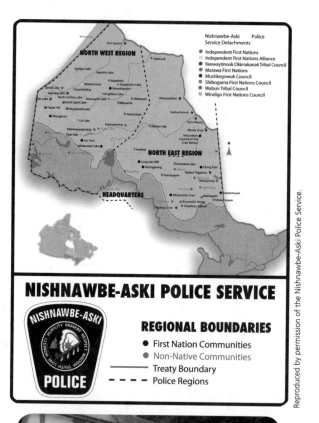

FIGURE 2.17
Many First Nations in Canada have self-administered police services.

FIGURE 2.18
The Nishnawbe-Aski Police Service is the largest First Nations police service in Canada and the second largest in North America.

Northern Ontario. The minimum requirements to become a police constable with NAPS are that the individual

- is a Canadian citizen or permanent resident of Canada;
- is at least 19 years of age;
- is physically and mentally able to perform the duties of the position;
- is of good moral character and habits;
- has successfully completed a Grade 12 diploma or equivalent;
- has a valid Class G driver's licence with a good driving record;
- has no unpardoned criminal convictions and no adult criminal charges pending;
- has no history of improper conduct, poor employment, or a military, educational, or driving record that would affect his or her suitability for policing duties; and
- has a valid OACP Certificate of Results.*

In addition, the following are preferred qualifications. The applicant

- has a university or college education;
- is a resident or has spent time in a northern community;
- resides in an area close to the posting or will be able to move upon being hired; and
- is a member of the Nishnawbe-Aski Nation (Nishnawbe-Aski Police Service, 2011).

The Nishnawbe-Aski Police Service selection process consists of six steps:

Step 1: Application package
Step 2: Selection process
Step 3: Background investigation
Step 4: Interview process
Step 5: Psychological testing
Step 6: Job offer (Nishnawbe-Aski Police Service, 2011)

POLICING ONLINE

For further information on the particulars of the recruitment and selection process for NAPS, refer to

http://www.naps.ca/

POLICING IN PRACTICE

SAMPLE PATI TEST ANSWERS

Section 1: Mapping

Item	Correct Answer	Explanation
Q1	a	It takes 2 minutes to drive one block.

Section 2: Arithmetic

Item	Correct Answer	Explanation
Q1	a	$4 - 3(14) = -(38)$ so "m" has to equal 13 [13 + 1 = 14]

(continued)

*Source: Nishnawbe-Aski Police Service, Hiring Information, available at http://naps.ca/index.php?option=com_content&view=article&rid=81&Itemid=69. Reproduced by permission of the Nishnawbe-Aski Police Service.

SAMPLE PATI TEST ANSWERS (Continued)

Section 3: Classification

Item	Correct Answer	Explanation
Q1	b	All the other faces are smiling; all other characteristics are the same.

Section 4: Word Problems

Item	Correct Answer	Explanation
Q1	b	6 firearms divided by 2 police officers.
Q2	c	Starting from the 1st to the 31st, there are 16 odd-numbered days (1st, 3rd, 5th, 7th, 9th, 11th, 13th, 15th, 17th, 19th, 21st, 23rd, 25th, 27th, 29th, 31st)

Section 5: Syllogisms

Item	Correct Answer	Explanation
1	a	All boys must be alive since they are people and all people are alive.

Section 6: Figure Series

Item	Correct Answer	Explanation
2	c	The handcuffs are increasingly spread out from the one another until the two cuffs are fully extended.

Source: Reprinted from Ministry of Community Safety and Correctional Services, "Policing Services: Constable Selection System: Constable Selection Information Package: Practice Test Answers" (2008). Retrieved from http://www.mcscs.jus.gov.on.ca/english/police_serv/const_select_sys/const_select_info/ testing_tips_practice/practice _exercise_answers/practice_exercise_answers.html. © Queen's Printer for Ontario, 2008. Reproduced with permission.

WCT SAMPLE SCENARIO ANSWER

Important Facts

Time

- June 13
- 10:52 a.m.—call received
- 10:20 a.m. Mazda parked
- 10:30 a.m. Chevette parked

Location

- parking space in front of 342 Elm St., Coarville

Evidence at the scene

- red Mazda parked behind grey Chevette
- driver's door scratched on Elogar's car
- shopping cart overturned in street
- a lot of people on sidewalk
- red paint evident on front right corner of shopping cart
- only 3 vehicles parked on street

Other

- windy day

Report

The damage to Ms. Elogar's car, a red Mazda, occurred between 10:30 a.m. and 10:52 a.m. on June 13, in front of the Coarville Pharmacy at 342 Elm Street. Since the shopping cart was overturned beside the Chevette, and was blocking the lane, the Chevette would have been unable to park around it. The owner of the Chevette said he had parked in front of the Mazda at 10:30 a.m. Therefore, the incident must have occurred after 10:30 a.m. since the call was received by the police at 10:52 a.m.

The most likely explanation for the damage is that the shopping cart had been left on the street, and the wind then pushed it into Ms. Elogar's car. The impact of this then slowed the shopping cart, and perhaps set it off balance, so that it fell over into the street, beside the Chevette. As there were a lot of people on the sidewalk, it is very likely that someone would have seen the incident, and could verify this theory.

CHAPTER SUMMARY

There is no magical formula that will guarantee success in the police constable selection process. The hiring process is very competitive across the country and could take anywhere from a few weeks to a year or more to complete. In that time, the candidate is put through some gruelling tests and interviews. This chapter has examined the various dimensions of the recruitment of police officers in Canada at the national, provincial, and municipal levels. Essential competencies and developmental competencies have been identified in policing as fundamental to be successful in the community. Some police services also look for various preferred competencies, such as additional languages and higher education. Physical fitness is a component of every police test in Canada.

LO¹ List and discuss the minimum requirements to become a police constable in Ontario.

In Ontario, the Ministry of Community Safety and Correctional Services has developed and implemented the following minimum requirements as outlined in the *Police Services Act*. Applicants for the position of police constable must meet be a Canadian citizen or permanent resident of Canada; be at least 18 years of age; be physically and mentally able to perform the duties of the position; be of good moral character and habits, meaning being an individual other people would look upon as being trustworthy and having integrity; and have successfully completed at least four years of secondary school education or equivalent. Additional requirements include possessing a valid Class G driver's licence with no more than six demerit points; possessing a standard first aid certificate and CPR certificate (Basic Rescuer Level C); holding a current OACP Certificate of Results; not having a criminal conviction for which a pardon has not been granted; and having vision and hearing within acceptable standards.

LO² Define essential competencies and development competencies.

Essential competencies are the knowledge, skills, and abilities a candidate must exhibit before becoming a police officer. Developmental competencies are specific skills and abilities that can be acquired through training and are preferred by some police services.

LO³ Explain the police recruitment and selection process in Ontario.

The steps in the application (hiring) process are in place to provide candidates the opportunity to demonstrate that they meet and/or exceed the required and preferred (developmental) competencies to become a police officer. The purpose of the hiring process is to provide police services with a tool not only to test candidates for their suitability for police work but also to screen out inappropriate candidates. The Constable Selection System has been developed as a standardized selection system for police services to use in selecting police recruits in Ontario. The following is an example of the hiring stages candidates may go through when they meet the minimum requirements and apply to a police service in Ontario: pre-interview assessment; application and résumé submission; pre-interview paperwork (including the Pre-Background Questionnaire); local focus interview; essential competencies interview; psychological testing; background investigation; and final selection.

LO⁴ Briefly describe commonalities in the police recruitment process across Canada.

The minimum requirements to be a police officer (excluding RCMP officers) in every province have been established and outlined in provincial legislation, normally in each province's police act. Although each province is sanctioned to establish specific parameters for the minimum requirements of police officers, similarities exist among the provinces. The similar minimum requirements to be a police officer in most provinces across Canada include that the candidate is a Canadian citizen or permanent resident of Canada; is at least 18 or 19 years of age; is physically and mentally able to perform the duties of the position; is of good moral character and habits; has successfully completed a Grade 12 diploma or equivalent (certain provinces require a postsecondary education or specific police training at an approved postsecondary institution); has a valid driver's licence with a good driving record; has no unpardoned criminal convictions and no criminal charges pending (certain provinces are specific in the requirement that the candidate must not have any criminal convictions); has no history of improper conduct, poor employment, or a military, educational, or driving record that would affect his or her suitability for policing duties; has a working knowledge of English; and has a functional knowledge of French (Quebec only). The selection process for police officers is similar across the country because police officers generally perform the same policing duties in every community. Therefore, most recruitment selection processes follow these steps: application package (résumé, police application, etc.); aptitude tests (written examinations); physical fitness testing (police specific); interview(s) (local focus, intake, behavioural, descriptive, etc.); psychological evaluation and medical examination; polygraph interview/examination; background investigation; and final review committee (selection panel, final approval, job offer).

The Police Role and Discretion

LEARNING OUTCOMES

After reading this chapter, you will be able to:

LO1 Discuss the historical role of police.

LO2 Define the role of police in modern society.

LO3 Explain the legislative authority for the duties of a police officer.

LO4 Define police discretion.

> *The people are the police and the police are the people.*
>
> —*Sir Robert Peel*

The role of the police in Canada is significantly different from what you might see on TV and on the big screen. The thrilling car chases, breathtaking actors, gripping suspense, spine-tingling moments, awe-inspiring speeches from supervisors, and glorious shootouts are few and far between. The fact of the matter is that police work in Canada is about 95 percent repetitive and mundane, with about 5 percent adrenaline-pumping excitement from time to time. This is the reality of policing in Canada, and for the most part police officers are okay with this. The goal for every police officer in Canada is to go home safe at the end of every shift; that doesn't always happen. You should be aware that the job has its inherent dangers, as shown in Boxes 3.1 and 3.2. A police officer is truly a hero day-in and day-out. When most people are running away from their fears, police officers are expected to turn and face them. When there is a dangerous or emergency situation, police officers are the first ones to assist. And when someone is in dire need of help and 911 is called, police officers respond no matter who the person or what the situation is. Police officers are called upon to deal with situations and people that most of us turn a blind eye to or don't want to believe exist. As shown in Figure 3.1, four RCMP officers faced a monster and paid the ultimate price.

LO¹ THE POLICE ROLE IN CANADA

Society's expectation of the police is that they will protect the public from harm and uphold the laws and Constitution of Canada in an unbiased manner by adhering to the *Canadian Charter of Rights and Freedoms*. Police officers have immense power and authority in society, and with this power comes even greater responsibility. Police have the legislated authority to arrest persons, to search, and to seize property, and they may use reasonable force in the execution of their duties. The expectations and demands put on the police today by the public are consistent with those Sir Robert Peel established in the mid-1800s. As discussed in Chapter 1, Peel introduced the world's first police force, the London Metropolitan Police Force, and drafted nine principles of policing, which continue to be implemented in police services all over the world. Peel's nine principles of policing are seen as guiding

BOX 3.1

YORK POLICE OFFICER DIES AFTER BEING DRAGGED 300 METRES BY VAN

In the last dramatic moments before York Regional Police Const. Garrett Styles died, his colleagues heard him calling for help over the police radio while pinned beneath a minivan.

Styles, who had been dragged 300 metres following a traffic stop east of Newmarket just before 5 a.m. Tuesday, was able to talk for several minutes with dispatchers until ambulance and fire arrived.

"I've got a car on top of me," he said. "Help. Help me." The dispatcher told him to hold on: "We've got help on the way, just sit tight."

Styles' breathing grew more difficult as the dispatcher kept the frantic officer in radio contact.

Another police officer joined in: "Garrett, keep talking to us," he told Styles. The dispatcher tried to assess the situation and the pain became almost too much for Styles to talk.

"I've got a van on my waist, I don't know . . . it hurts. And I've got some people inside the van. I don't know how they're doing." Styles' voice grew still just as emergency vehicles got to him.

Source: Reprinted from C. Rush, H. Stancu, & L. Casey. (2011, June 28), "York police officer dies after being dragged 300 metres by van," *Toronto Star*. Retrieved from http://www.thestar.com/news/crime/article/1015945--york-police-officer-dies-after-being-dragged-300-metres-by-van. Reprinted with permission - Torstar Syndication Services.

COBOURG POLICE SERVICE HERO IN LIFE, NOT DEATH

On May 15th, 2004 at approximately 03:00 hours, Constable Chris Garrett of the Cobourg Police Service responded to a call involving the alleged robbery of an 18-year-old Cobourg resident. Constable Garrett was unaware that in fact there was no robbery and he was being lured into a planned ambush.

When Constable Garrett arrived he began taking the details of the alleged robbery and radioed his colleagues a description of a suspect. This left Constable Garrett alone with the supposed victim while the other officers searched for a suspect. While trying to help this apparent victim, Constable Garrett was suddenly attacked with a knife and suffered a mortal wound to his throat. Although dying, Constable Garrett somehow managed to draw his firearm and pursue his attacker, firing off his entire clip of 17 bullets. Constable Garrett was able to wound his murderer with his last shot before he succumbed to his injury.

Constable Garrett's murderer, Troy Davey, was arrested at the Cobourg Hospital when he attended as a result of the gun shot injury.

It was later learned through the investigation that Davey's actions that night were part of a larger, detailed scheme. After killing the police officer, he planned to steal a car and kill two attendants at a local gas station, then go to the Cobourg Police Station and set off two home-made anti-personnel explosive devices. He also planned to shoot police officers and civilian employees at the police station using a shot gun in his possession and the firearm stolen from the officer he had initially murdered.

Constable Garrett's heroic actions while he was mortally wounded prevented a greater tragedy by halting this heinous chain of events.

Source: Reprinted from Cobourg Police Service. (2012). "The CPS Remembers our Hero...". Retrieved from http://www.cobourgpolice.com/hero.php. Reproduced with permission.

principles regarding the role the police have or should have in society.

The role of policing in Canada started in 1873 when Sir John A. Macdonald formed the North-West Mounted Police (NWMP) to aid in settling the Northwest Territory and prevent conflicts with the Native tribes (see Figure 3.4). Macdonald's intent was to abolish the NWMP once peaceful settlement was

FIGURE 3.2
Constable Garrett Styles.

Fred Lum/The Globe and Mail/The Canadian Press

The Canadian Press/Jeff McIntosh

FIGURE 3.1
The Mayerthorpe four were unfortunate and came face-to-face with a monster. The four RCMP officers paid the ultimate price associated with policing—their lives.

HEROES IN LIFE NOT DEATH

Courtesy of the Ontario Police Memorial Foundation

FIGURE 3.3
Heroes in Life Not Death.

Library and Archives Canada / C-042755

Dawson Y.T.1898
Back Row L to R Corpl. --------? Staff Sergeant G. Bates,
Corpl. Sidney Marshall, Staff Sergeant Stillman, F.? Corpl.
Bowdridge, W.J.
Sitting: Sergeant Major R.T.Tucker,

FIGURE 3.4
Personnel of the North-West Mounted Police.

achieved, but this did not happen. Instead, the NWMP would become Canada's national police force, known today as the RCMP.

The first police constables were called night watchmen and patrolled specific areas on foot. They were assigned to an area (or zone) and took on both a preventative and a reactive role in the community. The constables took ownership of their assigned area and focused on getting to know the community. With the evolution of the police role in modern society, officers were now able to cover a larger patrol area and became distant and removed from the communities:

> During the "Professional Era of Policing," three technological innovations radically altered the delivery of policing services, often in response to the growth of urban centres and communities: (1) the expansion of the telephone system into households, (2) the emergence of police patrol cars, and (3) the introduction of the two-way radio. All three innovations precipitated a fundamental change in how police services were delivered. Police officers became reactive, relying upon complaints telephoned in by community residents. Officers were dispatched to the scene of a crime by two-way radio in patrol cars. Motorized

police work: Any duty that is conducted by sworn members of a police service that they are legally mandated to perform and that will assist in the regulation and control of society and the maintenance of public order.

patrol began to emerge as the primary method of police patrol (Whitelaw & Parent, 2010, p. 11).

In policing today it is not uncommon for a police officer to be assigned a community area to patrol that has a geographical mass larger than some entire city boundaries. In some patrol areas in Canada, an officer's backup could be hours or even days away. This has had an enormous impact on the relationship between the police and the community and has created a disconnect between police officers and the communities they serve.

LO² THE ROLE OF THE POLICE TODAY

The role of the police in society today has changed both positively and negatively in many ways. For the most part, the role of a police officer is the same across Canada, with a similar philosophy on the definition of police work and the role of police in society. In fact, one could argue that this role is similar not only across Canada but all over the world, with a few exceptions. **Police work** is defined as any duty conducted by members of a police service that they are legally mandated to perform and that will assist in the regulation and control of society and the maintenance of public order (Figure 3.5). The legislative framework of policing is found in the *Criminal Code of Canada*; the *Canadian Charter of Rights and Freedoms*; the *Constitution Act, 1867*; other federal statutes (such as the *Youth Criminal Justice Act*); provincial and municipal legislation; and various police services acts across the country, such as the *RCMP Act* and the *Police Services Act* of Ontario.

According to section 4(2) of the *Police Services Act* of Ontario, there are five core functions of police work that are the minimum standards for adequate and effective delivery of policing: "crime prevention;

Toronto Star / GetStock.com

FIGURE 3.5
Police officers at work.

law enforcement; assistance to victims of crime; public order maintenance; and emergency response" (1990, s. 4(2)). Ontario Regulation 3/99 further regulates the level of services that every police service in Ontario must provide to be considered adequate and effective.

LO³ DUTIES OF A POLICE OFFICER

For the purpose of this book, we will explore the legislation that dictates the police role in Ontario and nationally for the RCMP. The *Police Services Act* of Ontario (PSA) is a provincial statute that regulates and guides all police services and police officers in Ontario. Section 42(1) of the PSA sets out the duties of a police officer, including

   (a) preserving the peace;
   (b) preventing crimes and other offences and providing assistance and encouragement to other persons in their prevention;
   (c) assisting victims of crime;
   (d) apprehending criminals and other offenders and others who may lawfully be taken into custody;
   (e) laying charges and participating in prosecutions;
   (f) executing warrants that are to be executed by police officers and performing related duties;

   (g) performing the lawful duties that the Chief of Police assigns;
   (h) in the case of a municipal police force and in the case of an agreement under section 10 (agreement for provisions of police services by O.P.P.), enforcing municipal by-laws;
   (i) completing the prescribed training. (PSA, 990, s. 42(1))

Section 2 of the PSA gives police officers the power and authority to act as such throughout Ontario. For example, if you are sworn in as a police officer in Ottawa, you have the authority to act as such in Toronto, Windsor, or anywhere else in the province. Basically, you are sworn in as a police officer for the province of Ontario and have authority to exercise those powers throughout Ontario. (See Box 3.3 for the oath or affirmation of office

Police Services Act of Ontario (PSA): A provincial statute that regulates and guides all police services and police officers in Ontario.

oath or affirmation of office: A statement that police officers, special constables, or First Nations constables promise to uphold the Constitution of Canada and, to the best of their ability, complete their duties faithfully, impartially, and according to law.

oath or affirmation of secrecy: A statement that police officers, auxiliary members of a police force, special constables, or First Nations constables promise to not disclose any information they have gained while performing the lawful duties of their position unless authorized or required by law.

BOX 3.3

OATH OR AFFIRMATION OF OFFICE

The **oath or affirmation of office** to be taken by a police officer, special constable or First Nations Constable shall be in one of the following forms set out in the English or French version of this section:

> I solemnly swear (affirm) that I will be loyal to Her Majesty the Queen and to Canada, and that I will uphold the Constitution of Canada and that I will, to the best of my ability, preserve the peace, prevent offences and discharge my other duties as (*insert name of office*) faithfully, impartially and according to law.
>   So help me God. (*Omit this line in an affirmation.*)
> or
> I solemnly swear (affirm) that I will be loyal to Canada, and that I will uphold the Constitution of Canada and that I will, to the best of my ability, preserve the peace, prevent offences and discharge my other duties as (*insert name of office*) faithfully, impartially and according to law.
>   So help me God. (*Omit this line in an affirmation.*)

The **oath or affirmation of secrecy** to be taken by a police officer, auxiliary member of a police force, special constable or First Nations Constable shall be in the following form set out in the English or French version of this section:

> I solemnly swear (affirm) that I will not disclose any information obtained by me in the course of my duties as (*insert name of office*), except as I may be authorized or required by law.
>   So help me God. (*Omit this line in an affirmation.*)

Source: Reprinted from the *Police Services Act*, 1990, O. Regulation 268/10, ss. 2 & 4.

FIGURE 3.6
Swearing in of new police recruits.

police officers must take in Ontario. Figure 3.6 shows new recruits taking the oath at a swearing-in ceremony.)

Section 44(1) of the PSA states that municipal police officers shall be placed on a **probationary period**

probationary period: When a newly hired police constable is monitored on his or her job performance and suitability for the position of police officer for one year from the date of appointment or on the date he or she completes training at the Ontario Police College.

Ontario Police College (OPC): A police training facility in Aylmer, Ontario, operated by the Ontario government. OPC offers training and education for police officers and police services in Ontario. The *Police Services Act* mandates that all police officers in Ontario must complete their initial basic constable training at OPC.

Chief of Police: Also known as the chief constable, the person responsible and accountable for the day-to-day operations of the police service. The Chief of Police is accountable to the police services board, which, in turn, represents the members of the community they serve.

RCMP Act: A federal statute that regulates and governs the RCMP and their police officers.

of one year from the date they are appointed or on the date they complete training at the **Ontario Police College** (pictured in Figure 3.7), whichever is the later of the two. The PSA also mandates that police officers can be on a probationary period only once during their career. Hence, if a person was hired as a police officer by the Toronto Police Service and after the probationary period applies for a position with the Barrie Police Service, that individual will have already completed the mandatory probationary period regulated by the PSA and cannot be placed on probation with the Barrie Police Service.

The role of the **Chief of Police** is outlined in section 41(1) of the PSA. The chief oversees the administration and operation of the police service and acts as the liaison with the police services board to establish objectives, priorities,

FIGURE 3.7
All police recruits in Ontario must attend the Ontario Police College in Aylmer, Ontario.

and policies. In addition, he or she ensures that all members of the police service carry out their duties in accordance with the PSA and provide community-oriented policing. The Chief of Police is responsible for the conduct of the officers and other members of the police service.

The RCMP is governed by the federal ***RCMP Act*** (1985). Part I of the *RCMP Act* states that "there shall continue to be a police force for Canada, which shall consist of officers and other members and be known as the Royal Canadian Mounted Police and that the Force may be employed in such places within or outside Canada as the Governor in Council prescribes" (*RCMP Act*, 1985, ss. 3–4). Section 18 of the act regulates the prescribed duties of a police officer:

> It is the duty of members who are peace officers, subject to the orders of the Commissioner,
>
> (a) to perform all duties that are assigned to peace officers in relation to the preservation of the peace, the prevention of crime and of offences against the laws of Canada and the laws in force in any province in which they may be employed, and the apprehension of criminals and offenders and others who may be lawfully taken into custody;
>
> (b) to execute all warrants, and perform all duties and services in relation thereto, that may, under this Act or the laws of Canada or the laws in force in any province, be lawfully executed and performed by peace officers;
>
> (c) to perform all duties that may be lawfully performed by peace officers in relation to the escort and conveyance of convicts and other persons in custody to or from any courts, places of punishment or confinement, asylums or other places; and
>
> (d) to perform such other duties and functions as are prescribed by the Governor in Council or the Commissioner (*RCMP Act*, 1985, s. 18).

Every police officer in the RCMP has the power and authority to execute those duties as prescribed anywhere in Canada. The provisions in the Royal Canadian Mounted Police Regulations, 1988, further state the following duties:

17. (1) In addition to the duties prescribed by the Act, it is the duty of members who are peace officers to

(a) enforce all Acts of Parliament and regulations made thereunder, and render such assistance to departments of the Government of Canada as the Minister may direct;

(b) maintain law and order in the Yukon Territory, the Northwest Territories and national parks and such other areas as the Minister may designate;

(c) maintain law and order in those provinces and municipalities with which the Minister has entered into an arrangement under section 20 of the Act and carry out such other duties as may be specified in those arrangements;

(d) guard and protect such buildings, installations, dock yards and other property of Her Majesty in right of Canada as the Minister may designate.

(e) protect, within or outside Canada, whether or not there is an imminent threat to their security,
    (i) the Governor General,
    (ii) the Prime Minister of Canada,
    (iii) judges of the Supreme Court of Canada,
    (iv) ministers of the Crown in right of Canada, and
    (v) any other person who may be designated by the Minister for the period designated by the Minister, those designations to be based on an actual or apprehended threat to the security of the person;

(f) protect, within Canada, whether or not there is an imminent threat to their security,
    (i) any person who qualifies under the definition "internationally protected person" in section 2 of the *Criminal Code*, and
    (ii) any other person who may be designated by the Minister for the period designated by the Minister, those designations

to be based on an actual or apprehended threat to the security of the person; and

(g) ensure, in accordance with any memorandum of understanding between the Commissioner and the Clerk of the Privy Council, the security for the proper functioning of
    (i) any meeting of the first ministers of the provinces and the Prime Minister of Canada that is convened by the Prime Minister of Canada, or
    (ii) any meeting of Cabinet that is not held on Parliament Hill.

(2) The duties described in paragraphs (1) (e) and (f) shall be carried out in accordance with the Force's assessment of the threat to the security of the person (*Royal Canadian Mounted Police Regulations*, 1988, s. 17).

In every province in Canada except for Ontario and Quebec, the RCMP officer's role is very similar to that of any other police officer. The RCMP provides frontline policing services at both the municipal and provincial level. In Ontario and Quebec, the RCMP is responsible only for policing duties that are of a federal nature—for example, security at international airports, the enforcement of illegal drugs, and investigation of terrorism. The RCMP is also mandated to conduct missions abroad. Internationally, the RCMP is well recognized for managing peacekeeping missions (Box 3.4), providing security at Canadian consulates around the world, and assisting in the training of police officers in troubled countries.

Now that we have discussed the legislative duties of a police officer, let's explore the changing role of the police in contemporary society. Changes in society bring about changes in policing and how services are delivered. As police services have moved toward a more community-based style of policing, the traditional mould of a hierarchical structure and paramilitary model has broken down (Griffiths, 2008).

The traditional method of policing is described as the *professional model* of police work and is based on the three Rs: random patrol, rapid response, and reactive investigation (Griffiths, 2008). In the professional model of policing, clearance rates of calls for service and statistics for charges or incidents are used to determine the effectiveness of not only the individual police officer but also the services provided to the public by the police.

BOX 3.4

RCMP INTERNATIONAL POLICE PEACE OPERATIONS PROGRAM

Canada has committed to the presence of qualified and trained police officers to assist in conflicts and emergency situations abroad (Figure 3.8). Most RCMP international operations are one year in duration and can be extended as required. Below is a list of RCMP police peace operations abroad in 2011.

1. Afghanistan: NATO Training Mission (NTM-A)

2. Afghanistan: European Union Police Mission (EUPOL)

3. Afghanistan: Ministry of the Interior

4. Afghanistan: Embassy of Canada in Kabul

5. Côte d'Ivoire: United Nations Operation in Côte d'Ivoire (UNOCI)

6. Democratic Republic of Congo: United Nations Stabilization Mission in the Democratic Republic of the Congo (MONUSCO)

7. Guatemala: Police Reform Commission

8. Haiti: United Nations Stabilization Mission in Haiti (MINUSTAH)

9. Netherlands (The Hague): Special Tribunal for Lebanon (STL)

10. Republic of South Sudan: United Nations Mission in South Sudan (UNMISS)

11. Sudan: United Nations African Mission in Darfur (UNAMID)

12. Sudan: United Nations Development Programme (UNDP) Rule of Law

13. West Bank: European Union Police Co-ordinating Office for Palestinian Police Support (EUPOL COPPS)

14. Canada's Permanent Mission to the United Nations in New York

Source: Retrieved from http://www.rcmp-grc.gc.ca/po-mp/missions-curr-cour-eng.htm. © 2012 HER MAJESTY THE QUEEN IN RIGHT OF CANADA as represented by the Royal Canadian Mounted Police (RCMP). Reproduced with the permission of the RCMP.

Source: **Canadian Forces Combat Camera, AR2010-0144-05. URL:** http://www.combatcamera.forces.gc.ca /netpub/server.np?find&catalog=photos&template=detail_eng.np&field=itemid&op=matches&value=219 14&site=combatcamera, Department of National Defence, 2010. Reproduced with the permission of the Minister of Public Works and Government Services Canada, 2012.

FIGURE 3.8
RCMP performing international police peace operations.

Carlos Osorio / GetStock.com

FIGURE 3.9
Community policing requires police officers to interact with the public.

Recently, the philosophy of **community policing** has increasingly been adopted (Figure 3.9). Community policing is policing which emphasizes crime prevention and problem solving. The principles of community policing are based on the three Ps: prevention, problem solving, and partnership and shared accountability with the community (Griffiths, 2008). **Problem-oriented policing** is a principal of

FIGURE 3.10
The duties of a police officer change from day to day.

community policing which addresses community problems at the root cause and develops sustainable solutions.

The role of today's police officer has become extensive, and the police are increasingly becoming generalists (see Figure 3.10). Police officers are required to possess a broad spectrum of knowledge and experience to enable them to perform the duties that are expected by the public, which go well beyond those set out in the PSA or the *RCMP Act*. A police officer is expected not only to enforce the law but to act as a mediator, social worker, and problem solver, while developing cooperative relationships in the community and meeting the challenges of policing a multicultural society. To meet these needs, police are moving away from a traditional reactive form of policing toward a proactive problem-solving model within the community. However, not all incidents involving the police or calls for service can be handled in a proactive manner. Some situations call for a reactive response from the police; therefore, the most effective role for the police in the community strikes a balance between the more traditional, professional model and the community-based policing model. Table 3.1 compares various models of policing. Included in this comparison is zero-tolerance policing, which is when a police service directs officers to have a zero tolerance approach to certain offences committed by the public. This means that an officer must charge everyone who commits the identified offence. For example, if a police service is having a problem with vehicles speeding in a certain area, such as a school zone, they will initiate a traffic enforcement blitz so that everyone who is observed speeding is charged with no exceptions or warnings.

LO⁴ POLICE DISCRETION

Many debates have taken place over the years regarding discretion and discretionary powers in policing. Should an officer be expected to follow the letter of every law and charge people appropriately? Is this a reasonable expectation? This grey area is where the concept of police discretion comes into play. **Discretion** is an individual's exercise of free will to make choices or judgments that are responsible decisions within the legal boundaries of the law. **Police discretion** is the judgment officers use both on the streets and within the administration of a police service, whether it's letting someone go with a warning, or arresting someone for a minor offence because that person may be a danger to him- or herself or others. Police officers are not the only members of the justice system with discretionary powers. Crown attorneys have discretion to decide to proceed with a charge and whether witnesses and evidence should be presented at a trial. Judges also possess discretionary power over sentencing of a convicted person and issuing of warrants, as do justices of the peace.

Decision making by police officers is based on individual situations and is governed by common law, federal and provincial statues, and case law. Police have the duty to enforce the law under common law but possess the authority to exercise discretion in any particular case. However, each province in Canada has its own statutes that define the obligations of police officers and their duties to enforce the law. Many influential factors may affect an officer's use of discretion on the job, but the main aspects are as follows:

- *Type of crime.*
  Frontline police officers possess the most discretion, but as the level of seriousness of the crime increases, the level of discretion decreases. An officer is more likely to use his or her discretion with a traffic violation than in an assault investigation.

community policing: A philosophy that emphasizes crime prevention and problem-solving techniques rather than a more traditional reactive approach to policing within a community.

problem-oriented policing: A principle of community policing that involves solving specific problems of crime and disorder at their root cause, with the intention of identifying and modifying the particular factors giving rise to each problem within the community.

discretion: An individual's exercise of free will to make choices or judgments that are responsible decisions within the legal boundaries of the law.

police discretion: The judgment police officers use both on the streets and within the administration of a police service.

TABLE 3.1
Social Interactions and Structural Components of Various Forms of Policing

Social Interaction or Structural Dimension	Traditional Policing	Community Policing	Problem-Oriented Policing	Zero-Tolerance Policing
Focus of policing	Law enforcement	Community building through crime prevention	Law, order, and fear problems	Order problems
Forms of intervention	Reactive, based on criminal law	Proactive, on criminal, civil, and administrative law	Mixed, on criminal, civil, and administrative law	Proactive, uses criminal, civil, and administrative law
Range of police activity	Narrow, crime focused	Broad crime, order, fear, and quality-of-life focused	Narrow to broad—problem focused	Narrow, location and behaviour focused
Level of discretion at line level	High and unaccountable	High and accountable to the community and local commanders	High and primarily accountable to the police administration	Low, but primarily accountable to the police administration
Focus of police culture	Inward, rejecting community	Outward, building partnerships	Mixed depending on problem, but analysis focused	Inward focused on attacking the target problem
Locus of decision making	Police directed, minimizes the involvement of others	Community-police coproduction, joint responsibility and assessment	Varied, police identify problems but with community involvement/action	Police directed, some linkage to other agencies where necessary
Communication flow	Downward from police to community	Horizontal between police and community	Horizontal between police and community	Downward from police to community
Range of community involvement	Low and passive	High and active	Mixed depending on problem set	Low and passive
Linkage with other agencies	Poor and intermittent	Participative and integrative in the overarching process	Participative and integrative depending on the problem set	Moderate and intermittent
Type of organization and command focus	Centralized command and control	Decentralized with community linkage	Decentralized with local command accountability to central administration	Centralized or decentralized but internal focus
Implications for organizational change/ development	Few, static organization fending off the environment	Many, dynamic organizations focused on the environment and environmental interactions	Varied, focused on problem resolution but with import for organization intelligence and structure	Few, limited interventions focused on target problems, using many traditional methods
Measurement of success	Arrest and crime rates, particularly serious Part 1 crimes	Varied, crime, calls for service, fear reduction, use of public places, community linkages and contacts, safer neighbourhoods	Varied, problems solved, minimized, displaced	Arrests, field stops, activity, location-specific reductions in targeted activity

Source: Reprinted from J. R. Greene. (2000). "Community Policing in America: Changing the Nature, Structure, and Function of the Police," *Criminal Justice, vol. 3: Policies, Processes, and Decisions of the Criminal Justice System*, p. 311. Retrieved from https://www.ncjrs.gov/criminal_justice2000/vol_3/03g.pdf

- *The suspect's attitude.* Police officers are expected to be impartial and unbiased toward the public, but they are only human.
- *Departmental policies.* Often police services will implement departmental policies that dictate an officer's course of action in a certain situation, thereby removing the officer's discretionary power. For example, with incidents of domestic assault, most police services have implemented a zero-tolerance policy in that the suspect *must* be arrested.

Police officers do not have **unfettered discretion** when dealing with crime. The police are obviously bound by the laws of Canada, just like any other person in our society. *R. v. Beaudry* is a good example of this principle. Beaudry was a police officer who was charged with obstructing justice for deliberately failing to gather evidence required to lay criminal charges against another police officer for impaired operation of a motor vehicle. At the trial, Beaudry stated that his decision was a proper exercise of police discretion. However, Beaudry was convicted, as the trial judge stated that this was not an incident of discretionary authority but a case of preferential treatment of another officer. The decision was upheld in the court of appeal based on the grounds that the use of discretion must be justified subjectively and in this case it was not.

Police officers are bound by the direction of the *Criminal Code of Canada*. Take, for instance, sections 495(1) and (2), where an arrest without a warrant by a peace officer is made. Section 495(1) specifically states that a peace officer may arrest without warrant and then goes on to list the conditions that must exist prior to arrest. Section 495(2) states the limitations of section 1, dictating that a peace officer shall not arrest a person without warrant for certain offences and in certain cases. The wording in this section is very specific, and police officers have no discretion in interpreting it. The word *may* means that you as a police officer have the discretion to arrest without warrant if the situation calls for it, and the words *shall not* are very specific in that you cannot arrest without warrant in the listed circumstances (Greenspan, Rosenberg, & Henein, 2012). With discretion comes scrutiny of your decisions as a police officer. You must be able to justify and articulate why and how you used your discretionary power in every situation and with every person. The public could easily misinterpret your actions and the actions of the police as racial profiling or some other discriminatory action based on your discretionary decision, and the issue may even progress into a human rights complaint. Racial profiling is when an officer uses a profile strictly based on race as a reasonable suspicion to stop a vehicle. The idea of racial profiling began as a tool for law enforcement officers in the United States to stop drug smuggling across the U.S. border, and later expanded to assist in the flow of drugs up the interstate of the southern states (Pollock, 2012). The question is, would you as a police officer have stopped the vehicle for the infraction regardless of the race of the persons inside the vehicle?

unfettered discretion: Unrestricted discretion. An unfettered discretion is an opportunity for corruption, discrimination, and an intrusive style of policing.

CHAPTER SUMMARY

This chapter has been an introduction to police discretion and the role police officers have in our society. The role of police officers in society has changed over time and will continue to change with our increasingly shifting, multicultural society. With the issue of the emerging fiscal crisis, greater expectation of police accountability, increasing social disorder, and globalization, it is inevitable that the role of a police officer will continue to evolve with society's challenges.

LO¹ Discuss the historical role of police.

Society's expectation of the police is that they will protect the public from harm's way and uphold the laws and Constitution of Canada in an unbiased manner by adhering to the *Canadian Charter of Rights and Freedoms*. Police officers have immense power and authority in society, and with this power comes even greater responsibility. Police have the legislated authority to arrest persons, to search, and to seize property, and they may use reasonable force in the execution of their duties. The expectations and demands put on the police today by the public are consistent with those Sir Robert Peel formulated in the mid-1800s when he introduced the world's first police force, the London Metropolitan Police. Peel also introduced his nine principles of policing—guiding principles as to what role the police have or should have in society—which continue to be implemented in police services all over the world.

LO² Define the role of police in modern society.

The role of the police in society has changed both positively and negatively in many ways. For the most part, the role of a police officer is the same across Canada, with a similar philosophy on the definition of police work and the role of police in society existing throughout the country. Police work is defined as any duty that is conducted by a sworn member of a police service that the police are legally mandated to perform and will assist in the regulation and control of society and the maintenance of public order.

LO³ Explain the legislative authority for the duties of a police officer.

The *Police Services Act* of Ontario (PSA) is a provincial statute that regulates and guides all police services and police officers in the province. Section 42(1) of the PSA sets out the duties of a police officer in Ontario. Section 2 gives police officers the power and authority to act as such throughout Ontario.

LO⁴ Define police discretion.

The *RCMP Act* is a federal statute that regulates and governs the RCMP and their police officers. Part I, sections 3 and 4 state that "there shall continue to be a police force for Canada, which shall consist of officers and other members and be known as the Royal Canadian Mounted Police and that the Force may be employed in such places within or outside Canada as the Governor in Council prescribes" (*RCMP Act*, 1985, ss. 3–4). Section 18 of the *RCMP Act* regulates the prescribed duties of a police officer. Every police officer in the RCMP has the power and authority to execute those duties as prescribed anywhere in Canada.

PART 2

Skills Required for Providing Police Service Excellence

This part of the text includes a review of communication skills required to be successful in the policing profession; customer service and police service excellence practices; and the culture, personality, and stress related to the policing profession.

CHAPTER 4:   Communication Skills

CHAPTER 5:   Customer Service

CHAPTER 6:   Police Culture, Personality, and Stress

4

Communication Skills

LEARNING OUTCOMES

After reading this chapter, you will be able to:

LO1 Describe the basic communication skills required for policing.

LO2 Define interpersonal and impersonal communication.

LO3 Discuss the various types of communication methodology used in policing.

LO4 Explain the various techniques in conflict management.

LO5 Describe the use of tactical communications in policing.

I never learned anything while I was talking.

—Larry King

We were given two ears but only one mouth, because listening is twice as hard as talking.

—Unknown Author

LO¹ BASIC COMMUNICATION SKILLS

As a police constable in Canada, you will be trained by some of the best instructors in the world on such elements of policing as firearms, police vehicle operations, defensive tactics, and criminal and provincial statutes, to mention a few, but the most valuable asset for your safety and security on the streets is your communication skills. A police officer will rely on his or her communication skills more often than any other policing tool including use of force options available. Excellent communication skills are the key to success in policing everywhere in the world—whether you're policing in Hong Kong or Australia, you are dealing with people on a daily basis and must be able to communicate effectively. Police officers constantly have to deal with situations involving people who are angry, upset, frustrated, hyper, passive, etc., and in order to be effective in their position they need to successfully communicate with people from various backgrounds, cultures, races, and religions in a diplomatic manner.

New police recruits are trained in *tactical communication skills*. The focus of this training is on enhancing the recruit's communication skills and redirecting these skills toward the issues and expectations in policing. Building on this foundation, the recruit will enhance his or her problem-solving skills by using simulated scenarios to learn skills in addressing grief and loss, hostage taking, crisis response, and conflict management. It is expected that new police recruits have already developed good communication skills by way of a higher education and/or extensive life experience, and these skills are examined and verified in the constable selection process outlined in Chapter 2. In order for applicants to be successful in the hiring process, they must be able to show that they possess excellent communication skills and have demonstrated this in the past and throughout the entire hiring process.

Communication can take many forms. In this chapter we will briefly introduce the basic concepts of communication between humans and explore the specific communication techniques and avenues used in policing.

There are many definitions for communication, but in the broadest sense, **communication** is a means of sending or receiving information in some sort of medium. "The exchanging of information by speaking or writing are presumed as the most employed and most effective way of communicating but in fact humans only use speech about 30% of their time and written communication only about 9% of their time. So which form of communication is utilized the most by humans? Listening is used about 45% of a person's time communicating" (Beebe, Beebe, Redmond, & Geerinck, 2011, p. 91; see Figure 4.1).

Communication in policing is broken down into verbal and nonverbal communication. A trained police officer will rely on his/her interpretation of these forms of communication in every investigation. Whether you are investigating the theft of a bicycle or a homicide, a police officer will rely on his/her training and expertise in "reading" people to decipher what they are telling you or not telling you. This skill is often referred to as being a "human lie detector," and some police officers are better at it than others. **Verbal communication** is essentially what is being said and the words that are being used to communicate the message. **Nonverbal communication** is the process of sending and receiving wordless messages by way of gestures, body language, touch, facial expression, and eye contact. These messages are just as vital or in some cases even more important than the words that are being

communication: A means of sending or receiving information in some sort of medium.

verbal communication: What is being said and the words that are being used to communicate the message.

nonverbal communication: The process of sending and receiving wordless messages by way of gestures, body language, touch, facial expression, and eye contact.

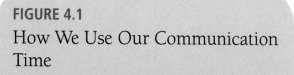

FIGURE 4.1
How We Use Our Communication Time

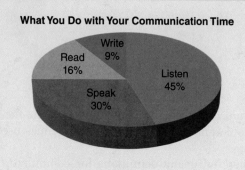

What You Do with Your Communication Time

- Write 9%
- Read 16%
- Speak 30%
- Listen 45%

Data sourced from Beebe, S., Beebe, S., Redmond, M., & Geerinck, T. (2011). *Interpersonal Communication: Relating to Others*, Fifth Canadian Edition. Toronto: Pearson Canada. P. 91. Reprinted with permission by Pearson Canada Inc.

paralanguage: Speech that also contains nonverbal elements such as pitch, tone, volume, rate, and stress.

kinesics: Elements of body language such as posture, stance, gestures, and movements.

haptic communication: A form of nonverbal communication involving the sense of touch.

active listening: Not only hearing the message but also understanding what is being said.

communicated—they are telltale signs or triggers that may tweak your suspicions as a police officer. For instance, a basic technique for determining if a suspect is lying is noting whether they fail to make or keep eye contact with the investigator. Lack of eye contact can be a hint that something is out of sorts with this person or that part of the story or all of it is a lie (it may be hard to believe, but people do lie to the police). However, a police officer cannot rely solely on this method of detection because of certain differences in our society. For example, in some cultures it is forbidden for a female to look directly at or make eye contact with a male who is not her husband. This behaviour could lead to a person being misinterpreted as someone who has something to hide or is lying.

Nonverbal communication is described as paralanguage and kinesics but is also communicated by way of material objects. How a person looks or presents him- or herself speaks volumes to other people. Speech also contains nonverbal elements known as **paralanguage**. This includes elements such as pitch, tone, volume, rate, and stress. **Kinesics** is body language,

including posture, stance, gestures, and movements. Another nonverbal form of communication is **haptic communication**, which is relaying information through touch. Forms of haptic communication that you may use every day include giving a high-five to express your excitement, kissing to express your love, and holding hands to express your relationship or closeness with a person.

The four components of effective communication are

- *Language:* The words and structure used to relay the message. The words you choose and the order you put them in can dramatically affect your message and the interpretation of the message.
- *Paralanguage:* The tone, cadence, volume, and speed used when speaking. Paralanguage includes the nonverbal elements of communication used to enhance the meaning and expression of emotion when relaying a message.
- *Kinesics:* The physical components of communications. Kinesics is the interpretation of body language such as gestures, posture, and facial expressions used when relaying a message. This is one of the most powerful ways that humans can communicate nonverbally. It is difficult for people to hide their emotions when communicating about something they are passionate about, and this is often evident in their body language when relaying the message. Police officers often rely more on this form of communication when interacting with people than on the actual words or language used in communication. Police officers are trained in how to pick up on these cues when speaking with people and after time become self-proclaimed experts in this form of communication. Most interviewing and interrogation courses for police officers build on this concept of "reading" a person's body language as a form of deceit detection.
- *Active listening:* Going beyond just hearing the message. **Active listening** requires that the listener *understand* what he or she hears (see Figure 4.2).

As noted earlier in the chapter, a police officer's primary role is to deal with people, and when doing so we use *human communication*. Human communication is the process of making sense of the world and sharing that sense with others by creating meaning through the use of verbal and nonverbal messages (Beebe et al., 2011). With human communication, we learn about the world and other people through our experiences and share our interpretations via multimedia channels, such as speeches, songs, radio, television, email, Internet, and books, just to name a few. Communication takes place when a message

© ZUMA Press, Inc. / Alamy

FIGURE 4.2

To understand is to listen. Effective communication involves active listening.

is sent and received (Beebe et al., 2011). The components of the human communication process are:

- *Source:* The person who has the idea or message.
- *Receiver:* The person or group to whom the source directs the sound or message.
- *Message:* The verbal and nonverbal elements of the message to which we assign meaning.
- *Channel:* The pathway through which the message travels between the source and receiver.
- *Noise:* Anything that interferes with the message (see Figure 4.3).
- *Encoding:* The translation of ideas, feelings, and thoughts into a code.
- *Decoding:* The interpretation of encoded ideas, feelings, and thoughts.
- *Context:* The physical and psychological environment.
- *Feedback:* The verbal and nonverbal responses to a messages (Beebe et al., 2011).*

Figure 4.4 summarizes the essential elements in the human communication process.

Stephen Coburn/Shutterstock.com

FIGURE 4.3

Communication can be simple if you filter out any interfering noise.

FIGURE 4.4

The Components of the Human Communication Process

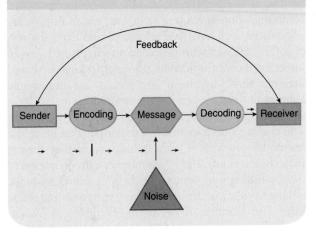

Source: PASSIA, Seminars: Conflict Resolution and Negotiations In Organizations, March – June 2000, http://www.passia.org/seminars/2000/conflict/wanis-6.html.

LO² INTERPERSONAL AND IMPERSONAL COMMUNICATION

There are two forms of human communication: **interpersonal communication** and **impersonal communication**. Interpersonal communication involves mutual influence and respect. This form of communication is most effective in managing relationships. "Interpersonal communication is a distinctive form of communication. Unless you live in isolation, you communicate interpersonally every day. It is impossible not to communicate with others" (Beebe et al., 2011, p. 4). "Interpersonal communication occurs not when you simply interact with someone, but when you treat the other as a unique human being"† (Beebe et al., 2011, p. 3). You would have this type of communication with someone you are close with and care about, such as a family member, intimate partner, or close friend, not with a stranger or an acquaintance. Interpersonal communication is based on respect and is a true dialogue between the two people.

> **interpersonal communication:** A unique style of communication involving mutual influence and respect. This form of communication is most effective in managing relationships.

> **impersonal communication:** An ineffective type of communication that occurs when we treat people as objects, or when we respond to their roles rather than to them as individuals.

---

*From Beebe, S., Beebe, S., Redmond, M., & Geerinck, T. (2011). *Interpersonal Communication: Relating to Others*, Fifth Canadian Edition. Toronto: Pearson Canada. P. 12. Reprinted with permission by Pearson Canada Inc.

†From Beebe, S., Beebe, S., Redmond, M., & Geerinck, T. (2011). *Interpersonal Communication: Relating to Others*, Fifth Canadian Edition. Toronto: Pearson Canada. P. 3-4. Reprinted with permission by Pearson Canada Inc.

Impersonal communication is the communication style that police officers would most likely have with the people they interact with in their daily duty. Impersonal communication occurs when we treat people as objects, or when we respond to their roles rather than to them as unique people (Beebe et al., 2011). Interpersonal communication is relating to others, which in policing is essential, but most police officers and even the rest of society interact with people in an impersonal way. In impersonal communication, nothing personal is shared between those involved. You would use impersonal communication when you communicate with a salesperson or waiter; in policing, an officer would use it in dealing with a member of the public that he or she has no history with or plans to have any further contact with (Beebe et al., 2011). You interact with people every day by listening to your co-workers or fellow students, talking to your teacher, and ordering your morning coffee from Tim Hortons; these are all examples of human communication. In policing, examples of impersonal communication include attending platoon briefings at the start of your shift, communicating with other officers, interacting with your supervisors, ordering your lunch, and communicating with the public in the form of answering calls for service, investigations, or community policing initiatives. Impersonal communication is impossible to avoid in policing due to the nature of the job. Police officers constantly interact with people with whom they have no emotional attachment and respond to them as objects that are part of their jobs rather than treating them as individuals.

In today's technological society, a more common form of communication is **mediated interpersonal communication**. Mediated interpersonal communication is used in the business world and for social interactions, mostly among the younger generations in society. Mediated interpersonal communication is communicating with others through a popular media source, such as instant messaging, texting, email, video exchanges (Skype), cellphones, Facebook, or Twitter.

"Social learning theory suggests that we can learn how to adapt and adjust our behaviour toward others; how we behave is not solely dependent on our genetic makeup. By observing and interacting with others (hence the name social learning), we discover that we can adapt and adjust our behaviour"* (Beebe et al.,

mediated interpersonal communication: Communicating with others through a popular media source, such as instant messaging, texting, email, video exchanges, cellphones, Facebook, or Twitter.

Photodisc/Thinkstock

FIGURE 4.5
Active listening is the key to being a good communicator.

2011, p. 25). One behaviour that is often worth changing is our style of listening.

Active listening was mentioned earlier in this chapter as one of the components of effective communication (see Figure 4.5). Active listening involves more than just hearing the message, but also understanding what we hear. If listening makes up 45 percent of our communication, as shown in Figure 4.1, then it is the most effective way of communicating. This means that we should understand what makes a good listener and how we can improve our listening skills.

"Listening is the process of selecting, attending, understanding, remembering, and responding to sounds and messages"† (Beebe et al., 2011, p. 92). When we listen we hear the words, but a good listener is able to accurately interpret the messages being delivered. In order to do that, the listener has to

- Select: Sort through various sounds that compete for your attention;
- Attending: Focus on a particular sound or message;
- Understand: Assign meaning to messages;
- Remembering: Recalling information that has been communicated;
- Responding: Confirming your understanding of a message (Beebe et al., 2011, p. 95).

"Researchers found that there are a variety of factors that influence your listening style but found

*From Beebe, S., Beebe, S., Redmond, M., & Geerinck, T. (2011). *Interpersonal Communication: Relating to Others*, Fifth Canadian Edition. Toronto: Pearson Canada. P. 25. Reprinted with permission by Pearson Canada Inc.
†From Beebe, S., Beebe, S., Redmond, M., & Geerinck, T. (2011). *Interpersonal Communication: Relating to Others*, Fifth Canadian Edition. Toronto: Pearson Canada. P. 92. Reprinted with permission by Pearson Canada Inc.

LISTENING STYLES

- People-Oriented: Listener who is comfortable with and skilled at listening to people's feelings and emotions.

- Action-Oriented: Listener who prefers information that is well-organized, brief, and error-free. They are more likely to be more skeptical when listening to information by questioning the ideas and assumptions underlying a message.

- Content-Oriented: Listener who is more comfortable listening to complex, detailed information than are those with other listening styles. This style of listener hones in on the facts, details, and evidence in a message.

- Time-Oriented: Listener that likes messages delivered succinctly. Their to-do lists and inboxes are often overflowing, so they want the messages delivered quickly and briefly.

Source: From Beebe, S., Beebe, S., Redmond, M., & Geerinck, T. (2011). *Interpersonal Communication: Relating to Others*, Fifth Canadian Edition. Toronto: Pearson Canada. P. 95-96. Reprinted with permission by Pearson Canada Inc.

that everyone tends to fall into one of four listening styles: people-oriented, action-oriented, content-oriented, or time-oriented"* (Beebe et al., 2011, p. 95). Take a look at Box 4.1 and determine which listening style you fall under. Which style of listener do you think a police officer should be?

American communication researchers Lyman Steil, Kittie Watson, and Larry Barker (1983) developed the SIER hierarchy of active listening based on their observation that people forget about 50 percent of a message immediately after hearing it and remember only 25 percent after two days. The SIER model (Figure 4.6)

is a hierarchical, four-step sequence of listening activities: sensing, interpreting, evaluating, and responding. The hierarchical aspect of this model is that each sequence of the listening activities is followed by another stage in a certain order. In the first stage of this hierarchy, *sensing*, the active listener starts to hear and observe the verbal and nonverbal characteristics of the message. The second stage of the hierarchy is *interpreting* the message. Once the message is received, the listener will put the message into some sort of meaningful context that will be influenced by the receiver's experience, knowledge, and attitudes. The third stage is *evaluating* the message. This is where the listener must sort through the message and distinguish between the facts of the message and the opinions of the sender. The listener will be influenced by the sender's logic as well as emotions. The final stage of the hierarchy is *responding* to the message. Responding to any message is considered two-way communication. The receiver can respond to the sender both verbally and nonverbally, and this feedback provides the sender with an understanding of how the message was received. The receiver can clarify the sender's message by paraphrasing it back to the sender for confirmation that the meaning behind the message is clearly understood and received.

With the SIER model, the receiver must use all of his or her senses during the sensing phase to improve the quality of the interpretation, evaluation, and response stages. When a misunderstanding occurs between the sender and the receiver, both participants need to restart their analysis at the bottom of the hierarchy (Steil et al., 1983). The SIER model of listening may prove to be a valuable tool in policing in order to avoid any misunderstandings of the message that may cause unchangeable reactions to the message being heard.

FIGURE 4.6
The SIER Model of Communication

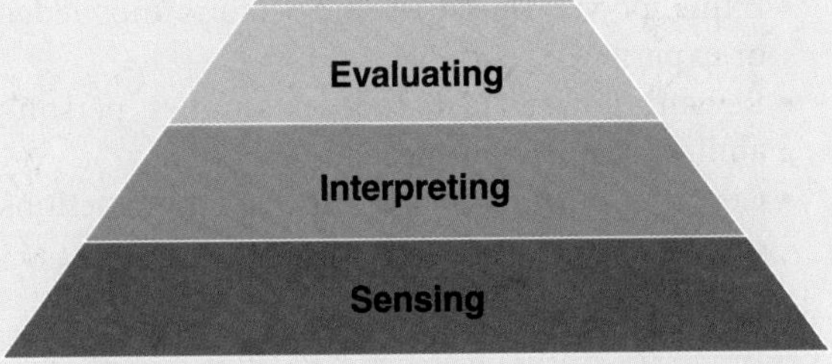

Source: Adapted from L. Steil, K. Watson, & L. Barker. (1983). *Effective listening*. Reading, MA: Addison-Wesley.

*From Beebe, S., Beebe, S., Redmond, M., & Geerinck, T. (2011). *Interpersonal Communication: Relating to Others*, Fifth Canadian Edition. Toronto: Pearson Canada. P. 95. Reprinted with permission by Pearson Canada Inc.

LO³ TYPES OF POLICE COMMUNICATION

Way too often police officers hear what people are saying but not often enough do they actually understand what is being said. Either you are concentrating and involved in the conversation or your mind is a hundred miles away and you're thinking about a million other things, like what's for dinner. Have you ever had a conversation with someone but were thinking about one or two other things at the same time because you were not that interested in hearing what the person was saying? This often happens in relationships, but when this happens in policing it has an impact on the interpretation of the message. Furthermore, the person who is talking often picks up on your lack of interest in the conversation by the words you use in response or your body language and may feel that you think the situation is unimportant or that you are minimizing what happened to him or her as the victim of a crime. "Researchers suggest that people who learn how to stop mental distractions can improve their listening comprehension"* (Beebe et al., 2011, p. 105). People (including police officers) can improve their listening, comprehension, and responding skills by adhering to the following:

1. *Stop:* To be a good listener you have to stop focusing on your own mental messages and be other-oriented (Beebe et al., 2011). When you are a police officer and you respond to an incident or a call for service, take the time to put your own thoughts aside and be 100 percent mentally there for that person. Take the time to listen to the speaker and not worry about what you have to do next, and most of all, be opened minded. As a police officer you are supposed to be open minded and impartial. You are expected to be unbiased and unprejudiced while on duty and to assist the public in various situations.

2. *Look:* Nonverbal messages in some instances are very powerful. Sometimes it is what is not being said that is important. If the nonverbal cues are contradicting the verbal message, we tend to disbelieve the words that are being said. It is hard for most people to hide or be deceitful in displaying their nonverbal messages even if they try. Don't be mistaken, though, as some people are very good at hiding their nonverbal communication or can mislead you as an investigator with these cues.

3. *Listen:* Just listen and do not interrupt. Most police officers have personalities that inherently lead them to try to control the situation and/or conversation. They feel that what they have to say is important and have a tendency to interrupt other people or finish their sentences. Respond appropriately both verbally and nonverbally (with eye contact, nodding your head, and facial expressions) to the person.

4. *Ask questions:* The first question a police officer should ask is "What happened?" and to clarify the information, "Then what happened?" This way the person will describe the situation in his or her own words and will be consistent if called to testify in court.

5. *Reflect content by paraphrasing:* You can also verify that you understand the message by reflecting on the information through paraphrasing. Once the person has finished telling his or her story, you should ask questions like "Are you saying…?" or "Here is what I understand you mean…" This will allow you to summarize the key events, details, or points of what the speaker has said. Not only will you understand the person's message better by clarifying the words, but the speaker will be satisfied that you heard what they were saying (Beebe et al., 2011).

A person's listening skills are influenced by who the person is that is speaking. If we respect the person speaking or he or she holds a position of power and authority, we have a tendency to be more attentive and to retain more information. With power comes respect. This is true in policing, for the most part. The majority of society respects police officers because of the power and authority they represent. There are certain types of power a person may hold, and for various reasons, they are directly correlated with our ability and willingness to actively listen. Police officers are no different from anyone else—they too alter their listening skills depending on the type of power the person has or appears to have. The various types of power in society are:

- Legitimate power: Comes from a respect for a position another holds.
- Referent power: Comes from our attraction to another person, or the charisma a person holds.
- Expert power: Derives from a person's knowledge or experience.
- Reward power: Is based on another person's ability to satisfy our needs.
- Coercive power: Involves the use of sanctions or punishment to influence others (Beebe et al., 2011, p. 276).†

Police officers' ability to communicate effectively is directly linked to the type(s) of power they possess

---

*From Beebe, S., Beebe, S., Redmond, M., & Geerinck, T. (2011). *Interpersonal Communication: Relating to Others*, Fifth Canadian Edition. Toronto: Pearson Canada. P. 105. Reprinted with permission by Pearson Canada Inc.

†From Beebe, S., Beebe, S., Redmond, M., & Geerinck, T. (2011). *Interpersonal Communication: Relating to Others*, Fifth Canadian Edition. Toronto: Pearson Canada. P. 276. Reprinted with permission by Pearson Canada Inc.

FIGURE 4.7
Good conflict management skills can prevent most situations from escalating.

or present. The police automatically present the notion of coercive power over the public; therefore, the majority of the public listens to police officers when directed to obey the law. Police officers also possess legitimate power simply because of their position and the uniform. The more power you assert or present, the more people not only will listen to what you are saying but will hear your message loud and clear.

Having power and authority as a police officer doesn't make you a good mediator. One of the primary roles of a police officer is to de-escalate situations and calm people down to avoid any further conflict. In order for police officers to efficiently and effectively perform their duties, they must possess exceptional conflict management skills (see Figure 4.7). Proficient communication skills and a good rapport with the community you serve will assist in fostering and developing outstanding conflict management skills, which are crucial to the position of police officer. A common type of conflict that police officers have to deal with is **pseudo-conflict**. Pseudo-conflict occurs when miscommunication triggers a conflict between people.

LO⁴ CONFLICT MANAGEMENT SKILLS

The five skills that are beneficial in conflict management are managing your emotions, managing information, being empathic, managing goals, and managing the problem (Beebe et al., 2011).

1. *Manage your emotions.* As a police officer you are expected to remain impartial and level-headed when dealing with various situations. Although this may be difficult at times, and may seem impossible in certain situations, your control of your emotions is

the key to success in conflict management. All too often police officers show up at an incident and escalate the situation by outwardly showing their emotions (fear, panic, anxiety, anger, annoyance, fury, resentment, grief, sorrow, happiness, etc.), thus prompting further conflict. Be conscientious that you are becoming angry or are about to express an inappropriate emotion. Make a conscious decision about whether to express your anger or step back and take a breath or remove yourself from the situation if you are able to. Plan your response based not only on what is being said but also on the nonverbal messages that are being conveyed, as we discussed earlier in this chapter. At all costs be professional and avoid personal attacks, name-calling, and emotional overstatements. Threats or derogatory names can escalate a simple situation (Beebe et al., 2011). In policing people are going to try and push your buttons (Figure 4.8), and your job is to keep your composure and complete the task at hand. Refer to Box 4.2 to see a list of "hot buttons" that people try to use to get you "off your game." When you are off your game you will make mistakes, and some of those mistakes could cost you your job or, even worse, somebody's life.

> **pseudo-conflict:**
> Conflict triggered by miscommunication.

2. *Manage information.* Validate and verify all information obtained in a conflict situation. The old saying goes, "there are three sides to every story," and in policing this misinformation may control and/or influence the actions of a police officer. As stated earlier in this book, police officers have the power and authority to take away a person's fundamental rights as guaranteed by the *Canadian Charter of Rights and Freedoms* when acting upon information; therefore, it is your sworn

FIGURE 4.8
People will try to get a reaction from the police by trying to push their "hot buttons".

BOX 4.2

IDENTIFYING HOT BUTTONS

The following are some phrases, words, and actions that you will hear often if you choose a career in policing and that may cause you to become emotionally charged. Check the boxes that are hot buttons for you, and try to think of any others that affect you both positively and negatively.

- "PIG!"
- Know-it-all attitudes
- "Shut up!"
- Being ignored
- Obscene language
- "I am going to get you and your family."
- Whining
- Being interrupted
- "What you should do is …"
- "Why aren't you out catching real criminals?"
- "The only reason you stopped me is because …"
- "Why me? The other cars are speeding too!"
- "I can do whatever I want."

- "What took you so long?"
- "How are you doin', babe?"
- "I pay your salary, ya know!"
- "Are you old enough to be a cop?"
- "Have you got your quota yet?"
- "I know the chief of police!"
- "Do you know who I am?"
- I make more money in a month then you make all year
- "What are you looking at, pig?"
- "Watch your back!"
- "I know where you live."
- "Hey babe, you can frisk me anytime."

This is just a small sample of some of the things you are going to hear as a police officer that may or may not push your hot buttons. Knowing what your emotional hot buttons are can help prevent you from overreacting when they are pushed.

---

duty and responsibility as a police officer to make sure the information you are receiving is accurate and relevant. Try not to jump to conclusions or put words into people's mouths when collecting information. Use effective listening skills.

3. *Be empathetic.* Taking the time to establish a rapport may provide significant help in settling the conflict. Use effective listening skills. Not only do you need to understand what the person is saying, but you need to put yourself in the person's place and try to understand what he or she is feeling. As humans we act on feelings, and if you understand someone's feelings you may be able to determine what that person will do next or how he or she may act. The more emotionally attached the person is to something, the more potential there is for the person to act out in

POLICING IN PRACTICE

Avoid jumping to conclusions. Try this brainteaser:
A blind beggar had a brother who died. What relation was the blind beggar to the brother who died? Brother is not the answer.

Answer: The blind beggar was the sister of her brother who died.

FIGURE 4.9

The Benefits of Being an Effective Communicator

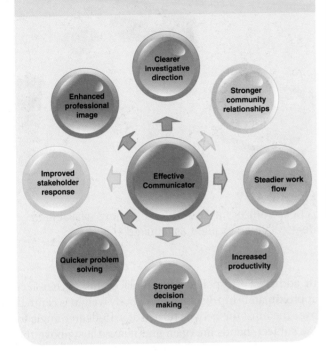

an irrational manner. This is where it is important to become other-oriented (Beebe et al., 2011).

4. *Manage goals.* When you are dealing with a conflict situation, it is best to identify your goal and attempt to recognize the goal(s) of the person you are dealing with. You will be able to manage the conflict with ease when these goals have been identified.

5. *Manage the problem.* Not all conflicts can be resolved, but once you realize that the conflict needs to be managed and not won or lost, your chances of success will be enhanced. Define the problem by finding out what the issue is. Analyze what the causes of the problem are and the obstacles to solving the problem. Determine the goals of everyone involved in the problem by finding out what everyone wants. If possible, create multiple solutions to the problem and then select the best solution and stick with it (Beebe et al., 2011). Try not to second-guess your decision, especially when you are in a potentially dangerous situation. Remember that as a police officer, for the most part, you are attempting to select the most amicable resolution to the problem whenever possible. Arresting everyone and taking them to jail is just not a realistic solution to every conflict.

As a police officer, not all conflicts you manage will be dealing with "bad guys." From time to time you will have to manage conflict of an internal nature as well. Police services are made up of people, and whenever you have people involved you are going to have conflicts. For example, you could have a conflict with another member of your shift or your shift supervisor, which will require a diplomatic way of resolving these situations. Policing is also a paramilitary organization with a rank-in-file structure. This means that the communication line is a top-down one, which may generate conflicts if you don't agree with every direction and/or order that is sent down from the senior command in the police service. Being an effective communicator has some significant benefits and advantages. Refer to Figure 4.9 for a quick view of some of these benefits.

> **tactical communication:** Any communication used by a police officer to resolve a situation. Tactical communication ensures that police officers adhere to a standard and professional approach when communicating with the public in order to prevent conflicts from escalating and ultimately de-escalate the situation.

LO⁵ TACTICAL COMMUNICATION

Tactical communication is any communication used by a police officer to resolve a situation, as shown in Figure 4.10. Tactical communication ensures that police officers adhere to a standard and professional approach when communicating with the public in order to prevent conflicts from escalating and

Sarah Dea/The Globe and Mail/The Canadian Press

FIGURE 4.10
Tactical communication should be used in every incident.

interview stance:
A position where a police officer angles his or her body so that the strong side (the side that the pistol is on) is away from the subject.

reactionary gap:
The distance (space) between the officer and the person(s) he or she is dealing with that will allow the officer to react to the situation if it escalates.

police challenge: A form of tactical communication used by police officers when they have assessed a situation and selected to draw their firearm to de-escalate a serious bodily harm or death situation. The police challenge is "Police—don't move!"

to ultimately de-escalate the situation.

Everyone has their own comfort level and preference when it comes to personal space. This isn't a place like under your bed, but rather the space between you and another person that you feel comfortable with. Your personal space is usually determined by the type and closeness of the relationship with the person you are interacting with. If you are interacting with an intimate partner or a close friend, your personal space may be closer than it would be while interacting with a complete stranger. All sorts of factors can influence your personal space, including size, gender, age, culture/racial background, emotional state, and so on.

If you intentionally or unintentionally invade someone's personal space, this may lead to anxiety and escalate the situation. Therefore, police officers are taught to employ the interview stance when dealing with the public. Shooters call it the "weaver stance." In the **interview stance**, a police officer positions his or her body so that the strong side (the side that the pistol is on) is angled away from the subject. The officer should never go face-to-face or toe-to-toe with a subject.

FIGURE 4.11
Police officers use the interview stance for their own safety.

FIGURE 4.12
A police officer has use-of-force options available to de-escalate an incident as required.

In addition, the police officer places his or her feet approximately hip distance apart, body weight is centred over the hips, the body is turned at a 45-degree angle to the subject, hands are open and relaxed just above the waist, and legs are relaxed and ready for any movement (see Figure 4.11). The interview stance is also vital in keeping a **reactionary gap** between the officer and the subject to allow the officer to react to the situation if it escalates. In this position, the officer will not be caught off guard if it's necessary to defend him or herself by selecting a use-of-force option (firearm, baton, pepper spray, Taser, and handcuffs—see Figure 4.12) or going hands-on with the subject. To summarize, the interview stance appears professional, respects the personal space of others, appears less threatening than squaring off face-to-face with a person, helps to maintain balance for the officer, and keeps the firearm away from the subject (for officer safety). Whether interacting with a suspect, a victim, or even a witness, an officer should always use the interview stance.

Communication is an integral tool in every situation that a police officer may encounter and, thus, is an essential component of the Ontario Use of Force Model (2004), as demonstrated in Figure 4.13. In the Use of Force Model, whenever a police officer has to deal with a situation that requires the use of force, the officer is trained to continuously use effective communication in attempts to de-escalate the situation. For example, when drawing their sidearm or firearm and pointing it at someone, all police officers in Ontario are trained to instinctively issue the **police challenge**, "Police—don't move!" Even at the

FIGURE 4.13

The Ontario Use of Force Model

Diagram of the Ontario Use of Force Model (2004)

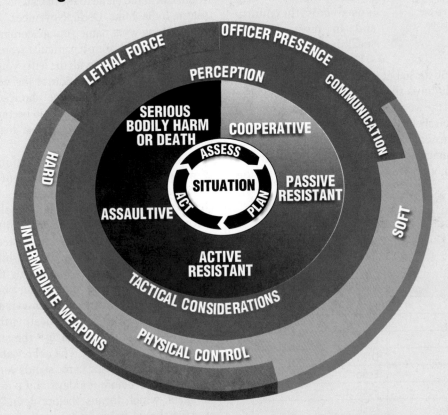

The officer continuously assesses the situation and selects the most reasonable option relative to those circumstances as perceived at that point in time.

Source: *Report of Conducted Energy Weapon Use in Ontario: Report of the Policing Standards Advisory Committee*, December 7, 2009. © Queen's Printer for Ontario, 2001. Reproduced with permission.

most critical and serious of times, communication is crucial. The officer has assessed the incident as a serious bodily harm or death situation and has selected the most reasonable response—drawing his or her firearm. This final attempt at communication with the suspect is made in hopes that the person will comply and the officer will not have to use his or her firearm. The police challenge is twofold: first, it informs the suspect that the person giving them directions/orders is the police and that this is a serious situation, and it gives the suspect one last chance to comply with the officer; and second, it notifies other officers on scene and members of the

public that you are a police officer and have given the suspect a chance to comply before the incident is escalated by the use of your firearm.

In policing, the common language used to clarify letters over the radio is called the phonetic alphabet. This system of substituting words for letters is used when spelling out names, words, and or vehicle licence plate numbers over the radio system to avoid any misunderstanding of what is being said. For example, often the letter *M* when spoken is mistaken for the letter *N*, or vice versa, causing inaccurate information about a suspect or a vehicle to be given out, which could be dangerous for police officers. The

International Phonetic Alphabet (IPA) is commonly used in most police services across Canada. Although there may be some minor differences, the IPA system is used across the country and in most English-speaking countries. Table 4.1 provides a look at how the phonetic alphabet is used in policing.

The first column is the letters of the alphabet. The second column is the word used to clarify which letter you are using when you spell out the name, place, or thing. The words used in this column are very specific and precise in terms of pronunciation and spelling. The meaning of these words has nothing to do with what you are talking about—each word simply starts with the same letter that you are communicating. For example, if you wanted to run a vehicle check on a licence plate attached to a particular vehicle and the plate number is MNNV 479, you would call in the plate as "Mike, November, November, 479." If you are checking a person with the name of Simon, you would call in the name to the dispatcher and spell it out as "Sierra, India, Mike, Oscar, November." This way there is no mistaking what name you are communicating. When you are communicating a particular word from the second column that correlates with the letter you are spelling, you emphasize the bolded section of the word. Try spelling out your own name using the phonetic alphabet. Keep practising and soon enough it will become second nature and you will be able to complete the entire alphabet without referring to the table.

Another form of communication in policing is identifying the correct time without any confusion or misunderstanding. Everything in policing is connected with the time of day. A police officer must account for every minute in every shift (tour of duty). Almost all police officers must keep a notebook detailing everything they do in a shift and the time they did it, so accurately identifying the time is vital. Therefore, to avoid any confusion, police officers use the 24-hour clock, otherwise known as *military time*, when recording and communicating the time of day.

Most people in Canada use the standard 12-hour clock with a.m. and p.m. The abbreviations of a.m. and p.m. are Latin phrases: a.m. stands for *ante meridiem*, which means "before midday," and p.m. stands for *post meridiem*, which means "before noon." The advantage of using the 24-hour clock in policing is that it avoids any confusion between a.m. and p.m. in documenting the time of day. The 24-hour clock distinguishes between before noon and after noon by continuously counting the numbers on the clock to correspond with the amount of numbers in the day. The day begins at midnight and continues for the next 24 hours in that day, so the clock starts at the first hour of the day, 00:00 hours. Then every second, minute, and hour is added to the clock. So 12:13 a.m. on the 12-hour clock would be 00:13 hours on the 24-hour clock, and 2:37 p.m. would translate to 14:37 hours. Basically, you add 12 to any number on the clock starting at 1:00 p.m. to get the appropriate time with the 24-hour clock. Refer to Table 4.2 for further examples on converting time from a.m./p.m. (12-hour clock) to the 24-hour clock used in policing.

Some people find it intriguing to listen in on police activity over the police radio frequency by using a scanner—a device used to monitor and listen to radio transmissions. The device that is generally referred to as a police scanner is a radio or communications receiver that can scan two or more frequencies and

TABLE 4.1

The International Phonetic Alphabet

Letter	Word
A	Alpha
B	Bravo
C	Charlie
D	Delta
E	Echo
F	Foxtrot
G	Golf
H	Hotel
I	India
J	Juliet
K	Kilo
L	Lima
M	Mike
N	November
O	Oscar
P	Papa
Q	Quebec
R	Romeo
S	Sierra
T	Tango
U	Uniform
V	Victor
W	Whisky
X	X-ray
Y	Yankee
Z	Zulu

TABLE 4.2
Converting from a.m./p.m. to the 24-Hour Clock (Military Time)

12 midnight to 12:59 a.m.	1:00 a.m. to 12:59 p.m.	1:00 p.m. to 11:59 p.m.
subtract 12 hours	straight conversion	add 12 hours
EXAMPLES: 12 midnight → 0000 12:13 a.m. → 0013 12:59 a.m. → 0059	EXAMPLES: 01:00 a.m. → 0100 08:00 a.m. → 0800 11:59 a.m. → 1159 12 noon —→ 1200 12:01 p.m. → 1201 12:45 p.m. → 1245 12:59 p.m. → 1259	EXAMPLES: 01:00 p.m. → 1300 03:30 p.m. → 1530 06:00 p.m. → 1800 09:00 p.m. → 2100 10:30 p.m. → 2230 11:05 p.m. → 2305 11:59 p.m. → 2359

Worldtimezone.com http://www.worldtimezone.com/wtz-names/wtz-am-pm.html

is primarily intended for monitoring police, fire, and ambulance communications by journalists, crime investigators, and tow truck operators.

For liability and safety reasons, most police services have developed or adapted communication codes for radio transmissions between its members. These codes replace key words in sentences or describe a situation without disclosing any personal or specific information about a person or an incident. This allows police officers to communicate with each other and with their communications centre on the open airwaves without being concerned about who is listening in on the transmission. These codes also provide the police with a way of communicating without taking up too much airtime on the radio as they are a quick and easy way to communicate without any unnecessary chatter. For example, the Durham Regional Police Service (DRPS) adapted a nine code system as a way of communicating over the police radio. This was a unique form of communication that all Durham Regional Police officers were trained to use in order to keep radio transmissions short, to the point, and confidential.

When DRPS upgraded their communication system and converted to an encrypted radio system (using cellphone-type technology), the nine code system became obsolete and unnecessary as the public was now unable to pick up any transmissions by way of radio waves on police scanners.

Several standard code systems have been adopted by most police services and have quickly become common radio communications across Canada and most of North America. The ten code communication system, or ten signal system, is an example of a standardized communication system used to communicate on the police radio system. Even with advancements in technology, most police services continue to use the ten code system. Refer to Table 4.3 for a breakdown of the ten code system. Most police services now use an encrypted radio system, which works off a digital system that blocks the public from eavesdropping on police communications. The purpose of an encrypted system is to ensure public safety, officer safety, operational security, and integrity in policing. In 2008, a report revealed that the Toronto Police Service made the transition to encrypted radios just in time for the G20 summit held in Toronto. Listening to police radio calls will soon be a thing of the past. The encrypted radio system is new to some cities and police services, but it has been used for decades in various parts of the world.

The standard ten codes can be found printed in the back of every police officer's notebook, along with some other pertinent information for quick reference—for example, arrest procedures and cautions, demands for roadside screening, breathalyzer tests, bloods samples and drug evaluations, first aid notes, and the use of force model, just to mention a few.

The **police notebook (memo book)** is an essential tool in policing. This is a daily journal (recording) of police officers' activity when they are on duty (see Figure 4.14). On-duty police officers are required to keep contemporaneous, concise, and complete notes of their daily activities. Although they should have an independent recollection of events, their notebooks will be used to refresh their memory when questioned about an incident in court or with

police notebook (memo book): A daily journal (recording) of police officers' activity when they are on duty.

TABLE 4.3
Standard Ten Codes/Ten Signals

10-1	Receiving poorly	10-35	Major crime alert
10-2	Receiving well	10-36	Correct time check
10-3	Stop transmitting	10-38	Investigation alert
10-4	Acknowledgment	10-45	Death or fatality
10-5	Relay message	10-51	Tow truck needed
10-6	Busy, unless urgent	10-52	Ambulance needed
10-7	Out of service	10-60	Subject negative
10-8	In service	10-61	Subject has record (not wanted)
10-9	Repeat	10-62	Subject possibly wanted
10-10	Request for common channel	10-63	Subject positive hit—person is wanted
10-15	Pick up prisoner at _____	10-64	Proceed with caution
10-18	Complete assignment quickly	10-65	Assist on 10-64
10-19	Return to your station	10-66	Subject in observation category
10-20	What is your location	10-67	Subject in parolee category
10-21	Call by telephone	10-68	Subject in charged category
10-26	Detaining subject, expedite	10-78	Need assistance
10-28	Vehicle registration	10-92	Person in custody
10-29	Canadian Police Information Centre (CIPC) check required	10-93	Set up road block
10-30	Improper use of radio	10-100	Bomb threat
10-33	Emergency assistance required		

© Can Stock Photo Inc. / Ivan_Sabo

FIGURE 4.14
A police officer's notebook is a vital tool in policing.

a public complaint, judicial review, or public inquiry that may take place years after the date of the incident. A police officer's notes will stand the test of time and will become one of the most important tools an officer can have.

Police officers are accountable to the public and must officially record details and incidents while on patrol in order to justify their actions for every shift. Police officers have to account for every minute of the day they are on duty in their notebook. Although they use their notebook as a journal of their actions, the notebook is the property of the police service they work for. Each police service has policies and procedures in place to regulate the use of notebooks, as discussed in Chapter 11. A police officer can never have too many notes, and an officer should establish a habit of determining what goes into his or her notebook. Police officers are responsible for the safekeeping and storage of their notebooks and are asked to make sure their notes are professional, legible, and objective and avoid subjective statements or opinions, as they can be subject to a request made under the *Municipal Freedom of Information and Privacy Act*. All police notebooks are subject to the same rules of disclosure as other confidential documents, and they must contain everything deemed relevant to police work.

FIGURE 4.15
Most police officers must record their daily activities and actions in their notebook.

As mentioned, police officers are also expected to be consistent with what goes into their notebook and what order it appears in. The format of the officer's notes is very specific (see Figure 4.15). Each new entry is marked with the day and date in capital letters, and ends with a line covering the entire width of the page, along with the officer's signature. No information may be removed, and all corrections must be made by striking the incorrect entry with a line and inserting the correct entry with the officer's initials. Time is recording using the 24-hour clock format (as discussed earlier in this chapter), and any gaps left at the end of a line must be filled by a horizontal line to show that the gap was not created by the removal of a word. Some basic required information is recorded on the front cover of every notebook: name of the police officer, rank and badge number, notebook number, date of first and last entry in the notebook, and serial numbers of issued equipment (firearm, handcuffs, ASP baton, OC spray, Taser, and other equipment).

In Ontario, all police officers are taught note-taking skills that are consistent with those set out by the Ontario Police College. Police officers must use a ballpoint pen (usually black ink) and notes are to be recorded in chronological order. The officer's notes start with the date and time of the shift and then proceed to record the weather, location, zone or assignment, assigned patrol vehicle, odometer reading of the assigned vehicle, name of partner for that shift or accompanying person, and any pertinent information contained in the shift briefing. When an officer is recording notes of an incident that occurred while on patrol, the following information must be entered into the notebook:

- time of day;
- exact or approximate location;
- offence or occurrence number;
- names, addresses, and date of births of offenders, victims, or witnesses;

FIGURE 4.16
Technology is even changing the police notebook.

- action taken by the officer or other officers involved (arrests, use of force used, etc.); and
- any other pertinent information that is related to the incident (charges, warning, CPIC check, etc.).

All notes *must* be recorded at the time of the incident or shortly thereafter and must be completed before the end of the officer's shift unless approved by a supervisor. All notes are to be completed independently from other officers, and only one set of notes is permitted from each officer. The officer's notes are to be stored at a work location except while on patrol or attending court. Technological advancements have had an impact on policing and note taking is no exception. An application is now available for the Apple iPhone called the Police Notebook iPhone (see Figure 4.16). The creators of the Police Notebook iPhone propose that police officers can use this application to make their iPhone their official police notebook. Maybe one day policing will take this route, but for now this application presents many challenges with regards to security, legal issues, and liability. This application or similar ideas will be reviewed in the future as technology advances in policing.

TECHNOLOGY AND COMMUNICATION

Policing is no different from any other business or organization in Canada—police services have to keep up with today's technology in order to do business. Police services rely on computers and technological advancements to keep up with society, and this has become an even greater struggle with diminishing budgets in policing and increasing numbers of criminals with seemingly endless amounts of money. Trying to stay ahead of the criminals in the area of technology is a constant struggle in policing, but the truth of the matter is that most police services are just trying to keep up or even catch up with the "bad guys." Canadian police services are starting to explore the idea of in-car video cameras. Although U.S. law enforcement agencies have been using this technology for many years, Canadian police services are recognizing the benefits of this technology and are starting to install in-car cameras in their patrol vehicles. Not only is this technology a benefit for police officers by providing video evidence for situations on the road, but it will also hold police officers more accountable for their actions in dealing with the public. As discussed throughout this book, police officers are held to a higher standard and must follow the rules and regulations that unequivocally dictate an officer's behaviour in public.

Sharing of resources and information is crucial in policing, and common databases are used across Ontario and Canada. The following are examples of some of these shared resources among police services.

DATABASES

Canadian Police Information Centre (CPIC)

The CPIC is a nationally operated computer database system that links all law enforcement and justice partners in Canada. The RCMP is responsible for operating and maintaining the CPIC system. Every police officer has access to this database that contains vital information on warrants, warnings, and other important information. Police officers can verify information or the status of a person or property by conducting a check on the CPIC system. The system will identify if a person has a criminal record or is wanted on a warrant across Canada or if a vehicle has been reported as stolen. Every police service in Canada has access to this system via a CPIC terminal in the police station or patrol vehicles.

Criminal Name Index (CNI)

The CNI is part of the CPIC system. A CNI is a query made within the CPIC system. A CNI query is a quick check on a person's name that will identify the presence of any criminal record history. If the check comes back positive, the officer will have to request a more detailed query to get more information on the criminal record.

Computerized Integrated Information Dispatch System (CIIDS)

CIIDS is the dispatch organization system of the RCMP. CIIDS is used for messaging, queries, and linking officers to various other databases.

Canadian Criminal Real Time Identification Services (CCRTIS)

CCRTIS is the nation's storage area of fingerprint and criminal record information. Canadian law enforcement and international partners use the system to assist in the identification of persons in criminal, civil, and immigration investigations.

Canadian Integrated Ballistics Identification Network (CIBIN)

CIBIN is a national network of Integrated Ballistics Identification System (IBIS) instruments that collect, analyze, and correlate fired bullets and cartridge cases in a central database to generate investigative leads for police.

Remote Office and Dispatch System (ROADS)

ROADS is the mobile version of CIIDS. It allows remote access to many of the same application functions as CIIDS and is accessible in patrol vehicles.

Police Automated Registration Information System (PARIS)

PARIS is a provincially maintained computer-based information system in Ontario used primarily for vehicle and driver's licence checks.

Police Information Retrieval System (PIRS)

PIRS is the archaic localized information recording and retrieval system containing details on all incidents reported to the RCMP across the entire service.

Police Reporting and Occurrence System (PROS)

PROS is the modernized replacement system for PIRS. It has been enhanced with advanced capabilities that allow in-depth searches for information across the RCMP.

Mobile Data Terminal (MDT)

MDT is an in-vehicle computer that is a fully functional PC used in patrol vehicles. This system is used for records management, CAD, links to warrants and vehicle registration databases, automatic vehicle location, word processing, in-field reporting, records management, photos and other graphics, video, fingerprints, and so on.

Police Records Information Management Environment (PRIME)

PRIME is a province-wide real-time database system that is used by law enforcement agencies in British Columbia to search for information involving incidents or contact with the police.

In policing, common terms are used in communicating with other police officers and patrol units or the communications centre (dispatcher). Box 4.3 outlines some of the general terms used across the country by police officers.

BOX 4.3

TERMS AND DEFINITIONS

Term	Definition
Air 1	Police helicopter
Bar	Bar check and walk-through
BTA	Breathalyzer test
Bus	Ambulance/paramedic
Caution Charlie	Communicable disease
Caution Echo	Escape risk
Caution Mike	Mental instability
Caution Sierra	Suicidal
Caution Victor	Violent
Caution Foxtrot	Family/firearms violence
CNI Check	Criminal Name Index (see databases)
CIIDS	Computerized Integrated Information Dispatch System
Code 1	Respond routine
Code 2	Respond ASAP, no emergency
Code 3	Respond ASAP, emergency
CPIC	Canadian Police Information System
DL	Drivers licence
DOA	Dead on arrival
DOB	Date of birth
EDP	Emotionally disturbed person
EMS	Emergency medical service
ERT	Emergency response team

Term	Definition
FTA	Fail to appear
GOA	Gone on arrival
Hook	Tow truck
MHA	Person with a mental illness
MVA	Motor vehicle accident
MVC	Motor vehicle collision
OD	Drug overdose
Operation	Road block or speed trap
Pointer Vehicle	Vehicle under observation
PC	Police constable
PO	Police officer
Priority 1	Emergency call
Priority 2	Immediate police attention but not life-threatening
Priority 3	Routine call for service
Priority 4	Low priority
PIRS	Police Information Retrieval System
PRIM	Police Records Information Management Environment
PROS	Police Reporting and Occurrence System
RO	Registered owner of vehicle
Routine	No emergency lights or sirens
RSD	Roadside screening device
RTO	Return to office
Servicing	Filling up with gas

CHAPTER SUMMARY

Communication in policing is vital with both the constant human contact and the changing technology. Police officers are expected to serve the needs of the community, and in order to do this effectively and efficiently, they must possess exceptional communication skills. Everyday police officers have to interact with people and communicate on both an impersonal and an interpersonal level. A good communicator is a good listener. Good listening skills can effectively change the outcome or results of an incident. In today's society people are always in a rush and policing is no exception. Often police officers are going from call to call and, with personal and family issues they may be constantly thinking about, they unfortunately might not always give the public the attention required to be an effective listener. In addition, police officers often get caught up in the bureaucracy of the justice system, which in turn affects the way they deal with an incident or the people involved. In a conflict situation, the main goal of a police officer is to de-escalate the situation with a positive outcome. Communication is always and has always been a consistent requirement in policing, especially with the changes in society with regards to multiculturalism in Canada and technological advancements in the world.

LO¹ Describe the basic communication skills required for policing.

There are many definitions for communication but in the broadest sense, communication is a means of sending or receiving information in some sort of medium. Communication in policing is broken down into verbal and nonverbal communication. Verbal communication is essentially what is being said and the words that are being used to communicate the message. Nonverbal communication is the process of sending and receiving wordless messages by way of gestures, body language, touch, facial expression, and eye contact. These messages are just as vital or in some cases even more important than the words that are being communicated. These are telltale signs or triggers that can tweak your suspicions as a police officer.

LO² Define interpersonal and impersonal communication.

Interpersonal communication is a unique style of communication involving mutual influence on one another and respect. This form of communication is most effective in managing relationships between people. Impersonal communication occurs when we treat people as objects, or when we respond to their roles rather than them as individuals.

LO³ Discuss the various types of communication methodology used in policing.

People (including police officers) can improve their listening, comprehension, and responding skills by adhering to the following five steps. *Stop:* To be a good listener you have to stop focusing on your own mental messages and be other-oriented. *Look:* Nonverbal messages in some instances are very powerful. Sometimes it is what is not being said that is important. If the nonverbal cues are contradicting the verbal message, we tend to disbelieve the words that are being said. It is hard for most people to hide or be deceitful in displaying their nonverbal messages even if they try. Don't be mistaken, though, as some people are very good at hiding their nonverbal communication or at misleading you as an investigator with these cues. *Listen:* Just listen and do not interrupt. Most police officers have personalities that will inherently try to control the situation and/or conversation. They feel that what they have to say is important and have a tendency to interrupt other people or finish their sentences for them. Respond appropriately both verbally and nonverbally (with eye contact, nodding your head, and facial expressions) to the person. *Ask questions:* The first question a police officer should ask is "What happened?" and then to clarify the information, "Then what happened?" This way the person will describe the situation in his or her own words and will be consistent if called to testify in court. *Reflect content by paraphrasing:* You can also verify that you understand the message by reflecting on the information by paraphrasing.

LO⁴ Explain the various techniques in conflict management.

The five conflict management skills that are beneficial in the development of good conflict management are manage your emotions, manage information, be empathetic, manage goals, and manage the problem.

LO⁵ Describe the use of tactical communications in policing.

Tactical communication is any communication used by a police officer to resolve a situation. Tactical communication ensures that a standard and professional approach is adhered to by police officers when communicating with the public in order to prevent conflicts from escalating and ultimately de-escalate the situation.

Customer Service

LEARNING OUTCOMES

After completing this chapter, you will be able to:

LO1   Describe the community consultation process and the reasons for conducting this process.

LO2   Summarize the business-planning process and the reasons for following this process.

LO3   Explain community satisfaction surveys and the reasons for conducting these surveys.

LO4   Discuss the evolution of community policing in Canada.

Most people spend more time and energy going around problems than in trying to solve them.

—*Henry Ford*

Customer service. When you hear those two words what comes to mind? Can you think of a time when you received good customer service? Was it at a restaurant, a gas station, a movie theatre, a hotel, or perhaps even at your college or high school? Is there a time you can look back on and say, "That was good customer service?" Conversely, you may be able to think of a time when you received terrible customer service, most likely at a restaurant, where perhaps your tip reflected the service. Do you ever think of police officers as providing a service? Well, they do—the community is the customer and the police are the service providers. The job of the police service is to find out what the customer wants and whether the customer is satisfied with the service.

Many businesses now send follow-up emails to people who dine at their restaurants or stay at their hotels or rent their cars to ask how satisfied they were with the service. Policing is no exception to this practice. Many police services consult closely with their communities and work with the community to solve issues rather than taking the position that police officers know best and will decide what the priorities are and how to tackle them. Many witnesses and victims of crimes are surveyed to see how the police services provided to them were received and how, if needed, the police can improve on these services. They are asked if they were treated with dignity and respect and if they were offered the necessities when they required them. This is a good quality control mechanism so that the police service knows how all people are treated by police officers. Police services need to know who their clients are—basically, they are all the people they come in contact with, including those who are arrested and prosecuted.

quality service standards: Policies that are followed by employees to meet standards the employer expects. These standards relate to timelines and procedures involved with emails, phone messages, correspondence, etc.

business plan: A document that addresses the key priorities of a police service and explains who's going to do what by when.

QUALITY SERVICE STANDARDS

Many government services and police organizations have **quality service standards**. These are standards that measure the quality of services provided by each organization. Some police services have telephone quality service standards, such as you will not have to speak to more than two people for each call, your call will be answered after three rings, etc.

Table 5.1 provides an example of quality service standards for the York Regional Police:

> It is the policy of the Regional Municipality of York Police Services Board that superior quality service is provided to all citizens whenever they contact York Regional Police.
>
> York Regional Police currently has 13 external Quality Service Standards. We hope that we will frequently exceed these standards, thereby narrowing the service gap. In the future, other standards may be set. (York Regional Police, 2009, paras. 1–2)

After you have reviewed the standards on the next page, consider how they are measured. Each standard is designed to be met or exceeded. These standards are communicated to the customer, being the public, so that if a standard is not met a discussion can take place to correct the problem. When you review these standards, also think about how you would feel as a client of this police service and how you would feel when receiving the service.

LO1 COMMUNITY CONSULTATION

Providing a service to a customer includes making sure you know what the customer wants. When the police discuss how to use their resources, they generally come up with a three to five-year strategic plan, sometimes called a **business plan**. Having a business plan is a requirement of the *Police Services Act* and is seen as a good business practice, not only in policing but also in any organization. When police managers discuss their plans they often review the input provided by the community. Community members who participate in the consultation process often have opinions on what the police should be doing, and their input is sought through surveys, meetings, committee participation, or day-to-day interactions.

TABLE 5.1
York Regional Police Quality Service Standards: External

Complaint areas	The Officer in Charge of the District Community Oriented Response Unit shall provide a file number to a complainant within five business days of receiving a complaint from a citizen regarding activity of concern. The Officer in Charge of the District Community Oriented Response Unit shall update the complainant regarding any action taken within 15 days of receiving the complaint.
Correspondence	All correspondence requiring a response shall be responded to within 15 working days.
Criminal background checks	Criminal background check applications will be processed and completed within one hour.
Emotionally-disturbed persons	The Community Services Bureau Mental Health Support Unit shall conduct follow-up with officers and support organizations, within five business days, for all occurrences involving emotionally-disturbed persons.
Email set up	When a member is not returning for their normal tour of duty, the member shall use the out of office assistant to set up a message advising the sender when they will be returning to work and who to contact for immediate assistance.
Front-desk reception	When a person comes to the Front Desk of a District, a member of the Front Desk staff shall address or acknowledge that person, go to the front counter where the person is standing, make eye contact, greet the person in a courteous and professional manner and make reasonable efforts to satisfy any enquiries.
Investigative follow-up	All assigned district Criminal Investigation Bureau cases classified as a "crime against persons" offence or "break and enter" shall receive at least one investigative contact. Investigative contact shall occur in all cases when a suspect has been identified, arrested or charged, stolen property is recovered or additional information is required to assist with the investigation.
Online reporting	Any person filing an online report will be contacted via email or telephone by the next business day.
Paid duties	Satisfaction surveys shall be conducted for all new paid duty customers and random sampling shall take place throughout the year for ongoing customers. All surveys will be reviewed by the Quality Assurance Bureau to ensure that York Regional Police is providing the highest quality of service.
Telephone inquiries	With the exception of a call received by a switchboard operator, a caller shall not be transferred more than once and every effort shall be made to satisfy any inquiries. All voice mail shall identify the name and assignment of the member and shall further indicate how a caller can obtain immediate assistance. Voice mail shall be checked during each member's assigned shift and responded to within one working day. When a member is not returning for their normal tour of duty, the member shall set up their voice mail with a message advising the caller when they will be returning to work and whom to contact for immediate assistance.
Training and awareness	Quality Service Standards shall be posted on the York Regional Police external website and on the YRPNet. All new members shall receive training in relation to Quality Service Standards.
Victims of crime	When an officer takes a report from a victim, they shall fill out a YRP384 Criminal Incident Information Pamphlet, explain the contents and leave the pamphlet with the victim.
Vulnerable sector screening	Vulnerable sector screening applications that require contact with an external police service will be processed within five business days of York Regional Police receiving a response. Those applications requiring a York Regional Police database search only will be processed within five business days.

Source: Reprinted from York Regional Police. (2009). Quality Service Standards. Retrieved from http://www.yrp.ca/qss.aspx

DECODING POLICE TERMS

Business plan: A requirement of the *Police Services Act:* Every board shall prepare a business plan for its police force at least once every three years.

(2) The business plan shall address,
- (a) the objectives, core business and functions of the police force, including how it will provide adequate and effective police services;
- (b) quantitative and qualitative performance objectives and indicators relating to,
  - (i) the police force's provision of community-based crime prevention initiatives, community patrol and criminal investigation services,
  - (ii) community satisfaction with police services,
  - (iii) emergency calls for service,
  - (iv) violent crime and clearance rates for violent crime,
  - (v) property crime and clearance rates for property crime,
  - (vi) youth crime and clearance rates for youth crime,
  - (vii) police assistance to victims of crime and re-victimization rates, and
  - (viii) road safety;
- (c) information technology;
- (d) resource planning; and
- (e) police facilities. (O. Reg. 3/99, ss. 30(1) & (2))*

*http://www.canlii.org/en/on/laws/regu/o-reg-3-99/latest/o-reg-3-99.html

In the past, the police took the position that they knew what was best for the community, and they imposed law and order as they saw fit. In proactive policing, the community is consulted and the input is seen as highly valuable. In the past, the police would spend their time catching the criminals after they committed a criminal act. Catching the "bad guy" has always been a priority within the policing community; this type of policing activity is sometimes called "**reactive policing**" as it takes place following the commission of a crime. Solving crimes and arresting the people who committed them was highly celebrated by police officers of all ranks and was the way to be recognized and rewarded. Following community input, additional issues were raised that the public wanted the police to focus on, such as youths loitering in the streets, public property being damaged, and other issues deemed to be of a low priority to the police. Over time, a trend toward consultation and crime prevention emerged.

The police started to collaborate and partner with other parts of the community, such as hospitals, social agencies, schools, municipal committees, volunteer committees, and community policing committees. As this trend continued, the people involved in these collaborations saw themselves as part of the solution to problems within the community. It became not just the responsibility of the police to address criminal activities—everyone could assist in this regard.

The Toronto Police Service places a high degree of emphasis on **community consultation**. They suggest that the outcomes of this consultation will assist in identifying, prioritizing, and problem solving community issues and concerns and will improve safety and quality of life in the city of Toronto. All police divisions in Toronto have Community Police Liaison Committees (CPLCs), which are made up of police officers and members of the community. In addition to the CPLC committees, the Toronto Police Service also has Community Consultative Committees. These specialty committees contribute to "wider policing issues such as training, recruiting, Professional Standards and community mobilization. Currently the service has created committees with the following communities, Aboriginal, Black, Chinese, French, Gay/Lesbian-Bisexual/Transgender/Transsexual, Muslim, South and West Asian" (Toronto Police Service, 2011, para. 8). This depth of consultation will improve communication and cooperation between different stakeholders so that when an issue does arise, speedy resolutions will be more attainable.

In addition to the above consultation committees, there are other community consultation bodies that assist the police service: "The Chief's Community Advisory Council (CAC) and the Chief's Youth Advisory Committee (CYAC) exist to provide a voice for various community representatives, from business through to social agencies and spanning the various diverse communities as well as youth on a wide variety of issues" (Toronto Police Service, 2011, "Chief's Community Advisory Council," para. 1).

reactive policing: A type of policing where the police respond to calls for service requiring immediate response. This traditional approach does not focus on preventing crimes from taking place.

community consultation: A process of engaging and mobilizing members of the community to work on solutions to areas of mutual concern.

All of this consultation and communication is designed to break down barriers and work with people to solve problems. This process also enables people to have a say in solutions, as well as providing information to the police that enables them to respond to issues before they become full-fledged concerns. This type of collaboration and two-way communication is proactive and builds on the relationships between members of the committees.

Another police service taking a similar approach is the Halton Regional Police Service. Each policing division of Halton Regional Police has community committees set up to discuss and review strategies to reduce crime, reduce victimization, increase public safety, reduce community conflicts, reduce social disorder issues, and ensure traffic management. The purpose of the committees is to "work towards creating a healthy and safe community environment for all who live and work within that given area or community. . . . Committees work in a proactive, creative and innovative way to solve problems, research and establish strategies for both prevention and resolution of such issues" (Halton Regional Police Service, 2011, para. 5). This approach is similar to that taken by the Toronto Police Service; however, it appears to be less focused on communication issues between the police and specialized groups and more focused on problem solving within the community.

Police services use another type of community consultation while developing a business plan. Box 5.1 provides an example of this type of community consultation. Here, the London Police Service advertised for members of the community to attend police headquarters on three separate dates in an effort to engage members of the public in a consultation process and to gain insight into the priorities of the citizens of London, Ontario.

In their 1996 research paper, "It's Good to Talk: Lessons in Public Consultation and Feedback," Elliott and Nicholls identified several goals of police/community consultation groups (PCCG). Additionally, they identified some of the problems and issues associated with those groups. It is interesting to note that although this study was conducted in England in 1996, the processes and issues are essentially the same in Canada. Elliott and Nichols identified several purposes of police/community consultation groups. These include reaching a representative cross-section of the population, identifying public priorities to influence the annual policing plan, providing the public with information on policing activities and initiatives, and developing partnerships with the public.

BOX 5.1

LONDON POLICE SERVICE SEEKING COMMUNITY CONSULTATION

The London Police Service advertised the following community consultation in a flyer (bold type in the original):

The **London Police Service** is seeking your input to assist us in formulating our next 3-year Business Plan for 2013–2015. The community consultation process helps us to determine the direction the London Police Service will take over the next three-year period. The intent of this consultation process is to ensure that the Business Plan is reflective of what you, the citizens of London, need in terms of service and programs. **We need to hear from you** as to what issues are important, and where our resources should be placed to ensure an effective and efficient police service. **The Community Consultations are open to all citizens including, but not limited to, business owners, neighbourhood associations, church groups, volunteer agencies, community organizations and other interested persons.**

Source: London Police Service. (2011). Community consultation meetings [Flyer]. Retrieved from http://www.police.london.ca/Headlines/ReadMore/London_Police_flyer .pdf. Reproduced by permission of the London Police Service.

CHALLENGES AND OPPORTUNITIES

Elliott and Nicholls also identified challenges and opportunities for improvement in the consultation and partnership process. In their research they found that "meetings are often poorly attended: commonly, the public number in the low tens, and there have been cases where they have been outnumbered by the officials present" (1996, p. 10). This is true of many community consultations held by politicians, business, and school boards. It is only when the issue being considered is volatile, such as a local landfill site proposal, that people attend in large numbers.

Elliott and Nicholls also found that due to the low attendance at these consultation meetings, the people who did attend were not comfortable speaking on policing priorities and this enabled the police to "steer the discussion according to their own priorities" (p. 11). This is a concern because it essentially defeats the purpose of consulting with the public if only the public are hearing from the police during the consultation process. The hope is that the public will start to understand the issues facing the police and the limited resources available to deal with these issues.

As can be seen in Box 5.2, the police have a limited amount of resources and they have to prioritize those

---

BOX 5.2

NEWSPAPER REPORT OF A COMMUNITY CONSULTATION MEETING, LONDON, ONTARIO

Lack of law enforcement presence in the community was the recurring theme at Wednesday's (Nov. 2) community consultation meeting at police headquarters.

Held every three years, about 50 people showed up for the public input meeting to voice what they want to see from the police between now and the next set of meetings.

Issues addressed ranged from police building precincts throughout the city all the way to the recent incident where a teen was tasered by an officer.

The one issue consistently brought up throughout the meeting was people wanting to see more blue in their neighbourhood....

London Police Chief Brad Duncan fielded most of the questions and concerns in the community meeting and admitted drugs are one of the city's biggest problems.

"If I could eliminate drugs I would probably be able to eliminate a great percentage of the criminal activity that we deal with," Duncan said. "Drugs, quite frankly, fuel much of the crime that occurs in our community."

Dundas Street business owners shared their wishes of a greater police presence during the meeting as well. Many expressed concerns with the constant drug deals and public urinations they see on a regular basis.

"Probably the worst drug problem in the city is here, right in front of the police headquarters," said Janelle Blankenship, a resident and business owner in the Old East area. "This is an incident I've reported on numerous occasions and I'm frustrated by what responses I get from the police.... No one has ever come to my house but the response I get is, 'Is there serious property damage?'"

The drugs and urination do more than just hurt the reputation of her business, added Blankenship.

"It destroys the community and the social fabric and we don't have pride anymore, we need to build pride and bring back Dundas Street in terms of its business potential," she said.

To remedy the problem Blankenship suggested police issuing more tickets for certain by-laws like loitering.

The police would like to help everyone, but just don't have the resources to blanket the city with officers, said Duncan.

"In a perfect world I would like to have a fulltime foot patrol in SoHo," he said. "The Hamilton Business District has also asked for foot patrol, I had the Argyle Business Improvement Association, the Richmond Merchant Association, the Downtown Business Association and the Old East Business Association all asked. You can see the problems that we have as a service."

Duncan added, historically police should be adding 16 officers to the force every year to help meet all the calls but that hasn't happened in the last five years.

"There are deficits in our frontline service delivery," he said. "Just having a cruiser in the neighbourhood I realize has a huge impact but I can tell you on any given day, night or afternoon, and we have beats that are not filled within our community."

Source: "Community meeting urges police to show presence," (2011, November 3). London Community News.com. Retrieved from http://www.londoncommunitynews .com/2011/11/community-meeting-urges-police-to-show-presence/. Reproduced with permission.

resources accordingly. The police chief speaks about the resources he'd like to have in a "perfect world"; however, currently resources are tight and the world is far from ideal, so the police service has to allocate resources based on the most pressing needs and the best anticipated outcomes. This is the main purpose of community consultation: to identify priorities and work with community partners to find solutions.

LO² THE BUSINESS-PLANNING PROCESS AND MEASUREMENT

Establishing a business or **strategic plan** is now a standard practice in policing. Police services boards are required by the Provincial Adequacy Standards Regulation to develop business plans every three years. These plans are often called strategic plans and, in the spirit of customer service, they are the result of extensive community consultation.

The Durham Regional Police Services Board Chair explains the value of its business plan:

> To ensure that our citizens had a prominent voice in how police services are delivered, this Business Plan was developed through extensive consultation with Durham Region residents, our Community Partners, and members of the Police Service. The Business Plan has established as priorities, Community Safety, Crime Prevention Through Law Enforcement and Organizational Excellence. (Durham Regional Police Services, 2011, p. 4)

The OPP breaks down the development of its business plan into four steps. This process is consistent with those followed by most police services and by most organizations. The first step is to gather data (see Box 5.3). Initially, police services conduct an environmental scan, which sometimes includes a SWOT analysis: strengths, weaknesses, opportunities, and threats. The environmental scan provides an update on relevant issues and trends locally, nationally, and internationally. According to the Toronto Police Services Board,

strategic plan: Also called a business plan, a plan required every three years that sets long-term goals, priorities, and initiatives.

> the Environmental Scan provides a review of the external factors affecting the needs and demands for police services and the internal challenges affecting the Service's ability to respond to such needs and demands. It [is] prepared as the result of an ongoing process of analysis of internal and external trends, with regular feedback from Service units and input from an extensive consultation process, which involve[s] both internal and external consultations. (2011, para. 2)

Internally, the organization looks at its strengths and its weaknesses; this process is subjective but is helpful when considering where to place resources. Strengths or weaknesses of an organization could include human resources, sick leave, number of vehicles, types of buildings, succession planning, and so on. Next, the organization looks at the opportunities and threats from outside the organization. These could be issues such as an aging population, industrial downsizing, or an increase in drugs in schools.

The business-planning process is a cycle that starts with community consultation. This consultation is ongoing and the information is compiled for the purposes of creating a plan. The Midland Police Service, for example, found that the community provided

BOX 5.3

STEP 1 OF THE BUSINESS-PLANNING PROCESS

1. Gather Data:
   - Environmental Scanning
   - External Stakeholder Consultations
   - OPP Employee Survey
   - Employee Discovery Sessions
   - Trend Analysis

Source: Reprinted from *Ontario Provincial Police Strategic Plan 2011–2013*, p. 5. Retrieved from http://www.opp.ca/ecms/files/259349814.2.pdf

SWOT EXERCISE

Conduct a SWOT analysis on yourself. Write down a list of your strengths and weaknesses. Now look at things that are in your society but outside of your control: what opportunities are there for you, and what threats or dangers do you see that could directly affect you?

Next, conduct a SWOT analysis on your college. What are its strengths and weaknesses? What opportunities are there for your college, and what are the threats or dangers that could directly affect it?

With the SWOT analysis, you are now able to develop a plan to take advantage of your strengths and correct your weaknesses. You can maximize the opportunities available to you and defend yourself from any dangers or threats you have identified. You can also do the same for your college.

---

valuable input during the consultation process, which led to the development of several strategies:

> Although hundreds of submissions were received, there was a great deal of commonality among the responses. Almost every respondent focused on the need for increases in: Police Visibility (in high crime and residential locations), Traffic Initiatives (enforcement of speeding, disobeying traffic signals, RIDE, distracted driving, and pedestrian crossing infractions), Drug Enforcement, and Community Partnerships. (Midland Police Service, n.d., p. 2)

The RCMP notes that environmental scanning "provides the organization with a solid understanding of external conditions; managers a context for decision making; and ultimately a launching pad for strategic planning and priority setting exercises" (2007b, para. 2). The Toronto Police Service, for example, conducted an environmental scan in 2008 to review the following topics: demographic trends, crime trends, youth crime, victims and witnesses, traffic trends, calls for service, technology and policing, police resources, urban trends, public perception, and legislation changes (Toronto Police Service, 2008).

In the second step of the business-planning process, senior police managers set the strategic direction of the police service (see Box 5.4). This process is often completed over a few days, with several people being tasked with incorporating the information into a readable plan. Strategies are developed by senior executives, as part of the "top-down" approach to the process. For each strategy, activities and targets or measurements are discussed.

So what would this mean to you as a frontline police officer? Your patrol area would be assigned with certain priorities, such as traffic enforcement and education, drug enforcement and education, proactive crime prevention initiatives, and so forth. If you review your police services business plan, you will see where you fit in as your activities are considered "inputs" and the results you achieve, such as reducing the number of fatalities, are considered "outcomes."

Whitelaw and Parent (2010) state that "in the traditional model of police work effectiveness is

---

BOX 5.4

STEP 2 OF THE BUSINESS-PLANNING PROCESS

2. Strategic Plan:
   - Goals
   - Strategies
   - Activities
   - Indicators

Source: Reprinted from *Ontario Provincial Police Strategic Plan 2011–2013*, p. 5. Retrieved from http://www.opp.ca/ecms/files/259349814.2.pdf

---

determined by the clearance rate. This rate is the percentage of cases in which an offence has been committed and a suspect identified, regardless of whether the suspect is ultimately convicted of the crime" (p. 47). This method of measurement is still in effect; however, Sir Robert Peel had a more effective measurement of success for policing. As discussed in Chapter 1, Peel's ninth principle stated, "The test of police efficiency is the absence of crime and disorder, not the visible evidence of police action in dealing with it" (New Westminster Police Service, 2011). Which of these two measures—clearance rates or the absence of crime and disorder—would you prefer? "Crime prevention is a core police service, mandated in the *Police Services Act* of Ontario. Effective crime prevention programs and initiatives rely on the intelligence-led approach of continuously analyzing and sharing information" (OPP, 2011, p. 6).

Following the creation of a strategy, the third step of the planning process, implementation, takes place (see Box 5.5). The plans have to be communicated to all stakeholders, including all participants in the plan. In the OPP, the plan is included in police officers' performance plan—the plan does not dictate that they must achieve a certain number of tickets or arrests, but it does outline activities each member must aim to complete. These activities may include attending mandatory training, working on initiatives to reduce traffic fatalities, or reducing property and violent crimes based on the priorities for each detachment. The local activities are devised by local people, including detachment commanders; this is the "bottom-up" part of the plan. The notion of this planning process is that what gets measured gets done!

The fourth step in planning is evaluation (see Box 5.6). Once plans are implemented they must be monitored to see if they are working. For example, a plan may call for an activity related to foot patrol on the main street during evening hours. The goal of the activity may be to reduce the number of acts of vandalism on that street. When measuring the outcome of the activity, a manager may find that it either is or is not effective. The manager finds this out by measuring the number of occurrences that take place during the police initiative—if the numbers don't go down, the activities may be seen as ineffective. If it is not effective, that activity should be discontinued and another strategy should be developed, such as installing more lighting in the area or having closed-circuit television

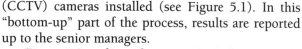
(CCTV) cameras installed (see Figure 5.1). In this "bottom-up" part of the process, results are reported up to the senior managers.

Figure 5.2 outlines the entire OPP planning process described above. Several steps are ongoing, such as monitoring, evaluating, reviewing, and environmental scanning. As a frontline police officer, you may be only vaguely familiar with the entire plan, but you will be aware of the initiatives assigned to you by your supervisor. It is good to know that there is a plan and that you are contributing to it. When announcements are made showing success, you will know that you contributed to that success.

LO³ COMMUNITY SATISFACTION SURVEYS

Another key element to providing customer service is to find out and evaluate how satisfied the customer is with the service. As mentioned in the introduction to this chapter, police services provide exactly that: a service. Twenty years ago, as community policing was emerging, many police services changed their names from police force to police service. The term *police force* implied the notion of using force, being a force, and enforcing law and order. The term *police service* is more reflective of the police as community partners rather than enforcers. So, just like other service providers, police services ask their customers how satisfied they are with the services provided. Most community satisfaction surveys take place over the telephone; people are called and asked to participate by answering a few questions. The majority of people contacted would have had little contact with the police service, while others would have been in contact with the police as a victim, a witness, or a person in need of some other service such as obtaining a criminal record check or a copy of an accident report. Box 5.7 provides an example of a public notice that a satisfaction survey will be issued to the community.

Volunteers are usually used to conduct the surveys, and professionals analyze the results and provide conclusions based on the results, as the OPP did in conducting its province-wide survey (see Box 5.8). It is interesting to note that the West Grey Police Services Board was using Police Foundations students to conduct their surveys.

© ZUMA Wire Service / Alamy

FIGURE 5.1

Closed-circuit television cameras, like those installed throughout downtown Toronto before the G20 summit, are one strategy that may be part of a strategic plan to reduce vandalism.

FIGURE 5.2
From Strategy to Action: The OPP Planning Process

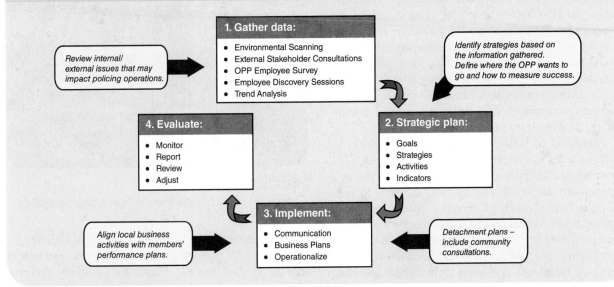

Source: *Ontario Provincial Police Strategic Plan, 2011-2013*, online at http://www.opp.ca/ecms/files/259349814.2.pdf. © Queen's Printer for Ontario, 2011. Reproduced with permission.

BOX 5.7

WEST GREY POLICE SERVICE COMMUNITY SATISFACTION SURVEY

The West Grey Police Services Board is preparing its 2011–2013 Business Plan. The plan will address the policing priorities and objectives of the police service for the next three years. In order to plan and implement some of these programs, the police services board needs input from the public with a community satisfaction survey. To complete this project the board has enlisted assistance of students from the Georgian College Police Foundations Program. These students will randomly contact residents and business owners either by phone, mail or in person to respond to the questionnaire. Students attending in person will have proper photo identification issued to them by the Police Service. Your input is very important and we hope you will take the time to complete this survey if contacted.

Source: Reprinted by permission from West Grey Police Service. (2011, January 27). Community satisfaction survey. Retrieved from http://www.westgreypolice.ca/node/237

BOX 5.8

OPP PROVINCE-WIDE COMMUNITY SATISFACTION SURVEY

In 2011, the OPP conducted its second community satisfaction survey to gather public opinions on the services of the OPP. "I know Ontarians are very busy, but we hope the people who are contacted will take the time to answer the survey questions. I promise that the OPP will use the information wisely to improve OPP service,*" said OPP Commissioner Chris Lewis. This survey is a way of providing the OPP with feedback on how well they are doing, and it provides input on safety and youth issues in each community. Following the analysis, the OPP uses the information to develop its business plan and reports on it in the annual report.

*Ontario Provincial Police, "Second Province-Wide Community Satisfaction Survey Helps OPP Assess Service to Ontarians," January 28, 2011. http://www.newswire.ca/en/story/815643/second-province-wide-community-satisfaction-survey-helps-opp-assess-service-to-ontarians. © Queen's Printer for Ontario, 2011. Reproduced with permission.

LO⁴ COMMUNITY POLICING

Some think of **community policing** as the warm and fuzzy side to policing; others think that it is the only effective means of providing safe and secure communities. As noted in Chapter 1, Sir Robert Peel suggested that the police are the public, and the public are the police, meaning that the safety of the community is a shared responsibility. "Community policing is a philosophy, management style, and organizational strategy centered on police-community partnerships and problem solving to address problems of crime and social disorder in communities" (Whitelaw & Parent, 2010, p. 51).

According to Whitelaw and Parent (2010), **traditional policing** operated under several key principles. For example, the police were seen as having the sole responsibility for crime control, and the way to control crime was through preventative patrols and rapid response times. Whitelaw and Parent suggest that "traditional models of patrol practice are premised on the three Rs: random patrol, rapid response and reactive investigation . . . . Patrol officers spend their shifts responding to calls, and the remaining is spent patrolling randomly, waiting for the next call for service" (p. 46).

Police services have evolved over the years to become more consultative with the community in looking at problems and finding solutions. The police are often only part of the solution, and other members of the community can work with the police to solve community problems, as demonstrated in Figure 5.3. According to the Winnipeg Police Service (2011), the four cornerstones of community policing are community consultation, problem analysis, problem solving,

Courtesy of Port Coquitlam Community Police

FIGURE 5.3
Community policing partners in Port Coquitlam, B.C.

and call management. Whitelaw and Parent (2010) propose the PARE problem-solving model as a system and process for tackling all community problems: *p*roblem identification, *a*nalysis of the problem, *r*esponse to the problem, and *e*valuation of the outcomes of your response. The RCMP use a model called CAPRA, which stands for *c*lients, meaning knowing who your direct and indirect clients are; *a*cquire/analysis of information; *p*artnerships, or who can you work with to solve the problem; *r*esponse; and *a*ssessment of action taken. Both models take similar approaches that involve figuring out the problem, figuring out a solution, deciding who is going to do what and by when, and assessing and evaluating the outcomes.

Take a look at the following problem of graffiti involving the Halifax Police Service and consider how you would use the PARE problem-solving model to deal with it.

THE COMMUNITY APPROACH TO GRAFFITI IN HALIFAX

Most people view graffiti as a criminal offence involving vandalism and mischief. Often gang

> **community policing:**
> A form of policing that is based on the police working with the community to solve problems and provide solutions. Police work and consult with community partners to resolve issues either before or as they arise.

> **traditional policing:**
> A reactive approach to policing that focuses on making arrests after a crime has been committed. This approach limits community consultation and involvement in solutions. The responsibility for problem solving is entirely that of the police service.

DECODING POLICE TERMS

Graffiti: A problem that, if not addressed, contributes to the decline of a community. The application of paint to private or public property without the consent of the owner is a *Criminal Code* offence (s. 430—Mischief to Property).

Halifax Regional Municipality

FIGURE 5.4
The Halifax Regional Municipality targeted graffiti to avoid urban decay.

members mark or "tag" areas as their turf to serve as a warning to others. Community members and business owners view graffiti as an indication of social decline and a lack of law enforcement in the area (see Figure 5.4). These perceptions indicate a problem within the community, and the Halifax Regional Municipality worked together with the police and the community to come up with a solution.

The Halifax police service responded to this problem by creating a proactive crime prevention strategy following a complete analysis of the issues. This is a comprehensive solution to the complex problem of graffiti. If the problem were ignored it would not go away and the city of Halifax would be overwhelmed with graffiti, leading to further problems with crime. According to the broken windows theory, if small issues are not addressed they will only get worse. American criminologists James Wilson and George Kelling developed this theory in 1982, in an article entitled "Broken Windows: The Police and Neighborhood Safety" published in *The Atlantic*. According to Kelling and Wilson, broken windows in New York were a metaphor for neighbourhood deterioration. The main idea of this theory is that "the existence of unchecked and uncontrolled minor incivilities in a neighborhood—for example, panhandling, public drunkenness, vandalism and graffiti—produces an atmosphere conducive to more serious crime" (Burke, 1998, in Griffiths, 2008, p 346).

The Halifax Regional Municipality provided property owners with a removal kit to assist in the rapid removal of any graffiti. The Halifax Regional Police partnered with key corporate and municipal agencies to take a proactive approach to the problem, including the Halifax Regional School Board, Canada Post, Nova Scotia Power, the Business Improvement District Commissions, Halifax Water, residents' associations, community watch groups, parents and youth, and the Nova Scotia Justice Department (Halifax Regional Municipality, 2009).

This community problem illustrates a community response that included the police as a key member of the team; in other words, this was a community policing approach. It was also a proactive approach that included "the *three P's*, prevention, problem solving and partnership (with the community)" (Griffiths, 2008, p. 230). Traditional policing would have taken on the issue with a reactive approach, hoping to catch graffiti artists in the act,

POLICING ONLINE

To read the Halifax Regional Municipality graffiti management plan, go to

http://www.halifax.ca/corporate/Graffiti/GraffitiManagementPlan.html

arresting them, charging them, and releasing them. This reactive approach would not have been as effective as the comprehensive one taken by the Halifax Regional Municipality.

CHALLENGES AND OPPORTUNITIES

One of the challenges with community policing initiatives is to encourage community members to participate in meetings and discussions and to review issues or concerns in the community. Most often an issue has to be pressing and highly visible (e.g., graffiti) before people become motivated to participate and offer their services as part of the analysis and solution. Once a motivated group is formed, another problem is sustaining the group and maintaining the motivation of the community members and partner agencies. Volunteer burnout is common after a committee or group has been running for a number of months. Some people are unable to maintain the enthusiasm they initially had to complete the initiative.

There are many opportunities for the police to engage community members in new ways that make public participation easier. For example, social media provide a great opportunity for the police to conduct community consultation online rather than requiring people to attend meetings to provide input. Police services are using Facebook, Twitter, YouTube, and other methods of communication to get their messages out and to receive information from the public. Additionally, the police are using the same social media to conduct investigations and monitor criminal activity.

CHAPTER SUMMARY

In this chapter we discussed quality service standards and the community consultation process, along with the sound reasons for consulting with the public and finding out what issues are priorities. In addition, we discussed community satisfaction surveys and the value of finding out if members of the public are satisfied with the policing services they receive. This chapter also reviewed the concept of community policing and the reasons why this policing philosophy evolved. Finally, this chapter described the business planning process and the legal and practical reasons for following this process. As customer service and working with community partners are key components of modern-day policing, it is important to understand the processes involved in making partnerships successful.

LO¹ Describe the community consultation process and the reasons for conducting this process.

This chapter described the types of community consultation and the benefits of police services working *with* members of the community. Asking community members what they deem to be priorities is a good way to ensure customer satisfaction and to make sure policing resources are directed the way community members appreciate. The police benefit from having collective problem-solving approaches to find resolutions rather than being solely responsible for outcomes.

LO² Summarize the business-planning process and the reasons for following this process.

In Ontario, all police services are required to create a business or strategic plan. Prior to creating a plan, data are collected through a consultation process. A plan is then developed identifying goals, objectives, and initiatives. Next, the plan is implemented and operationalized. All plans are consistently monitored, reviewed, and evaluated to ensure the goals are being met.

LO³ Explain community satisfaction surveys and the reasons for conducting these surveys.

Most police services conduct community satisfaction surveys using various methods to find out what they are doing well and where they can improve their service to the public.

LO⁴ Discuss the evolution of community policing in Canada.

This chapter discussed different approaches to policing, including proactive and reactive activities. Community policing involves working with the community to solve problems and provide solutions. Community policing uses problem-solving models such as the PARE and CAPRA models to find solutions to combat community issues.

Police Culture, Personality, and Stress

LEARNING OUTCOMES

After reading this chapter, you will be able to:

LO1   Define the police culture or subculture.

LO2   Describe the personality of police officers.

LO3   Describe organizational characteristics of police services.

LO4   Explain stress and its impact on policing.

LO5   Summarize the services of employee assistance programs for police officers.

The word culture refers to patterns of human activity or the way of life for a society. It includes informal codes or rules of manners, dress, language, behavior, rituals, and systems of belief.

—J. Dempsey and L. Forst (2011, p. 81)

A diamond is merely a lump of coal that did extremely well under pressure!

—Author Unknown

In this chapter we will discuss the culture of policing, the personalities of police officers, and the nature of stressors that affect police officers. Many researchers agree that a police culture or subculture exists; they also agree that there is a certain "police personality" that is distinct to the occupation. Have you ever looked at someone and thought, that person must be a cop? Was it the way the person carried him- or herself, or the way the individual looked, positioned him- or herself in a room, or spoke? These are all indicators of both the police culture and the police personality. Dempsey and Forst (2011) describe academic studies that "have indicated that the nature of policing and the experiences officers go through on the job cause them to band together into their own subculture, which many researchers call the police culture or police subculture" (p. 81).

LO¹ POLICE CULTURE

Policing has many similarities to other occupations where employees are members of a large organization, wear identifying clothing, and drive vehicles that are marked to identify the organization. These organizations include delivery services, taxi companies, military organizations, and security companies.

The policing organization is similar in its hierarchical structure to organizations or companies with a president at the top and the entry-level employee at the bottom. As mentioned in Chapter 1, policing is a paramilitary organization with a chain-of-command reporting structure. The culture of policing starts with the notion of the chain of command, the uniform, use-of-force weapons, marked vehicles, and the powers of the position. Police officers are the only people in our society who can legally take a life—this civil legal authority is one that no other occupation has and is essentially where the similarity with other organizations ends. Police officers have legislative authority over citizens in society, and this authority is an important aspect of the identity and culture of the policing occupation (Figure 6.1).

The police subculture, like most subcultures, is characterized by clannishness, secrecy, and isolation from those not in the group. Police officers work with other police officers during their tours of duty. Many socialize together after work and on days off, often to the exclusion of others—even old friends and family. When socializing off-duty officers tend to talk about their jobs (Dempsey & Forst, 2011, p. 82).

Acceptance into the police subculture is a natural evolution, as is the development of police-like characteristics. With shift work police officers are on their days off when many other people are working, so they tend to socialize with their colleagues who have similar schedules.

New recruits, like those shown in Figure 6.2, are socialized into the culture of policing. According to Janet Chan, this socialization is a "process through

FIGURE 6.1
Police officers perform nonuniform duties.

FIGURE 6.2
Toronto police recruits.

which a novice learns the skills, knowledge and values necessary to become a competent member of an organization or occupation" (2004, p. 328). Think of your first week attending your college courses. How did you feel when you sat in the classroom for the first time? What did you have to learn in order to function within the new college culture? In the policing world socialization involves "not only learning the laws, procedures and techniques of law enforcement and order maintenance, but also acquiring a range of organizational skills, attitudes and assumptions that are compatible with other members of the occupation" (Chan, 2004, p. 328). This socialization is affected by many variables, such as generational issues, where the senior police officers are significantly older than the recruits and were introduced themselves to policing by people who were significantly older than they were (see Figure 6.3). Chan states that "police culture [is] a system of shared values and understandings which is passed on from one generation of police to the next"

FIGURE 6.3
Graduating OPP Constable Matt Starzecki receiving his warrant card and badge from Georgian College Police Foundations Coordinator, retired Sgt. Peter Maher.

(2004, p. 328). For example, a recruit who is hired in 2012 will be learning the policing culture from people who were hired up to 30 years earlier. The paramilitary nature of policing is passed on from generation to generation, and the culture tends to be conservative, cynical, and suspicious of members of society who are not police officers.

LO² THE PERSONALITY OF POLICE OFFICERS

When you think of the type of person who would want to become a police officer, what type of personality do you envision? Is there a "type" of personality going into the profession, or is there a "type" of personality that develops over time while in the profession? Van Maanen (1981) asserts that "the police personality is developed through the process of learning and doing police work. In a study of one urban police department he found that the typical police recruit is a sincere individual who becomes a police officer for the job security, the salary, the belief that the job will be interesting, and the desire to enter into an occupation that can benefit society" (p. 85). The personality of the new recruit is certainly affected by the stressors of the occupation. Working shifts with a high volume of work, including phone calls, calls for service, and mounds of paperwork, can have an impact on the once enthusiastic employee. Thibault, Lynch, and McBride state that "most studies have found that the police working personality derives from the socialization process in the police academy, field training and patrol experience" (p. 85).

When people think of a police officer they often think of a stoic, conservative person dressed in a uniform and driving a marked police vehicle. New recruits work very hard to be accepted into police agencies, and their goal is most often to help people. The police culture encourages people to develop a police personality or traits that are common to many police officers. According to Skolnick (1966), "Scholars have reported that this personality is thought to include such traits as authoritarianism, suspicion, hostility, insecurity, conservatism and cynicism" (p. 84). This description seems incongruent with the goal of the police recruit, which is to help people. Recruits often find themselves in a difficult position as their goal is also to be accepted into the police culture. "By adopting the sentiments and behaviour of the older officers, the new recruits avoid ostracism and censure by their supervisors and colleagues" (Van Maanen, 1981, p. 85). Once recruits become seasoned officers themselves, they are often able to combine the two goals and work within the police subculture to attain some of their own goals and apply their own perspectives.

The goal of helping people may be attained by going into different lines of police work, such as becoming a crime prevention officer or a school liaison officer. Other people may want to specialize in areas such as tactics and rescue or work to become a canine officer. All of these options require hard work and dedication; however, they also foster a sense of accomplishment and satisfaction in helping people. A study conducted by Toch found that

> as the officers described what they saw as the "high points" of their police careers, they recalled a variety of incidents they had effectively resolved, with citizens receiving needed assistance. What the officers said they valued was the experience of "walking in and making a difference," "helping somebody who really desperately could use some help," "affecting somebody in some way"—in other words, the opportunity to make a humane contribution (2002, p. 2-2).

This description goes back to the recruit's goal of "helping people." Many officers find their own ways of meeting that goal.

Toch's research captured some revealing comments by the respondents:

> "You know, we have the greatest job in the world. It is the biggest secret. It really is! It's like you live on it. You need it."
> "You look forward to going to work."
> "You get out there and you're playing cops and you're having a real good time."
> "I just feel the joy of this job."
> "Every emotion that you could ever think of happens to you on this job" (2002, p. 2-2).

When discussing the various police personalities, the best way to do so is to look at the job from two perspectives: that of the new recruit and that of the seasoned veteran. According to Chan (2004), "Research studies have consistently shown that while most recruits join the police with high expectations and lofty ideals, by the time they graduate as police constables, many have become disillusioned and cynical about police work and the police organization" (p. 328). New recruits must make a transition from a life outside of policing to a new life within the culture. This transition is influenced by the people the recruit is working with during this critical time. If the recruit has a nurturing, caring, interested, and progressive coach officer and shift supervisor, he or she will acclimate well to the profession and to the shift. Conversely, if the recruit is paired with a cynical, dishonest, hostile coach officer and a disconnected shift supervisor, he or she will suffer accordingly. There have been many instances of dismissal of probationary constables based at least partially on personality conflicts. Although this is unfortunate, it is the nature of the occupation and the nature of all organizations. This may be seen as an issue to be solved systemically; however, as humans are involved in these transactions, no organization can remove all instances of this type of behaviour. When a recruit finds him- or herself in a situation with difficult superiors, the best way to handle it is to stick it out. A key ingredient to being a successful police officer is managing relationships, and this includes the people on the platoon.

Kevin Gilmartin (2002) has stated that "for almost all law enforcement officers, their career begins from a position of enthusiasm, motivation and idealism, but the journey over the years from new recruit to experienced officer produces changes" (p. 3). These changes are influenced by issues that are both internal and external to the policing organization. "Idealism can become cynicism, optimistic enthusiasm can become pessimism, and the easygoing young recruit can become the angry and negative veteran police officer" (Gilmartin, 2002, p. 3). The dedication and the requirements of the policing profession have an impact on both the personal and the professional life of a member. Often police officers regret missed opportunities in their family lives and their professional lives. These missed opportunities can cause anger and resentment, further perpetuating the problems these officers face.

"Law enforcement personnel, like all other human beings, form their worldviews and predictions about life from the situations and events they see every day. Who calls the police to their home because things are going well?" (Gilmartin, 2002, p. 23). The officer's worldview is affected by the calls for service attended. Many officers attend calls for domestic violence, drugs, robberies, assaults, frauds, drunkenness, and so on. Over the years, these interactions with people sometimes create cynicism in officers, which may carry over into their day-to-day activities and social gatherings (Gilmartin, 2002).

A good way to offset this cynical worldview is to change your job function every three to five years. If you are a frontline general duties officer, move over to being a traffic officer, then a canine officer or a polygraph officer. If you change your job functions and follow your interests, your worldview will reflected your experiences. Those officers who work at one location for their entire careers may find that they are negatively influenced by that experience. Officers are affected differently, and some officers find working in one location beneficial to both their working and personal lives as they gain the security and expertise of specializing in one area of policing. The key is to be aware of what is affecting you, and if you are unhappy with your situation, work on changing it. If you are happy where you are, don't change a thing! Finally, always keep in mind a work–life balance—make sure you spend time with people who are not associated with policing, such as your family and friends from school.

LO³ ORGANIZATIONAL CHARACTERISTICS OF POLICE SERVICES

According to McKenna and Murray (2007), traditional Canadian policing is based on military and bureaucratic organizational principles, and each policing organization reflects the following organizational characteristics:

- rank-based authority structure—authority resides solely in rank assigned; position power;
- highly centralized administration and authority structure—all important decisions are made at the top;
- command and control management philosophy—reliance on rank based authority, use of formal orders, reward rule following, punishment of rule violation;
- hierarchical decision-making structure that controls and directs police operations from the top; pyramid-shaped organizational structure; top down management;
- formalized—with a heavy reliance on formal, written communication: rules procedures, policies etc.;
- specialization of many police administrative and operational functions;
- emphasis on technology and technique—generally rigid and inflexible organizational structure; resistant to change; and
- insular and closed—organization resistant to outside political or community influence (McKenna & Murray, 2007, p. 9).*

McKenna and Murray use the RCMP as an example of the organizational characteristics of a traditional police service; however, the fact is that most police services in Canada emphasize these characteristics. The larger the police service, the more centralized the authority structure tends to be. New recruits

are taught that they must respect rank and seniority. There is a time and a place to discuss options, but when you are given an order by a superior officer, your job is to carry out the order, not to debate the merits of the request. A good analogy is when an officer is involved in a gun fight and the sergeant tells the recruit to duck—this is not the time to discuss the merits of the order! Conversely, if there is a problem involving break and enters in a neighbourhood and the sergeant asks for input from the platoon members, this is the time for the recruit to express an opinion.

When new recruits arrive at their new work location following their training, they may not immediately notice some subtle cues. Recruits are not expected to offer their opinions, as their lack of experience leads their input to be deemed useless. Senior members of the platoon need to feel superior and valued, and this pecking order quickly becomes evident to each new recruit; until they are seen as equal members, recruits would be well served to observe and make notes of conversations. Van Maanen discusses the experience of recruits once they complete their formal academy education and begin to work with a coach officer: "the recruits listen to the folklore, myths, and legends about veteran officers and start to understand police work in the way that older officers desire them to" (1981, p. 85). Sometimes there are friendly hazing rituals, with senior platoon members setting up the new recruits in embarrassing scenarios as a way of having fun at their expense and seeing how they handle the situation.

LO⁴ STRESS AND ITS IMPACT ON POLICING

Stress—we've all heard about it. There's good stress, such as winning a million dollars, and bad stress, such as a death in the family. "Stress is a transactional construct, which means that it refers to a process that links features of the human environment (stressors) with reactions to these features by persons (stress-related behavior)" (Toch, 2002, p. 2). Many people handle stress well, but some people do not handle it well at all. Police officers are trained both in the classroom and through experience to handle stress better than the average person. "Law enforcement officers face a number of sources of stress particular to their field, ranging from organizational demands (e.g., shift work) to the nature of police work itself (e.g., exposure to violence and suffering)" (Finn & Tomz, 1996, p. 13). Many stressors affect police officers, from the obvious ones, such as dealing with physical abuse or death, to the not-so-obvious ones,

*Rethinking Police Governance, Culture & Management. URL: http://www.publicsafety.gc.ca/rcmp-grc/_fl/eng/rthnk-plc-eng.pdf, Department of Public Safety Canada, 2007. Reproduced with the permission of the Minister of Public Works and Government Services Canada, 2012.

such as striving for promotion or dealing with internal politics. "The stress of belonging to the law enforcement profession affects every officer. It is just a matter of degree" (Toch, 2002, p. 1). Toch lists the following consequences of police stress: higher divorce rates, marital discord, disruption of family life, child-rearing problems, alcoholism, suicide, performance anxieties, overachievement, callousness, absenteeism, emotional detachment, and post-traumatic stress disorder (PTSD).

The study of the policing profession is accurately described by Fin and Tomz (1996):

> Law enforcement officers face a number of unusual, often highly disturbing, sources of stress, including organizational stresses (e.g., the hierarchical, autocratic structure of the agency), stresses inherent in law enforcement work (e.g., frequent exposure to violence and human suffering), frustration with other parts of the criminal justice system (e.g., perceived leniency of court sentences), and personal difficulties (e.g., not having enough time with their families) (p. 1).

This is the reality faced by many members of police services. Some members resign their positions, while others discover ways to find a work–life balance. Unfortunately, some end up depending on alcohol or develop other forms of dependency in order to cope with the stressors of the job.

Stress can have an impact on police officers' mental and physical health (see Table 6.1) "Stress weakens and disturbs the body's defense mechanisms and may play a role in the development of hypertension, ulcers, cardiovascular disease and as research indicated, probably cancer" (Dempsey & Forst, 2011, p. 87).

Most people perceive the danger of law enforcement work to be the most serious stress for officers, but more common sources of stress result from the policies and procedures of law enforcement agencies. Finn and Tomz (1996) list the following as the most common sources of stress:

- unproductive management styles
- equipment deficiencies and shortages
- inconsistent discipline and enforcement of rules
- perceived excessive or unnecessary paperwork
- perceived favouritism by administrators regarding assignments and promotions
- lack of input into policy and decision making
- second-guessing of officers' actions and lack of administrative support
- inconsistent or arbitrary internal disciplinary procedures and review

TABLE 6.1
Mental and Physical Problems Associated with Stress

Cardiovascular Problems
Heart attacks
Coronary artery disease
Hypertension
Stroke

Gastrointestinal Problems
Ulcers
Genitourinary problems
Failure to menstruate
Impotence
Incontinence

Immunology Problems
Reduced resistance to infection
Tumours

Psychiatric Problems
Post-traumatic stress disorder
Transient situational disturbances

From DEMPSEY/FORST, POLICE (with Review Cards and Printed Access Card), 1E. © 2011 Cengage Learning.

- lack of career development opportunities (and perceived unfairness of affirmative action), with resulting competition among officers, especially in small departments, for the few available openings
- lack of adequate training or supervision
- lack of reward and recognition for good work (p. 7)*

These sources of stress are not necessarily unique to the policing profession; most occupations suffer from the same stressors. Review the list above and consider, for example, your own college professors, who are affected by administrators and college policies and procedures. They must adhere to a code of conduct and they are evaluated by their supervisors. They may complain about a lack of training or developmental opportunities, and they may feel that their work is not recognized or rewarded.

Police officers, by the nature of their work, are exposed to critical incidents. Toch explains that critical incidents are "certain tragic events [that] are … dramatic, shocking and disturbing to our collective psyches" (2002, p. 2). These incidents might include extreme danger, deaths or serious incidents involving children, shootings, traffic fatalities, major disasters, or catastrophic events. One of

*Finn, P., Tomz, J., (1996), The National Institute of Justice (NIJ), Developing a Law Enforcement Stress Program for Officers and Their Families. Retrieved from https://www.ncjrs.gov/pdffiles/163175.pdf , p. 7.

FIGURE 6.4

The police funeral for Sgt. Ryan Russell.

the most traumatic critical incidents for police officers is the death of one of their own on the job (Figure 6.4).

At the time of writing, the Ontario Ombudsman was commencing an investigation into complaints about the way the OPP handles members suffering from psychological injury as a result of being exposed to traumatic events on the job. The bulk of the complaints allege that affected officers were ostracized and stigmatized. Other issues raised include a lack of training and education for serving officers about operational stress injuries and a lack of support systems for those who need help (Ombudsman Ontario, 2012).

CUMULATIVE STRESS

In an article by the OPP Human Resources Bureau (2006) called "The Impact of Stress on Officers and the OPP Response," the authors identified that "it is difficult to calculate the effects of continued exposures to motor vehicle accidents, murders, suicides, kidnappings, rapes and other violent acts that assault the sensibilities of law enforcement officers" (p. 3). Practices prior to 2005 were described as offering assistance only after "officers displayed maladaptive behaviors such as excessive drinking, domestic violence, or even suicide" (Sheehan & Van Hasselt, 2003, p. 12). The OPP Human Resources Bureau article identified that "cumulative stress results from a buildup of stressors that may be work-related or non-work-related. Each of the stressors or incidents, in and of themselves, may not necessarily overwhelm the individual's coping mechanisms. However, the combined effect of many events can overwhelm the individual" (p. 3). Cumulative stress reactions build up over a period of months or even years. "This type of stress can cause permanent psychological or physical damage because the stress builds up slowly over time and consequently goes unnoticed until the individual becomes sick or exhibits significant and observable behavioral changes" (Sheehan & Van Hasselt, 2003, quoted in OPP Human Resources Bureau, 2006, p. 3). The notion of stress building up over time makes it difficult for a policing organization to understand and recognize the need for assistance. Consequently, the allegations made against the OPP that affected officers "were ostracized and stigmatized" would have merit on the surface, as the policing culture would not accept the notion of cumulative stress. Members suffering from cumulative stress may be labelled troublemakers or malingerers. Furthermore, if they are on sick leave or long-term disability, they will not be offered much support from their former colleagues and friends.

POLICING ONLINE

Duxbury and Higgings's 2012 study of work–life issues in Canadian police departments seeks to focus attention on the important topics of work/life conflict and role overload within Canadian police organizations. The authors of this study anticipate that their work will prompt Canadian police organizations to take action and assist employees to reduce the impacts of role overload, stress, and work–life conflict.
Summary of key findings:

- **http://sprott.carleton.co/wp-content/files/Duxbury-Higgins-Police2012_keyfindings.pdf**

  Summary of key differences associated with rank and gender:

- **http://sprott.carleton.co/wp-content/files/Duxbury-Higgins-Police2012_rankgender.pdf**

  Full report:

- **http://sprott.carleton.co/wp-content/files/Duxbury-Higgins-Police2012_fullreport.pdf**

LO⁵ EMPLOYEE SUPPORT

Most policing agencies have employee assistance programs (EAPs) in place for police service members and their families. This service is confidential and free to the members and their families. One widely used EAP provider is Shepell·fgi (see Figure 6.5); this company helps clients (the employer) to "improve workplace productivity and engagement, reduce employee absences, lower health, drug and disability benefits costs and attract and retain employees"* (Shepell·fgi, 2012, para. 2). These types of companies offer the following services: "professional counselling, support for family, financial, career and legal issues, nutrition, naturopathic and health coaching services, traumatic event support, workplace support programs focused on mental health and addictions, workplace training including wellness seminars and workshops, intercultural solutions, health management services and online programs" (Shepell·fgi, 2012).*

When these types of services were first introduced to police officers, they were reluctant to take advantage of them, as there was a feeling that the information shared with a company representative or a counsellor would be relayed to the police service. As time progressed, more members tried the EAP services and were satisfied with the results. Currently it is an accepted practice for members who are struggling with stress to seek counselling services. Family members of police personnel frequently use the services at no cost. The employer is assisted by having a productive employee at work rather than one off on stress leave, and the employee is obviously better off as he or she is better able to function and contribute to both work and family environments.

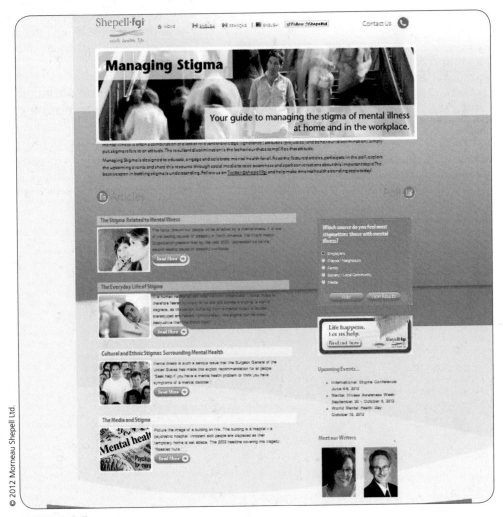

© 2012 Morneau Shepell Ltd.

FIGURE 6.5
Mental health is as important as physical health, and there are employee support programs in place to assist employees suffering from mental health issues.

*Shepell·fgi website, http://www.shepellfgi.com. © 2012 Morneau Shepell Ltd.

CHAPTER SUMMARY

The policing profession is an honourable one that enables recruits to become fulfilled, mature people once they have found their way around the organization. The benefits of a career in policing, including job security, an above-average salary, and an interesting job that benefits society, are attainable for every police officer in Canada. The impacts of the police culture, coupled with the inherent dangers and stress, are the price officers pay for the benefits of the job. Most people involved in policing come to the conclusion that the benefits far outweigh the negatives. The negative aspects of the profession discussed in this chapter are not designed to keep you away from policing; rather, they are discussed to increase your awareness of the issues of stress so that you will be informed and go into a career in policing with your eyes wide open.

LO¹ Define the police culture or subculture.

The culture of policing starts with the notion of the chain of command, the uniform, use-of-force weapons, marked vehicles, and the powers of the position.

LO² Describe the personality of police officers.

New recruits are influenced by the people they are working with during this critical time. If recruits have a nurturing, caring, interested, and progressive coach officer and shift supervisor, they will acclimate well to the profession and to their shift.

LO³ Describe organizational characteristics of police services.

The larger the police service, the more centralized the authority structure tends to be. Policing organizations are structured on a command-and-control model.

LO⁴ Explain stress and its impact on policing.

Many stressors can affect police officers. The consequences of police stress include higher divorce rates, marital discord, disruption of family life, child-rearing problems, alcoholism, suicide, performance anxieties, overachievement, callousness, absenteeism, emotional detachment, and post-traumatic stress disorder.

LO⁵ Summarize the services of employee assistance programs for police officers.

Most policing agencies have employee assistance programs (EAPs) in place for police service members and their families. This service is confidential and free to the members and their families.

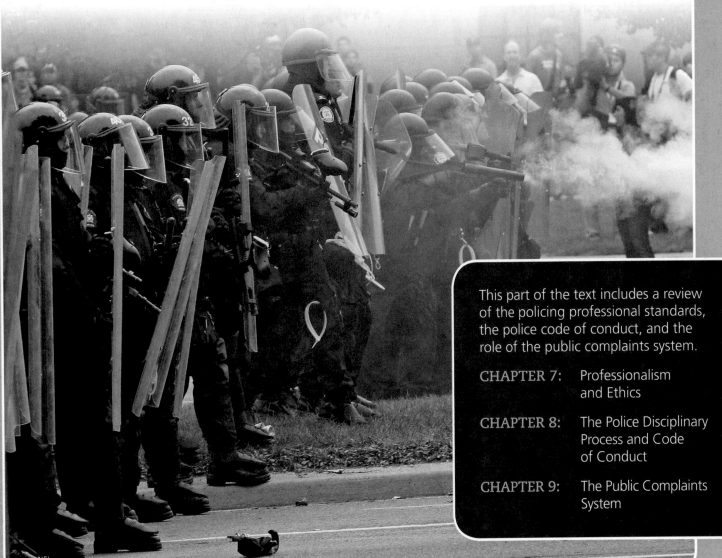

PART

3

Legislation Affecting Policing Conduct

This part of the text includes a review of the policing professional standards, the police code of conduct, and the role of the public complaints system.

CHAPTER 7:   Professionalism and Ethics

CHAPTER 8:   The Police Disciplinary Process and Code of Conduct

CHAPTER 9:   The Public Complaints System

Professionalism and Ethics

LEARNING OUTCOMES

After reading this chapter, you will be able to:

LO1   Describe what professionalism is in policing.

LO2   Explain why police officers should study ethics.

LO3   Summarize the ethical values identified in the Canadian Association of Chiefs of Police Ethical Framework.

LO4   Discuss the Six Pillars of Character.

LO5   State the five standards and principles of ethical policing.

LO6   Discuss how the ethical decision-making model is used in resolving an ethical dilemma.

Policing is a duty of the highest honour—also of the highest responsibility, the highest visibility, and the greatest challenge. Excellence in carrying out the policing mission to protect and serve inspires trust. The people of law enforcement are and must be the best, the brightest, and the most dedicated in defending the laws, the ideals, and the citizens that make this country great. More than anything else, law enforcement must be trusted to carry out these duties with the highest level of ethics and character. The reason is because in many ways, law enforcement embodies and represents the ideal of the rule of law that governs civilized society.

—Stephen M. R. Covey, cofounder and global practice leader, Franklin Covey's Global Speed of Trust Practice, Alpine, Utah

In this chapter we will take a practical and applied approach to the subject of professionalism and ethics in policing. We will examine the oath of office and oath of secrecy for a police officer, the code of conduct that governs their behaviour, and applicable codes of ethics that influence their everyday lives and work. Along with key definitions, we will discuss practical tools to assist police officers in ethical decision making when confronted with ethical dilemmas.

LO1 WHAT IS PROFESSIONALISM IN POLICING?

Carter and Wilson describe professionalism as "having an internal set of standards of performance and behaviour. Professionals aspire to high ideals: altruism; honour and integrity; respect; excellence and scholarship; caring, compassion, and communication; leadership; and responsibility and accountability" (2006, pp. 42–43).

For our purposes, we can define **professionalism** in policing as ethical and legal behaviour that contributes to the vision, mission, supporting values, goals, and objectives of the police service. Police officers demonstrate professionalism by adhering to the oath of office and oath of secrecy they took when sworn in as police officers (see Chapter 3); following their police service's mission statement and supporting values, including the *Canadian Association of Chiefs of Police* (CACP) code of ethics, the code of conduct, and the *Police Services Act*, which governs their conduct as public servants; and

being accountable for what they do or neglect to do as required by their profession while on duty (see Figure 7.1), and in some instances, off duty.

A key word in the definition of professionalism in policing is *accountable*, which means being responsible for one's own actions in accordance with the organization's mission, values, and objectives. Being accountable is a core part of professionalism in policing because the courts hold police to a higher standard, given the extraordinary powers extended to them by the federal and provincial governments and through the courts in interpreting the laws. "Police officers are granted extraordinary powers at law. As a result, they are subject to a strict Code and a legislative regime that holds them accountable" (*Precious and Hamilton Police Service*, 2002, p. 10). Being accountable may include off-duty conduct if there is a "connection between the conduct and either the occupational requirements for a police officer or the reputation of the police force" (*Police Services Act*, 1990, s. 80(2)).

Policing is a profession governed by legislation that includes a code of ethics and a code of conduct, as well as minimum training requirements. The Canadian Association of Chiefs of Police (CACP) has its own code of ethics, which police services have adopted in various forms. In Ontario, the legislation that governs policing is the *Police Services Act* (PSA) and its regulations. In this act, the duties of a police officer are prescribed, including minimum hiring and training

> **professionalism:** Ethical and legal behaviour that contributes to the vision, mission, supporting values, goals, and objectives of the organization that employs the professional.

FIGURE 7.1

Police Chief Bill Blair promised to hold officers accountable for their conduct at the G20 in Toronto.

Kevin Van Paassen/The Globe and Mail/The Canadian Press

requirements. Ontario Regulation 268/10 consists of the oath of office and oath of secrecy for police officers, as well as the code of conduct. Penalties (also referred to as dispositions) for professional misconduct can range from a reprimand up to and including immediate dismissal. Ceyssens (2005), in discussing principles relating to disposition of police misconduct, reinforces that the courts and police disciplinary tribunals have held police officers to a higher standard.

The PSA and its regulations describe the legal responsibilities of the Minister of Community Safety and Correctional Services (Solicitor General) in Ontario, the police service boards, the police services, and the members of police services. The PSA also contains a set of guiding principles for policing in Ontario, which are described in Chapter 11. Part V of the PSA in Ontario describes in detail the public complaints procedures against police, with some flexibility being provided for less serious complaints to be resolved locally in an informal way (O. Reg. 263/09). Regulations under

the PSA, particularly the Adequacy and Effectiveness of Police Services (O. Reg. 3/99), mandate the minimum police services required. Police services also develop their own policies and procedures with respect to how certain aspects of policing are to be carried out.

LO² WHY STUDY ETHICS?

Regardless of the profession, professionals should be held to a higher standard in society, and this is particularly true for policing. Ethics is perhaps the most important aspect of police training and education for police officers. The CACP Professionalism in Policing Research Project devoted an entire section to recommendations for training in ethics (Maguire & Dyke, 2011a, pp. 15–16). In an excellent article, Gleason (2006) speaks to the requirements of ethics training in policing, noting that not only should it be a stand-alone topic, but also it should be integrated into all other police-related topics. According to Gleason,

> An officer develops his or her moral compass, character, or ethical base, from interacting with other individuals and studying ethics. Ethics training for police professionals helps them do the following:
>
> - Readily recognize an ethical problem or dilemma
> - Identify various options to address the particular issue involved
> - Make a rational and ethically sound choice of which option to choose
> - Take prompt action based upon that choice
> - Accept responsibility for the outcome
>
> Police professionals cannot simply think ethically; they must also act ethically. Ethics training provides tools for addressing ethical problems, but the police professional must have the courage to act.* (2006, paras. 3–4)

To answer the question "Why study ethics?" in an informed manner, we need to examine the role of the police officer as a professional. In February 2012, the CACP released the first-ever study of ethics and professionalism in policing (Maguire & Dyke, 2011a). In 1997, the International Association of Chiefs of Police (IACP) Ethics Training Subcommittee identified ethics as their "greatest training and leadership need today and into the next century" (Maguire & Dyke, 2011b, p. 15).

Police officers have extraordinary powers, including the legal right to take away the liberty of a person

---

*Tag Gleason, Ethics training for police, *The Police Chief*, November 2006, v. 73, no. 11. http://www.policechiefmagazine.org/magazine/index.cfm?. Reproduced by permission of the International Association of Chiefs of Police.

FIGURE 7.2
Two RCMP officers demonstrating professionalism in making an arrest.

by way of arrest (see Figure 7.2), charge the person if reasonable grounds exist, and be a key player as part of the criminal justice system in gathering and placing evidence before the courts to determine the person's guilt or innocence. Given the mass media coverage of police conduct, police officers often find themselves under the public microscope. The police code of conduct governs not only the specific duties of a police officer, which we discussed in Chapter 3, but also, to some extent, the off-duty conduct. Police officers face ethical dilemmas on a daily basis, and it is important to understand that public trust and confidence depend on how police conduct themselves. This is why the values of every police organization are the standard that police officers must live up to every day.

In his 2003 report into various aspects of police misconduct within the Toronto Police Service, Justice Ferguson made a number of recommendations related to the importance of integrity and ethics training in policing. Often police services pay lip service to integrity and ethics by including them within the core values of their organizations but failing to address them in police training (Ferguson, 2003). Justice Ferguson recommended that ethics and integrity training be a condition for a promotion to a supervisory or management position within the Toronto Police Service. He also recommended ethics and integrity training be incorporated in all aspects of training, and that "all members of the [Toronto] police service be required to attend a one-day course on ethics, integrity, and corruption" (Ferguson, 2003,

p. 25). Ferguson saw ethics and integrity training as one way to increase the Toronto Police Service's "ability to maintain integrity and prevent corruption" (2003, p. 25). This view is consistent with those of Maguire and Dyke (2011b) and Gleason (2006) mentioned above.

Ethics are taught at the Ontario Police College and integrated into many of the college's core programs, including recruit training. Of interest, in the mid-1970s, recruits who graduated from the Ontario Police College received, in addition to their diploma, a copy of the *Law Enforcement Code of Ethics* signed by the director of the college on behalf of the International Association of Chiefs of Police (IACP), the Canadian Association of Chiefs of Police (CACP), the Police Association of Ontario (PAO), and the Ontario Chief Constable's Association, now known as the Ontario Association of Chiefs of Police (OACP). This practice has since been discontinued, but the college has strongly demonstrated through its code of honour that ethics and integrity are an integral part of the college's mission and vision statements (Ministry of Community Safety and Correctional Services [MCSCS], 2011f). These statements note that integrity "guides people to exemplify high ethical and moral behaviour" (p. 2). Integrity includes accountability, diversity, empowerment, and professionalism. The college describes courage as "the inner strength that enables a person to do what is right and commit themselves to a higher standard of personal conduct." This includes leadership by demonstrating "the dignity of our profession by conducting ourselves honourably while assuring the worth of others" and being "devoted to justice incorporating ethical and moral behaviour."

Evans and MacMillan define integrity as "the quality of acting in accordance with ethical values" (2008, p. 8). Police officers must remember that they are not entitled to public trust and that their conduct is under the microscope at all times. Officers need to understand the importance of integrity in upholding this public trust both on and off duty. In describing integrity, Edwin Delattre, a well-known scholar on the topic of ethics, states, "To me, integrity—in a person or an institution, in a police officer or a police department—means the settled disposition, the resolve and determination, the established habit 'of doing right where there is no one to make you do it but yourself'" (1989, p. 482).

Police ethics training in Canada is also available for police officers online. The Canadian Police Knowledge Network (CPKN) offers an online course called Police Ethics and Accountability. In addition, Georgian College, through its four-year Bachelor of Human Services—Police Studies degree program, offers the online courses Ethics in Policing and Professional Standards in Policing. Each course is a credit toward the degree program.

MISSION AND VISION STATEMENTS OF POLICE ORGANIZATIONS

A number of police organizations, including the IACP, the CACP, the Ontario Association of Chiefs of Police (OACP), individual police services, and the Ontario Police College, have adopted mission and value statements through working groups that address the issue of ethical conduct. Some of the common values for these organizations include professionalism, integrity, accountability, leadership, courage, honesty, respect, diversity, and community partnerships. These values continue to evolve, as demonstrated by the Ontario Provincial Police, who in 2010 added leadership to their organizational values (OPP, 2011). The OPP organizational values are "professionalism, accountability, diversity, respect, excellence, and leadership" (OPP, 2011, p. 4). These values are consistent with the Declaration of Principles within the *Police Services Act* (s. 1). Police organizations, through their recruitment processes (Figure 7.3), make every effort to ensure that their "police forces are representative of the communities they serve" (s. 1, para. 6, PSA).

LO3 ETHICAL VALUES IN THE CACP ETHICAL FRAMEWORK

Through the CACP Ethical Framework (provided in Box 7.4 on page 107), Canadian police chiefs and heads of police organizations demonstrate leadership in ethical values. These values include caring, courage, equity, integrity, openness, respect, transparency, and trustworthiness. The conduct of police officers should reflect these ethical values both on and off duty. In 2003, the Canadian Association of Police Boards (CAPB) adopted the framework, with some modifications (CAPB, 2003). See Appendix A for the full text of CAPB's Ethical Framework.

POLICE ACCOUNTABILITY AND THE COURTS

Another example of police being held accountable comes from the highest court, the Supreme Court of Canada (see Figure 7.4), which indicated that section 11 of the *Charter* does not apply to police discipline proceedings and that police officers must be held accountable to both society and their professions. In *Wigglesworth*, an RCMP officer was charged with a criminal offence of assault and a police misconduct offence arising from the same set of circumstances. The Honourable Madame Justice Wilson, in rejecting the argument that the two charges amounted to double jeopardy in violation of section 11 of the *Charter*, stated,

> I would hold that the appellant in this case is not being tried and punished for the same offence. The "offences" are quite different. One is an internal disciplinary matter. The accused has been found guilty of a major service offence and has, therefore, accounted to his profession. The other offence is the criminal offence of assault. The accused must now account to society at large for his conduct. (*R. v. Wigglesworth*, p. 566)

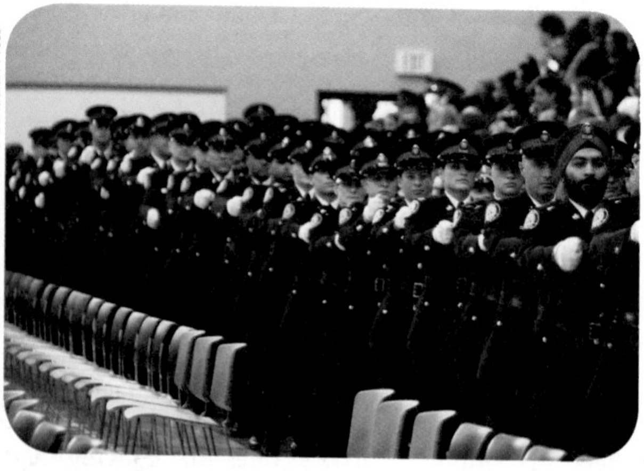

Fernando Morales/The Globe and Mail/The Canadian Press

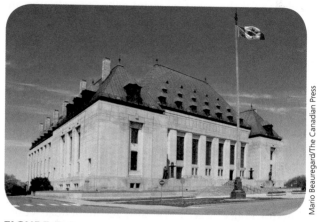

FIGURE 7.3
Toronto Police Recruit Class, May 10, 2011.

Mario Beauregard/The Canadian Press

FIGURE 7.4
Although not directly related to policing, the Supreme Court of Canada is not shy in holding the state and its agents to a higher legal and ethical standard.

The theme for the 2010 CACP conference was "Policing Excellence through Performance and Accountability." The CACP conducted a research project "to help law enforcement organizations identify what constitutes professionalism in policing, and learn what types of programs, policies and practices best support members and contribute to professionalism" (Blair, 2010, p. 1). Once again, we see the association of the words *professionalism* and *accountability* with quality policing. This research led to the production of the first-ever study of ethics in policing, which resulted in 52 recommendations being made to police services across Canada (Maguire & Dyke, 2011a).

THE RELATIONSHIP BETWEEN PROFESSIONALISM AND ETHICS

According to Michael Josephson of the Josephson Institute of Ethics, ethics "is a code of values which guides our choices and actions, and determines the purpose and course of our lives. Ethics is about the character of the individual as a person and as professional" (Institute for Law Enforcement Administration [ILEA], 2005, p. 2.7).

The Honourable René J. Marin states, "Police officers are the front door to the justice system. Professionalism cannot exist without ethics. The distinguishing feature of professions is the importance they place on the conduct of their members" (1997, p. 35). The Ontario Provincial Police Professional Standards Bureau lectures to OPP officers on the topic of ethics survival, and as part of that lecture, speaks to the topic of the top ten career-ending mistakes for police officers (see Box 7.1). This outstanding lecture clearly shows the relationship between professional standards and ethics (Whitton, 2011).

Pollock (2012) defines ethics as "the discipline of determining good and evil and defining moral duties" (p. 8). According to Pollock, morals are the "principles of right and wrong." These definitions lead into the definition of professional ethics, which Pollock describes as "applied principles of right and wrong relevant to specific occupations or professions." For the purposes of this chapter, **ethics in policing** is defined as on- and off-duty conduct consistent with a police officer's oath of office and code of conduct.

How do professional ethics enter the picture of law enforcement? As part of their extraordinary powers, police officers have the use of discretion. Discretion is the latitude a police officer has with respect to enforcing the law without the use of fear, political interference, or favouritism. This discretion must be used properly within the boundaries of the law, taking into account the officer's oath of office, code of conduct, and code of ethics. Discretion can be best described as the lawful options a police officer may have in making a law enforcement decision. As discussed in Chapter 3, the Supreme Court of Canada *R. v. Beaudry* addressed the issue of discretion. There was no question that a police officer had discretion to enforce the law but the Court made it clear that the discretion is not absolute ([2007] 1 S.C.R. 190, p. 209). The majority of the Court concluded,

> A police officer who has reasonable grounds to believe that an offence has been committed, or that a more thorough investigation might produce evidence that could form the basis of a

ethics in policing:
On- and off-duty conduct that is professional and consistent with a police officer's oath of office and code of conduct.

BOX 7.1

TOP TEN CAREER-ENDING MISTAKES

1. Deceit
2. Greed
3. Lust
4. Peer pressure
5. Anger

6. Misuse of social media
7. Alcohol and drug abuse
8. Domestic violence
9. Guns
10. Misuse of police records

Source: *Ethical Survival*, presented by Inspector P. Whitton of the Ontario Provincial Police Professional Standards Bureau in 2011. © Queen's Printer for Ontario, 2011. Reproduced with permission.

criminal charge, may exercise his or her discretion to decide not to engage the judicial process. But this discretion is not absolute. The exercise of the discretion must be justified subjectively, that is, the discretion must have been exercised honestly and transparently, and on the basis of valid and reasonable grounds; it must also be justified on the basis of objective factors. In determining whether a decision resulting from an exercise of police discretion is proper, it is therefore important to consider the material circumstances in which the discretion was exercised. The justification offered must be proportionate to the seriousness of the conduct and it must be clear that the discretion was exercised in the public interest. (*R. v. Beaudry*, [2007] 1 S.C.R. 190, p. 191)

There may be occasions where police officers do not have discretion. Discretion can also be influenced by government policy. In Ontario, police services have policies relating to mandatory charging in cases of domestic violence where reasonable grounds exist.

Doing the right thing is not always easy, and what one officer does in one situation may be totally different from what another officer will do in the same situation. The values and integrity of an officer will greatly influence how an officer makes a moral or ethical judgment. One of the recommendations in the *CACP Professionalism in Policing Research Project* was that "values need to be well defined and discussed in recruit and ongoing training to generate a shared understanding of how values appropriately guide discretionary judgement" (Maguire & Dyke, 2011a, p. 3).

Oliver defines values as "enduring beliefs that influence opinions, actions and the choices and decisions we make" (2008, p. 15). The Treasury Board of Canada Secretariat states that ethical values are reflected in the way professionals perform their duties while "acting at all times in such a way as to uphold public trust" (2003, p. 9). Professional values include serving the public with "competence, excellence, efficiency, objectivity, and impartiality" (p. 8). As will be discussed in Chapter 12, police officers even have the right to use lethal force when justified in accordance with the *Criminal Code.*

Noble cause corruption and **tunnel vision** are serious ethical issues relating to policing and have led to wrongful convictions. In a civil case before

the Ontario Superior Court of Justice, Justice Dyson quoted from Dianne Martin's paper "The Police Role in Wrongful Convictions: An International Comparative Study" in defining noble cause corruption:

> The conduct that is explained in this way may include everything from disregard for due process safeguards, to overt pressure on witnesses to give evidence that will support a conviction of the selected suspect and falsification of evidence, all in the name of securing a conviction of someone police have decided is guilty. (*McTaggart v. Ontario*, 2000, para. 203)

In this case, the court awarded civil damages against the police for withholding evidence that led to the accused being charged, convicted, and incarcerated. The court went on to say,

> It is difficult to imagine more egregious behaviour within the justice system than the withholding of relevant, exculpatory information by a police officer. Such behaviour makes it more likely that an accused person will be deprived of a fair trial and his liberty. Such acts strike at the very heart of the criminal justice system. (para. 200)

Police officers refer to noble cause as the ends justifying the means, but in a democratic society police must remember that noble cause cannot be justified. This is reinforced by Justice Marin: "The end cannot, and should not, justify the means. What counts is respect for the rule of law and ethics" (1997, p. 42). A famous case often quoted in police circles is *R. v. Allen* (1979), in which Allen was charged with first-degree murder. In this case, police officers used a false affidavit to obtain a statement from the accused. The statement was ruled to be inadmissible because of this tactic. The two police detectives were subsequently charged with falsifying an affidavit and were convicted (*R. v. Stevenson and McLean,* 1980).

Bruce MacFarlane, who has written extensively on wrongful convictions in Canada, describes noble cause corruption "as an ends-based culture that encourages investigators to blind themselves to their own inappropriate conduct, and to perceive that conduct as legitimate in the belief that they are pursuing an important public interest" (n.d., p. 6). In his review of the wrongful conviction of Guy Paul Morin (see Figure 7.5), Justice Fred Kaufman (1998) concluded that noble cause corruption and tunnel vision played a role in charging and convicting Morin.

According to the Federal/Provincial/Territorial Heads of Prosecution Working Committee Working

FIGURE 7.5
Guy Paul Morin was wrongfully convicted of the abduction and murder of a nine-year-old girl in 1984 as a result of noble cause corruption and tunnel vision.

Group, tunnel vision is one of the leading causes of wrongful conviction. In their report (2004), the committee quoted Commissioner Peter Cory (2000), who was head of the enquiry into the wrongful conviction of Thomas Sophonow (see Figure 7.6):

> Tunnel vision is insidious. It can affect an officer or, indeed, anyone involved in the administration of justice with sometimes tragic results. It results in the officer becoming so focussed upon an individual or incident that no other person or incident registers in the officer's thoughts. Thus, tunnel vision can result in the elimination of other suspects who should be investigated. Equally, events which could lead to other suspects are eliminated from the officer's thinking. Anyone, police officer, counsel or judge can become infected by this virus. (p. 37)

Police officers must remember their professional obligations in conducting impartial investigations and gathering evidence against and for the accused. This is also prescribed within the police code of conduct (O. Reg. 268/10, Schedule, 2 (1) (c) (vii)—neglect of duty), as well as in their duties as a police officer. These responsibilities are summarized by Justice

FIGURE 7.6
Thomas Sophonow was wrongfully convicted of the murder of a 16-year-old woman in Winnipeg in 1981. He spent four years in prison.

Marin in his book *Policing in Canada* (1997):

> Police ethics must lead to the impartial enforcement and respect of all laws, even those which appear to limit the police officer's ability to do his or her job. Police officers must recognize that they have the responsibility to ensure that the rights of all citizens are respected by, among other things, ensuring that their actions are within the limits prescribed by law and ethics. (p. 43)

ETHICAL DECISION-MAKING TOOLS

A number of ethical decision-making tools are available for police officers who are faced with an ethical dilemma. Before we examine these tools, we need to understand some basic terms, such as *ethical issues* and *ethical dilemmas*. According to Pollock (2012), ethical issues are "difficult social questions that include controversy over the right things to do, while ethical

DECODING POLICE TERMS

Tunnel vision: "The single-minded and overly narrow focus on a particular investigative or prosecutorial theory, so as to unreasonably colour the evaluation of information received and one's conduct in response to that information" (Kaufman, 1998, p. 26).

dilemmas are situations in which it is difficult to make a decision, because either the right course of action is not clear or the right course of action carries some negative consequences" (p. 18). There is no simple solution to many dilemmas. In making a decision, individuals may find themselves in conflict with their personal values versus the values in the unwritten code of conduct. In this case, they are in a no-win situation (Jones, 2005).

An example of an ethical issue might be the topic of abortion, which is a heated topic with two very strong opposing sides. What happens when a police officer has been ordered to keep the peace at an abortion clinic and guarantee safe access to women and staff but this order conflicts with the officer's values and religious beliefs? The ethical dilemma in this case is the difficult decision for the officer because of the competing obligations of the officer's personal values and his legal obligation to his profession. In one such case in Ontario, an officer refused to perform his duty at the Morgentaler Clinic in Toronto (see Figure 7.7). A disciplinary tribunal held that the officer was required to follow orders and dismissed him from his job for insubordination. The dismissal was later overturned on appeal, but the

John Lehmann/The Canadian Press

FIGURE 7.7

Dr. Henry Morgentaler, a long-time advocate for access to legal abortion in Canada. His clinic in Toronto was the subject of a police discipline case involving insubordination.

appeal tribunal still held that the order was lawful and the officer was convicted of insubordination (*Packer and Toronto Police Service*, 1990).

For police officers facing an ethical dilemma, they must consider their both legal and moral obligations to act, taking into consideration their options and the consequences of the decision they make. Officers must remember that they must accept responsibility for their actions, and to do nothing in itself may constitute misconduct depending on the circumstances.

Another issue facing officers within the policing profession is what is referred to as the *code of silence* or *blue curtain of secrecy*. Pollock defines these terms as "the practice of police officers of keeping silent and not coming forward to report the ethical transgressions of other officers" (2012, p. 409).

What do officers do when they see a fellow officer commit an unprovoked assault on a handcuffed prisoner sitting in the back seat of a cruiser? In one case, fellow officers who witnessed such an assault reported it immediately to a supervisor. The officer who assaulted the prisoner was subsequently suspended and charged with a number of misconducts under the code of conduct governing the police in that jurisdiction, and also with a criminal offence. At his disciplinary hearing, the officer pled guilty. In dismissing the officer from the police service, the adjudicator described the assault as "very serious; shocking and egregious; a significant lapse of judgment; a breach of public trust warranting both general and specific deterrence; and conduct that had caused serious damage to the reputation of the Police Service" (*Venables and York Regional Police Service*, 2008, p. 9). It is worth noting that on appeal to the Ontario Civilian Commission on Police Services (OCCPS), the commission stated that the conduct of the officer resulted in a criminal conviction, and

that this crime took place while the constable was on duty, in uniform and in the presence of other officers who were put in the difficult position of having to do their sworn duties and report the event. On the latter point, the

DECODING POLICE TERMS

Ethical dilemma: a situation in which

You are unsure of the right thing to do.

Two or more of your values may be in conflict.

Some harm may be caused, no matter what you do. (Oliver, 2008, p. 15)

Hearing Officer observed "this assault has caused problems with the officers on this shift; they are uncomfortable for having been brought into this situation. (*Venables*, 2008, p. 10)

In his book *Character and Cops: Ethics and Policing*, Delattre (1989) describes the moral and legal duties of police officers who witness fellow officers mistreating prisoners:

> The very habits of character that inspire good policing—a spirit of service, integrity, moral seriousness, devotion in friendship, intolerance for betrayals of the public trust—may also lead to questions of conscience. Officers may find themselves torn between their loyalty to a partner who mistreats suspects and their duty to refuse to tolerate such wrongdoing. Although such tensions can be extreme, they cannot justify allowing a friend to violate the trust of public office. It is not betrayal to expect a friend to live up to the known duties of office. Still, decent people are seldom free of conflict when they face questions of conscience. (p. 333)

Besides their moral and ethical duty to report behaviour such as that described above, police officers in Ontario are reminded of their legal obligations under the code of conduct and the principles of the PSA.

LO⁴ THE SIX PILLARS OF CHARACTER

The Six Pillars of Character is a concept that was developed through the Josephson Institute of Ethics (see Figure 7.8) in 1992 under the leadership of Michael Josephson. Josephson brought together 30 national

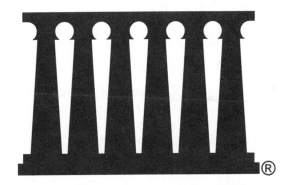

FIGURE 7.8
Logo of the Josephson Institute of Ethics, California.

leaders with strong backgrounds on the subject of ethics, and the group developed universal values that they felt would be applicable to any professional (Josephson Institute of Ethics, 2012). These Six Pillars of Character, outlined in Box 7.2, are just as applicable today as they were in 1992. Many of the pillars and what they represent are included in the mission and value statements of police and training organizations. The courts, police disciplinary processes, and legislation governing police conduct emphasize that police are to be held to a higher standard, given their extraordinary powers through government. The Six Pillars of Character should serve as benchmarks that police officers should strive to meet in carrying out their duties in accordance with their oath of office, their code of conduct, and the mission, vision, and supporting values of their organizations.

BOX 7.2

SIX PILLARS OF CHARACTER

1. *Trustworthiness*, including integrity, promise-keeping, and loyalty.

2. *Respect* and equal treatment of all members of society.

3. *Responsibility*, including accountability for decisions of everyday actions, pursuit of excellence, and self-restraint to understand that the ends cannot always justify the means.

4. *Fairness* to emphasize the importance of upholding the law and constitutional rights of all citizens.

5. *Caring* for how decisions and conduct affect citizens and the reputation of the policing.

6. *Citizenship* and civic virtue beyond self-interest, and for the greater good of the community both on and off duty.

Source: Based on materials from the Josephson Institute of Ethics, 1992 (the Aspen Declaration), and handouts from the Ethics Train-the-Trainer course, Institute for Law Enforcement Administration [ILEA], 2005, pp. 2.7–2.9.

LO5 STANDARDS AND PRINCIPLES OF ETHICAL POLICING

According to the Honourable René Marin, "All police forces have discipline codes. These are not codes of ethics though" (1997, p. 42). Marin takes the position that police officers understand that they have a legal obligation dictated through legislation and the courts to uphold the law, and that they are fully accountable to their employer, to oversight bodies, and to the courts when they fail to do this. Equally important is that police officers have a moral responsibility to respect the rights of all citizens (Marin, 1997).

We have already identified how our values influence our everyday personal and professional lives. This is important to note when considering the Six Pillars of Character because we need to understand that "our values are primarily caught, and not taught" (The Institute for Law Enforcement Administration (ILEA), 2005, p. 2.6). New recruits are highly influenced by their instructors and coach officers. Leadership by every member of the police community is critical, and the need for management and supervisors to demonstrate ethics and integrity is reinforced throughout the Justice Ferguson's report on police misconduct (2003). All police officers must lead by example both on and off duty. In order to do their jobs effectively, the police must have the trust of the public they are sworn to serve.

When making ethical decisions, police officers can consider the Six Pillars of Character and the five standards and principles of ethical policing (see Box 7.3), which are taught in the ILEA's Ethics Train-the-Trainers course at the Center for American and International Law in Texas (Figure 7.9). These principles reflect police values and ways of policing, and

Courtesy of The Institute for Law Enforcement Administration (ILEA).

FIGURE 7.9

ILEA has developed the Ethics Train-the-Trainer course, which has been delivered internationally, including at the Ontario Police College.

BOX 7.3

STANDARDS AND PRINCIPLES OF ETHICAL POLICING

1. *Fair and open access.* As a social resource, police must provide fair and open access to all services. This is consistent with the Honourable René Marin's statement, "I believe that the concepts of professionalism and ethics can be summed up in two words: social responsibility" (1997, p. 46).

2. *Public trust (accountability).* Public trust is sacred and the public expect the police to honour this trust.

3. *Safety and security (including discretion).* Police should use discretion in balancing the goal of maintaining order and security with the goal of law enforcement. Should all laws be enforced blindly? Is noble cause ever acceptable? The Honourable René Marin states, "Failure to stop at a stop sign is a violation but does it justify a high speed chase through a school zone? The end cannot, and should not, justify the means. What counts is respect for the rule of law and ethics" (1997, p. 42).

4. *Teamwork (coordination, cooperation, communication).* Police are part of a larger system of justice officials, and they all must work together for the greater public good. This was evident in the Paul Bernardo/Karla Homolka investigation. The review of the Bernardo investigation, the Campbell report (1996), emphasized that multi-jurisdictional crimes demanded that these investigations include coordination, cooperation, and communication between police agencies.

5. *Objectivity (impartial, loyal to oath of office).* In accordance with the rule of law, police officers must understand that the law applies equally to everyone. Officers need to understand that they can never use their office for their own personal gain. As Marin points out, the values reflected in various codes of conduct can be summarized as "integrity, impartiality, dignity and the need to set a standard to be looked up to, respect for law and the judicial system, and respect for individuals" (1997, p. 46).

Source: Based on The Institute for Law Enforcement Administration. (2005). Course Materials from "Ethics Train-the-Trainer" Course. Dallas, TX: The Center for American and International Law p. 2.10

equally important, how the public perceives the police in their communities (ILEA, 2005).

In Canada, policing is a public service accessible by all members of the public. This is consistent with Sir Robert Peel's nine principles of policing, discussed in Chapter 1. Public trust is essential for police to be effective, and that is why accountability in policing is essential through police governance and oversight bodies (see Chapter 12).

Safety and security of the public is a priority, and this is evident in how offenders are apprehended by the police. Police prioritize the risks associated with apprehending offenders with the overriding principle that public safety is paramount. Here, discretion is important. This is evident in high-speed pursuits (see Figure 7.10), where guidelines are regulated (O. Reg. 266/10). Police will not put the safety of the public at risk for the sake of pursuing a suspect who committed a minor traffic violation in the absence of any other information.

Teamwork in policing is critical, as was made clear by the Campbell report (1996). Coordination, communication, and cooperation between police agencies are essential if the police are to avoid the mistakes made during the Bernardo investigation. Some of the good to come out of this review was the development of mandatory reporting of sexual assault–related offences in a database to assist in identifying sexual predators and their behaviours (O. Reg. 550/96) and the establishment of minimum investigative standards for managing and investigating defined major cases (O. Reg. 354/04).

Police officers are bound by the *Police Services Act* and its regulations, including upholding the Canadian Constitution. Police officers must remain objective and impartial in accordance with their oath of office and prescribed duties. An example of this requirement was provided earlier in this chapter in the discussion on the ethical issue of abortion.

FIGURE 7.10
Police officers block in a vehicle with their cruisers following a high-speed chase.

LO6 THE ETHICAL DECISION-MAKING MODEL

The ethical decision-making model is designed to assist police officers to make the best, and hopefully correct, decision when faced with an ethical dilemma.

IS THERE AN ETHICAL ISSUE, PROBLEM, OR DILEMMA?

The first question you need to ask yourself is whether there is an ethical issue, problem, or dilemma. If there is an ethical issue with the situation, we then briefly explain what it is. For instance, police communications receives a call from a local bar that there is a disturbance that involves a fight between off-duty police officers and local citizens, and that one of the off-duty officers has assaulted a citizen.

In this case (unlike the case involving the abortion clinic, which is a broader social issue that is usually but not always a reflection of government policies), we have an allegation of discreditable conduct by off-duty police officers, and allegations against citizens and off-duty officers engaged in criminal conduct. The ethical dilemma is how the officers who receive this call are going to respond to this occurrence, since these allegations are criminal in nature, and some of the involved parties are off-duty officers to whom they will have a sense of loyalty. The other ethical dilemma is how the off-duty officers are going to react and respond to the investigation.

THE ETHICS CHECK QUESTIONS

Next, you need to ask yourself the following questions (ILEA, 2005) in relation to the situation and your proposed course of action:

1. Are there any existing laws or regulations?
2. Are there any existing professional codes of conduct?
3. Are there any existing policies and procedures?
4. Are there any constitutional issues?
5. Are the oaths of office and oath of secrecy applicable?
6. Are there any other issues that may be applicable, such as conflict of interest, personal gains or benefits, or a conflict of loyalty to the police organization?

For instance, in the above case of the disturbance and assault, these questions would be applicable to both the on-duty officers responding and the off-duty officers allegedly involved in the bar fight and assault. Assuming the allegations are true, in answer to question 1, we at least would have criminal charges of cause disturbance and assault. Regarding question 2, the on-duty police officers would be governed by the code of conduct (O. Reg. 268/10) and the *Police*

Services Act to conduct an impartial investigation. The off-duty officers would have a responsibility to answer for their conduct. Regarding question 3, we would have to determine if the premises the off-duty officers were in were "off limits" for any reason. The on-duty officers would have to carry out the investigation and reporting procedures in accordance with the policies and procedures of their police service. Regarding question 4, there are constitutional issues given that the allegations against the off-duty officers are criminal in nature, and there are also equality issues. Regarding question 5, there are significant "oath of office" issues for both the on-duty and the off-duty officers. Police officers are expected to obey the laws, not break them. They are expected to preserve the peace, not participate in violating the peace. The on-duty officers are expected to carry out their duties in accordance with their oath of office. Regarding question 6, there is the principle that the law applies equally to all persons. Furthermore, the on-duty officers need to be loyal to their chief of police/commissioner in upholding the law.

ETHICAL VALUES

What ethical values are relevant to the ethical issue, problem, or dilemma you have identified? The ethical values, Six Pillars of Character, and principles/standards have already been discussed in this chapter. Police officers need to ask themselves which of the ethical values described in Box 7.4 apply to the problem based on the definitions provided.

Police officers should be guided by these values, the Six Pillars of Character, and standards and principles of ethical policing in reaching decisions when confronted with an ethical issue. They should form part of the core values of every police officer.

When confronted with an ethical problem, police officers need to ACT by doing the following:

- carefully examine the *alternatives* by identifying all options;
- in examining the alternatives, be aware of possible *consequences* by projecting outcomes; and
- *then* make a decision and *tell* your story justifying your decision (ILEA, 2005).

BOX 7.4

THE CANADIAN ASSOCIATION OF CHIEFS OF POLICE ETHICAL FRAMEWORK

Whether an ethical decision made by a police officer is right or wrong can be guided by the following ethical values:

- Caring
- Courage
- Equity
- Integrity
- Openness
- Respect
- Transparency
- Trustworthiness (CACP, 2011, "Ethical Values")

The following are considerations for ethical decision-making:

1. Consistency with the law, police policy and regulations.
2. Consistency with the CACP Ethical Framework
3. Identification of those potentially affected by the decision.
4. Probable consequences of the decision.
5. Potential for good over harmful outcomes from the decision.
6. Potential for a conflict of interest or the perception of personal gain.
7. Ability to justify the decision in terms of the public trust. (CACP, 2011, "Considerations for Ethical Decision-Making")

Source: David R. Evans and Craig S. MacMillan (2003, 2008). *Ethical Issues in Law Enforcement*, 2nd and 3rd Editions, (p. 140; p.132). Reproduced by permission of Emond Montgomery Publications Ltd; Canadian Association of Chiefs of Police, Ethical Framework, retrieved from http://www.cacp.ca/index/aboutus

Officers must be prepared to tell their story and present their arguments for the decisions they made by explaining their actions to those to whom they are accountable. Michael Josephson's book *Making Ethical Decisions* is an excellent source of information on this process (see Figure 7.11).

Once officers have examined the above values, Six Pillars of Character, and standards and principles of ethical policing, they needs to answer the questions provided in Box 7.5 in a risk–benefit analysis (alternative/consequences) chart. This is a template officers use to record their responses related to an ethical issue or dilemma. The responses are in answer to the questions identified in this chapter related to stakeholders, alternatives, and the risks and benefits associated with the consequences of officers' decisions when faced with an ethical dilemma.

THE BELL, THE BOOK, THE CANDLE: AN ETHICAL DECISION-MAKING TOOL

In addition to answering the questions in the risk–benefit analysis, the ethical decision-making tool known as "the bell, the book, the candle" (ILEA, 2005) will assist police officers when facing an ethical dilemma.

The bell: Are any warning bells going off? If yes, why? Have you taken some additional cautionary measures? Do you need to go to a supervisor or another person for a second opinion?

The book: Is there a violation or potential violation of any laws (statutes or regulations), ethical codes or codes of conduct, policies and procedures, constitutions, oaths of office, etc.?

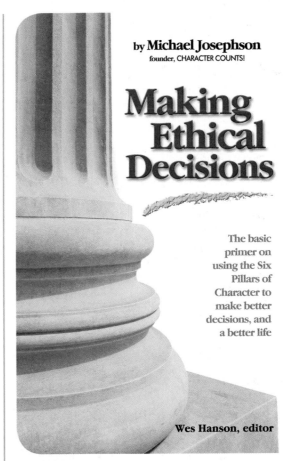

by **Michael Josephson**
founder, CHARACTER COUNTS!

Making Ethical Decisions

The basic primer on using the Six Pillars of Character to make better decisions, and a better life

Wes Hanson, editor

FIGURE 7.11
Making Ethical Decisions explains the step-by-step process of making ethical decisions that will hold individuals accountable.

The candle: Will the decision, if exposed to the light of day, withstand public scrutiny? Will you continue to feel good about your action, and will you continue to feel justified in what you did?

BOX 7.5

QUESTIONS TO DETERMINE THE RISK–BENEFIT ANALYSIS WHEN FACING AN ETHICAL DILEMMA

1. Who are the stakeholders? Identify those who may be affected by this dilemma. "**Stakeholders** are any person, organization, or entity that may be affected by what you do" (ILEA, 2005, p. 2.11).

2. What are the alternatives? Identify all choices that are available to each stakeholder facing the identified ethical dilemma(s).

3. What are the consequences of any decision each stakeholder makes as it relates to each alternative identified? What are the benefits and risks associated with each alternative?

4. Based on the answers to the above questions, what will the individual facing the ethical dilemma do? Will his or her decision be fair to everyone affected? Is it a balanced decision that will withstand public scrutiny? Most important, how will the individual who has to make the ethical decision feel about him- or herself?

CHAPTER SUMMARY

Ethics and professionalism go hand in hand with professional standards. Police officers must understand, given their extraordinary powers and their role in society, that they will be held accountable to the public they serve, to their employers, and ultimately by the courts. Personal ethics in off-duty conduct and professional ethics while on the job are the best examples of leadership in policing today. We are all judged by our actions.

LO1 Describe what professionalism is in policing.

Professionalism in policing is defined as police officers adhering to their oath of office and the oath of secrecy they took when sworn in as police officers; following their police service's mission statement and supporting values, including the CACP code of ethics, the code of conduct, and the *Police Services Act*, which governs their conduct as public servants; and being accountable for what they do or neglect to do as required by their profession while on duty, and in some instances, off duty.

LO2 Explain why police officers should study ethics.

Police officers have extraordinary powers, including the legal right to take away the liberty of a person by way of arrest, to charge the person if reasonable grounds exist, and to be a key player in the criminal justice system by gathering and placing evidence before the courts to determine the guilt or innocence of a person. Police officers find themselves facing ethical dilemmas every day, and it is important to understand that public trust and confidence depend on how police conduct themselves.

LO3 Summarize the ethical values identified in the Canadian Association of Chiefs of Police Ethical Framework.

The ethical values include caring, courage, equity, integrity, openness, respect, transparency, and trustworthiness.

LO4 Discuss the Six Pillars of Character.

The Six Pillars of Character are trustworthiness, respect, responsibility, fairness, caring, and citizenship.

LO5 State the five standards and principles of ethical policing.

These include fair and open access (providing equal access to all services); public trust (ensuring accountability); safety and security (using discretion in balancing the goal of maintaining order with public safety); teamwork (working with other justice officials); and objectivity (being impartial and loyal to the oath of office).

LO6 Discuss how the ethical decision-making model is used in resolving an ethical dilemma.

The officer should ask him- or herself following ethics check questions:

1. Are there any existing laws or regulations?
2. Are there any existing professional codes of conduct?
3. Are there any existing policies and procedures?
4. Are there any constitutional issues?
5. What are the oaths of office and oath of secrecy that may be applicable?
6. Are there any other issues that may be applicable such as conflict of interest, personal gains or benefits, or a conflict of loyalty to the police organization? (ILEA, 2005)

In addition to answering the questions above, "the bell, the book, the candle" decision-making tool (ILEA, 2005) will assist police officers when facing an ethical dilemma.

The bell: Are any warning bells going off? If yes, why? Have you taken some additional cautionary measures? Do you need to go to a supervisor or another person for a second opinion?

The book: Is there a violation or potential violation of any laws (statutes or regulations), ethical codes or codes of conduct, policies and procedures, constitutions, oaths of office, etc.?

The candle: Will the decision, if exposed to the light of day, withstand public scrutiny? Will you continue to feel good about your action, and will you continue to feel justified in what you did?

When confronted with an ethical problem, police officers need to ACT (*alternatives, consequences, tell* your story) by doing the following:

- carefully examine the *alternatives* by identifying all options;

- in examining the alternatives, be aware of possible *consequences* by projecting outcomes; and

- then make a decision and *tell* your story justifying your decision (ILEA, 2005).

The Police Disciplinary Process and Code of Conduct

LEARNING OUTCOMES

After reading this chapter, you will be able to:

LO**1**   State the legislation that governs police officers and police services in Ontario.

LO**2**   Define discipline and state the four purposes of discipline.

LO**3**   State the four principles of the common law duty of procedural fairness.

LO**4**   Describe the investigative process for allegations of police misconduct, including tunnel vision, and the impact of section 11 of the *Canadian Charter of Rights and Freedoms*.

LO**5**   Describe the code of conduct offences and unsatisfactory work performance under Ontario Regulation 268/10 and the *Police Services Act*.

LO**6**   Explain the disciplinary hearing process, including the standard for holding a hearing, the standard of proof for conviction, and sentencing principles for assessing penalty during disposition.

> *Although the main purpose of discipline is to assist a police force in providing effective and efficient police services to the community, this aim can only be pursued within the context of what otherwise constitutes a just and fair sanction.*
>
> —RCMP External Review Committee, 1991, p. 12

In this chapter we are going to discuss the legislation that governs police discipline in Ontario. We will examine what discipline is and analyze the purposes of discipline, especially in the context of police conduct relating to internal complaints. Given the extraordinary powers of police officers, they are held to a higher standard through a code of conduct. When officers are alleged to have breached that code of conduct or fail to perform to an acceptable standard, there is an investigation. We will discuss the investigative process and the standard to substantiate a complaint. Where the complaint is substantiated, officers are held accountable to their employer. Officers can be dealt with through a formal process or an informal process, depending on the seriousness of the misconduct. In a formal process, there is a tribunal and certain rules must be followed. We will address the impact that section 11 of the *Charter* has had on police discipline hearings, the rules of procedural fairness and natural justice for police discipline hearings, the standard of proof, and sentencing principles for assessing penalty where there is a finding of misconduct.

LO¹ POLICE DISCIPLINE LEGISLATION

Police services in Ontario are governed by the *Police Services Act* (PSA, 1990). This chapter will primarily deal with Part V of the PSA (Complaints and Disciplinary Proceedings) as it relates to the OPP and to municipal and regional police services. Other oversight bodies such as the Ontario Civilian Police Commission (OCPC), the Special Investigations Unit (SIU), and the Office of the Independent Police Review Director (OIPRD) are discussed in depth in Chapter 12; dealing with and investigating public complaints is discussed in Chapter 9; and civilian governance, including the role and responsibilities of police services boards, is discussed in Chapter 10.

Internal complaints about the conduct of a police officer can be made by the chief of police (s. 76, PSA, 1990; Figures 8.1 and 8.2) or by the police services board if the complaint involves a municipal chief of police or municipal deputy chief of police (s. 77). The

FIGURE 8.1
Chief of Police Mark Neelin, Barrie Police Service.

OCPC also has the oversight power to intervene at any stage of the investigation of these complaints (s. 78). Internal complaint investigations are not subject to review by the OIPRD. This chapter will deal only with internal complaints against a police officer including where an internal complaint may arise under *Ontario Regulation 263/09*.

LO² THE PURPOSE OF DISCIPLINE

There are numerous meanings of the word *discipline*, many of which have been associated with the words *to teach*. In the context of policing, the word *discipline* is associated with a police officer failing to

Source: Ontario Provincial Police (http://www.opp.ca/ecms/files/262221350.8.pdf). © Queen's Printer for Ontario, 2009. Reproduced with permission.

FIGURE 8.2

Commissioner Chris D. Lewis, Ontario Provincial Police.

follow the prescribed rules of conduct identified in statutes, regulations, standards, standing orders, policies, and procedures. The RCMP External Review Committee, in their discussion paper *Sanctioning Police Misconduct—General Principles*, states that **discipline** in policing "is what happens when

> **discipline:** A response, positive or negative, by an employer to an employee within an organization for failing to follow standards or rules, including governing regulations and laws.

one breaks the rules. Discipline is used to impose order or control over someone" (1991, p. 2). Discipline is essential within a police service to ensure accountability, and how it is implemented must take into consideration the police service as the employer, the police officer as the employee, and the public interest.

Police officers are held to a higher standard than members of the public through their own code of conduct and are accountable for their conduct at all times, even when they are not on duty (off-duty conduct, subs. 80 (2), PSA). The higher standard view has been reaffirmed in a number of disciplinary hearings and has been highlighted by the OCPC. The commission states, "Given the nature of their office, police officers must be held to a higher standard of conduct than members of the public" (Reilly and Brockville Police Service, 1997, p. 3). The code of conduct for police officers in Ontario is found in the schedule of Ontario Regulation 268/10, General (Code of Conduct). Regulations under the *Police Services Act* are made in response to decisions by the commission and the courts, or as a result of policy directions by the government flowing out of reviews or public inquires or commissions. Examples of this are discussed further in this chapter.

LO³ PROCEDURAL FAIRNESS

One of the leading authorities on police disciplinary matters in Canada is Paul Ceyssens, author of *Legal Aspects of Policing* (Figure 8.3). Police officers being investigated for discipline matters are entitled to be dealt with in accordance with the four principles of common law duty of procedural fairness (Ceyssens, 2005), as well as any legislative requirements regarding the investigation of their conduct and any subsequent allegations of misconduct (*Police Services Act*).

DECODING POLICE TERMS

Four purposes of discipline:

1. Protect the employer's interest in maintaining integrity and discipline in the police workplace,

2. Protect the rights of police officers suspected of misconduct,

3. Ensure a high standard of conduct within the police constabulary, and

4. Ensure the interests of the public are protected whether or not they register a formal complaint. (Ceyssens, 2005, p. 5-44)

Source: Ceyssens, 2005, p. 5–44

FIGURE 8.3
Legal Aspects of Policing by Paul Ceyssens.

FIGURE 8.4
Retired Superintendent Joe Wolfe, Toronto Police Service, a qualified adjudicator under the *Police Services Act*, sitting in a hearing office.

Adjudicator Joe Wolfe, retired superintendent of the Toronto Police Service (Figure 8.4) excluded conversations from a wiretap in a police disciplinary hearing. In suppressing the evidence in the PSA trial, Retired Superintendent Wolfe stated, "I want to make it clear, I am not making this decision based on a '*Charter*' argument, my decision is based on the concepts of fundamental fairness and natural justice, that to accept this evidence would damage the integrity of the system and offend the concepts of fair play and decency" (*Rose v. Sault Ste. Marie Police*, 2010, p. 39). Background to the wiretap evidence was "the wiretap evidence was being challenged at a Preliminary Hearing, once the preliminary hearing was concluded the Federal

DECODING POLICE TERMS

Principles of the common law duty of procedural fairness:

1. A formal notice must be served advising of the proposed action.

2. Reasons must be provided.

Source: Ceyssens, 2005, p. 5–23

3. The affected party must be provided with a meaningful opportunity to make representation before the decision is made.

4. The decision must be made in good faith. (Ceyssens, 2005, p. 5-23)

FIGURE 8.5

The *Canadian Charter of Rights and Freedoms.*

Prosecutors decided not to pursue the criminal charges, all seized money and property were returned to the accused and the charges stayed. Although there is no record of the basis for the Prosecutor's decision an inference can be drawn from an extensive review of the transcripts from the preliminary hearing that he/she determined that the chances of the wiretap evidence being admissible at trial was extremely unlikely." The adjudicator was very firm that the exclusion of this evidence was not based on a *Charter* argument (*Charter of Rights and Freedoms*; see Figure 8.5).

Police Service Act hearings are disciplinary hearings between an employee and employer conducted in a police disciplinary hearings room. This is supported in a number of judgments, including appeals heard by the Ontario Civilian Commission on Police Services (OCCPS), now referred to as the Ontario Civilian Police Commission (OCPC). In *Williams* (1995), the commission took the position, as it has in many other cases, that PSA disciplinary hearings are not criminal proceedings but rather are administrative in nature, involving the police service and officer.

In a judgment that is often quoted throughout police discipline cases, Justice Morden, pictured in Figure 8.6, stated that "a police discipline matter is a purely administrative internal process. Its most serious possible consequence makes it analogous to a discipline matter in ordinary employer-employee relationships, even though the procedure governing it is clearly more formal" (*Trumbley and Pugh and Fleming*, 1986, p. 589).

FIGURE 8.6

Retired Ontario Court of Appeal Justice John W. Morden.

FIGURE 8.7
The Supreme Court of Canada, Ottawa.

Other rulings from the Supreme Court of Canada (Figure 8.7) have struck down any suggestion that section 11 of the *Charter* applies in police disciplinary hearings (*Burnham v. Metropolitan Toronto Police*, 1987; *R. v. Wigglesworth*, 1987; *Trimm v. Durham Regional Police*, 1987). These provisions under section 11 of the *Charter* included the right to "an independent and impartial tribunal" (s. 11(d)), which the Supreme Court of Canada ruled was not applicable in police disciplinary proceedings.

In *Wigglesworth*, a disciplinary case involving an RCMP officer charged with the *Criminal Code* offence of assault and a major service offence under the *RCMP Act*, the defence argued the principle of double jeopardy under paragraph 11(h) of the *Charter*. *Double jeopardy* in terms of police discipline refers to being charged and convicted of similar offences arising from the same set of circumstances under one piece of legislation, and then under the officer's code of conduct. A ruling of double jeopardy would indicate that where police officers are being investigated for criminal offences, the *Charter* would have application and they would be entitled to the same protections as any other citizen. The *Wigglesworth* judgment argues that the principle of double jeopardy should *not* apply in police discipline hearings, given the nature of disciplinary hearings. The Supreme Court of Canada finally put this matter to rest in a judgment that made it perfectly clear that PSA matters and criminal matters are two distinct and separate issues. The court went on to say,

> Nevertheless, the appellant does not have the benefit of s. 11(*h*) because he was not being tried and punished for the same offence. The "offences" were quite different. One was an internal disciplinary matter where the accused was found guilty of a major service offence and has accounted to his profession. The other was the criminal offence of assault where the accused must account to society at large for his conduct. The accused cannot complain, as a member of a special group of individuals subject to private internal discipline, that he ought not to account to society for his wrongdoing as a member of the public at large. (*R. v. Wigglesworth*, 1987, p. 4)

Although the above judgments from the Supreme Court of Canada eliminate the section 11 *Charter* defence in police disciplinary proceedings, the principles of the common law duty of procedural fairness still apply (Ceyssens, 2005). The Supreme Court of Canada's decision in *R. v. Conway* (2010) has opened the door for some *Charter* arguments outside of section 11. The discussion around that judgment is beyond the scope of this chapter.

In a discussion paper, *Sanctioning Police Misconduct—General Principles* (RCMP External Review Committee, 1991), the role of police discipline was described as essential in order for the police service to meet its mandate of delivering adequate and effective police services to advance the organization's mission, vision, values, and goals and objectives. All discipline must be carried out in a manner consistent with procedural fairness and natural fairness, taking into consideration all the

POLICING ONLINE

For further information on police discipline cases that have been appealed to the OCPC, refer to

http://www.ocpc.ca/english/index.asp

relevant factors (RCMP External Review Committee, 1991). This position is supported in *Nicholson v. Haldimand-Norfolk Regional Board of Commissioners of Police* (1979), a Supreme Court of Canada decision involving a probationary constable who was dismissed from office. The court stated,

> The appellant should have been told why his services were no longer required and given an opportunity, whether orally or in writing as the Board might determine, to respond. The Board itself, I would think, would wish to be certain that it had not made a mistake in some fact or circumstance which it deemed relevant to its determination. Once it had the appellant's response, it would be for the Board to decide on what action to take, without its decision being reviewable elsewhere, always premising good faith. Such a course provides fairness to the appellant, and it is fair as well to the Board's right, as a public authority to decide, once it had the appellant's response, whether a person in his position should be allowed to continue in office to the point where his right to procedural protection was enlarged. Status in office deserves this minimal protection, however brief the period for which the office is held....

> . . . although the appellant clearly cannot claim the procedural protections afforded to a constable with more than 18 months' service, he cannot be denied any protection. He should be treated "fairly" not arbitrarily. (pp. 312 & 324)

Simply put, although Part V of the *Police Services Act* does not apply to a probationary police officer, the officer cannot be dismissed without just cause and must be given an opportunity to respond. To do otherwise would be a denial of natural justice.

The term of probation for municipal police officers is 12 months after the officer is appointed or has completed recruit training at the Ontario Police College, whichever is longer (subs. 44(1), PSA), unless the officer is a member of the OPP, where the time limit is up to one year after his or her appointment (subs. 37(1). A probationary officer could be dismissed only in accordance with the *Nicholson* case. The Supreme Court of Canada, in referring to *Nicholson*, as well as to comments made at the Divisional Court level, was of the opinion that the police service had a "duty of compliance with the rules of natural justice in their traditional sense of notice and hearing, with an opportunity to make representations, and with reviewability of the decision as much as a less onerous duty of acting fairly" (1979, p. 317).

LO4 INVESTIGATION OF INTERNAL COMPLAINTS

Part V of the *Police Services Act* places an onus on the chief of police to investigate all complaints. In the case of an internal complaint, sometimes referred to as a chief's complaint, the chief of police (who has initiated the complaint) must have the complaint investigated and the results of the investigation reported in writing (s.76(1)). The chief of police is not a public complainant for the purpose of Part V of the PSA (s. 76 (2)). Notice of investigation, unless it fits one of the exceptions, must be provided to the officer which is discussed further in this chapter. There are occasions where the chief of police or Commissioner of the OPP may request another police agency to investigate the internal complaint provided that certain conditions are met (s. 76 (4), (5)). At the end of the investigation the chief of police will review the written report and decide if the complaint is substantiated. If the complaint is unsubstantiated, then the chief of police will take no action and will give the respondent officer the decision in writing along with a copy of the written report (s. 76 (8).

If at the end of the investigation, the chief of police believes on reasonable grounds that misconduct as defined in section 80 (PSA) or unsatisfactory work performance is established, then the chief of police shall hold a hearing unless the chief of police chooses to resolve the matter informally if the misconduct or unsatisfactory work performance is deemed to be less serious. Reasonable grounds are addressed further in this chapter and what constitutes less serious is addressed in detail in Chapter 9. The informal resolution provided for in subsection 76 (10) must be on consent of the respondent police officer. This consent may be withdrawn in writing by the respondent officer within 12 business days after the day of the consent being given (s. 76 (11)). The chief of police may give a disposition to this matter provided the respondent officer receives sufficient information concerning the relevant issues and is given an opportunity to respond orally or in writing (s. 76 (12)). The chief of police may then impose a penalty in accordance with the provisions of clauses 85 (1) (d), (e) or (f) or any combination thereof and may take any other action described in subsection 85 (7). These dispositions are discussed in further detail in this chapter. The chief of police may also place documentation in the officers file for two years subject to certain conditions (76 (12)). This documentation is expunged after two years provided there is no other documentation in the respondent officer's employment file related to misconduct or unsatisfactory work performance under Part V. If the respondent officer refuses to accept this disposition, then the chief of police shall hold a hearing. Hearings are addressed further in this chapter.

Another informal complaint resolution process is found in section 93, *Police Services Act*. This process is discussed in further detail in Chapter 9. A key word in this section is the misconduct must be *obviously* less serious.

Although this chapter deals only with internal complaints, similar wording is found at section 66 of the PSA for public complaints referred to the chief of police by the OIPRD to be investigated by the chief of police, or at section 68, for public complaints investigated by OIPRD and then referred to the chief of police.

Part V of the *Police Services Act* deals with complaints, including public complaints and disciplinary proceedings. Although Part V allows for informal discipline/informal resolutions, a less rigid process for handling public complaints that are less serious is available at the local level at a police service under Ontario Regulation 263/09. This is also known as a local resolution. Ontario Regulation 263/09 became effective October 19, 2009, with the implementation of the *Independent Police Review Act, 2007*. This is discussed in further detail in Chapter 9.

However, if a chief of police is taking a local complaint that meets the criteria for a Part V complaint, the chief must not accept the complaint as a local complaint (clause 3 (3) (b) and must advise the complainant to make a complaint under Part V of the PSA (subs. 3(7), O. Reg. 263/09). Or if the chief of police is attempting to resolve a local complaint and subsequently determines that the complaint does not meet the necessary criteria, the chief cannot take the local complaint and must ask the complainant to make a complaint under Part V of the PSA (s. 4(8), O. Reg. 263/09). The chief of police must report this with his or her reasons in writing to the OIPRD, the complainant, and the respondent officer (s. 3(6) or 4(10), O. Reg. 263/09). Although this chapter deals with internal complaints, the purpose of discussing *O. Reg. 263/09* is if the complainant refuses to make a complaint under Part V of the PSA, the chief of police must make an internal complaint in accordance with Part V (s. 3(7) or 4(11), O. Reg. 263/09). Remember, the chief of police is not a complainant in this case as defined by s. 58, PSA in accordance with subsection 2 (1), *O. Reg. 263/09*.

Ontario Regulation 3/99, *Adequacy and Effectiveness of Police Services*, provides that police services in Ontario must have in place procedures for investigating public complaints (s. 34). The Professional Standards Bureau (PSB) of the OPP has trained its investigators in conducting investigations, Major Case Management, and electronic case file management. The composition of the bureau includes an inspector with a Major Case Management background. As a result of a review of an internal discipline matter, former OPP Commissioner Gwen Boniface directed "that major case management principles will be applied to Professional Standards investigations" (Boniface, 2001).

NOTICE OF INVESTIGATION

When an internal complaint is made, the chief has to give the officer immediate notice, unless the chief believes the notice will be detrimental to the investigation (s. 76(3), PSA). This subsection makes it clear that the officer under investigation is entitled to know the nature of the complaint up front unless the notice might jeopardize the investigation.

NATURE OF INVESTIGATION

As previously indicated, police discipline matters are between an employer and employee. Investigations must be conducted *fairly*.

Lorna Boyd, former legal counsel with the Ontario Provincial Police Association (OPPA), has expressed serious concerns about how complaints against police officers are investigated. A public or internal complaint against a police officer does not mean that misconduct or unsatisfactory work performance has occurred. PSB investigators, as in any investigation by police, must keep an open mind. The public and respondent officers are entitled to an objective and thorough investigation. PSB investigators must be aware of policies and procedures, as well as any standard operating procedures (SOPs) (Boyd, 2005). Many police services, including the OPP, have policies in place with respect to the rights of police officers, including having a lawyer or representative of their police association present.

Investigations involve interviewing all witnesses, including the officer who is the subject of the chief's complaint; collecting physical evidence, including documents; checking out any alibis; and consulting experts before the laying of any misconduct under the *Code of*

DECODING POLICE TERMS

Fairly: "Police have a duty to investigate fairly. They are not entitled to pay attention only to what might incriminate a person and disregard anything that might exonerate the person" (*Chartier v. the Queen*, 1979, as cited in *Rose v. Sault Ste. Marie Police Service*, 2010, p. 13).

Conduct (O. Reg. 268/10). Police officers need to be aware that in police discipline matters, and depending on the circumstances, the officers can be ordered to submit duty reports and answer questions from PSB investigators. Refusal to do so amounts to insubordination. A number of judgments have reinforced this, as demonstrated in a police discipline case where the OCPC stated,

> It is critical for the operation of a police service that a police officer obeys orders and account for his or her actions in the course of performing their official duties. For this reason the Commission would view the failure to obey an order without a lawful excuse as a serious offence. (*Orr v. York Region Police*, 2001, p. 15)

Investigators who conduct internal investigations must carry out these investigations in an objective manner, avoiding tunnel vision and taking the necessary steps to collect all the evidence, both inculpatory and exculpatory. As noted in Chapter 7, tunnel vision has been a factor in many cases of wrongful conviction (Figures 8.8–8.10).

Michael Stuparyk/Toronto Star/ZUMA Press/Newscom

FIGURE 8.9
Mr. Justice Peter Cory, retired Supreme Court of Canada judge and commissioner of the Sophonow Inquiry.

Fred Lum/The Globe and Mail/The Canadian Press

FIGURE 8.8
Guy Paul Morin was wrongfully convicted of murder. One of the contributing factors was tunnel vision.

Andrew Vaughan/The Canadian Press

FIGURE 8.10
Mr. Justice Fred Kaufman, retired judge and commissioner on proceedings involving Guy Paul Morin, 1998.

LO5 CODE OF CONDUCT OFFENCES AND UNSATISFACTORY WORK PERFORMANCE

MISCONDUCT AND UNSATISFACTORY WORK PERFORMANCE

Misconduct and unsatisfactory work performance are found in Ontario Regulation 268/10. The code of conduct offences are outlined in the schedule, and unsatisfactory work performance is found in sections 28 and 29. These apply to both OPP and municipal police services (ss. 28–29). Unsatisfactory work performance involves a comprehensive assessment of an officer's performance, with a significant onus placed on the performance management practices of a police service.

Unsatisfactory work performance can be best described as an officer's inability to meet minimum performance goals and objectives within a police organization. Subsection 29(1) (O. Reg. 268/10) states, "Every chief of police shall establish policies for the assessment of police officers' work performance" and "these policies shall "be available to police officers" (s. 29(2)). Regarding internal complaints, the steps outlined in s. 29 (O. Reg. 268/10) should be followed.

Misconduct is defined in sections 80 and 81 of the *Police Services Act*. Ontario Regulation 268/10, *Code of Conduct*, provides the exact wording and requirements of each charge of misconduct. As noted in this chapter, often it is the OCPC and the courts that interpret the law. The facts in issue depend on which form of misconduct is being examined. For instance, there are nine categories of misconduct in the schedule of the *Code of Conduct*:

- discreditable conduct;
- insubordination;
- neglect of duty;
- deceit;
- breach of confidence;
- corrupt practice;
- unlawful or unnecessary exercise of authority;
- damage to clothing or equipment; and
- consuming drugs or alcohol in a manner prejudicial to duty.

In addition, section 3 of the schedule in the *Code of Conduct* states, "Any chief of police or other police officer also commits misconduct if he or she conspires in, abets or is knowingly an accessory to any misconduct described in section 2" (O. Reg. 268/10).

There are numerous reported decisions of police misconduct at the first level of appeal, which is the OCPC (formerly the OCCPS). An example of an appeal dealing with the misconduct of deceit is outlined below.

DECODING POLICE TERMS

Unsatisfactory work performance:

29. (1) Every chief of police shall establish policies for the assessment of police officers' work performance. O. Reg. 268/10, s. 29 (1).

   (2) The chief of police shall make the policies available to the police officers. O. Reg. 268/10, s.29 (2).

   (3) Before the chief of police may make a complaint against a police officer of unsatisfactory work performance,

   (a) the police officer's work performance shall have been assessed in accordance with the established procedures;

   (b) the chief of police shall advise the police officer of how he or she may improve his or her work performance;

   (c) the chief of police shall accommodate the police officer's needs in accordance with the Human Rights Code if the police officer has a disability, within the meaning of the Human Rights Code, that requires accommodation;

   (d) the chief of police shall recommend that the police officer seek remedial assistance, such as counselling or training or participation in a program or activity, if the chief of police is of the opinion that it would improve the police officer's work performance; and

   (e) the chief of police shall give the police officer a reasonable opportunity to improve his or her work performance. (O. Reg. 268/10, s. 29(3))

Source: Ontario Regulation 268/10. s. 29 (3). Retrieved October 21, 2011, from http://www.e-laws.gov.on.ca/html/regs/english/elaws_regs_100268_e.htm

---

Deceit

The *Code of Conduct* outlines a number of different ways of committing each form of misconduct. For example, in the schedule of the *Code of Conduct*, the misconduct of **deceit** can be committed in one of three ways:

> (d) Deceit, in that he or she,
>   (i) knowingly makes or signs a false statement in a record,
>   (ii) wilfully or negligently makes a false, misleading or inaccurate statement pertaining to official duties, or
>   (iii) without lawful excuse, destroys or mutilates a record or alters or erases an entry in a record (O. Reg. 268/10, 2(1)(d), ss. i–iii).

In the misconduct of deceit, tribunals and courts have ruled that there must be some form of intent.

The OCPC defines deceit as "a fraudulent and cheating misrepresentation, artifice or device, used by one or more persons to deceive and trick another, who is ignorant of the true facts, to the prejudice and damage of the party imposed upon" (*Perry and York Regional Police,* 1972, p. 92).

In *Geske and Hamilton Police* (2003), the OCPC goes on to say,

> It is clear from the cases that in order to establish a charge of deceit that the prosecution must prove that an officer wilfully or negligently makes a false, misleading or inaccurate statement pertaining to official duties. Therefore, an inaccurate statement by itself in the absence of proof of wilfulness or intent will not support a conviction of deceit. Furthermore, the evidence must be weighty, cogent and reliable. (p. 10)

Furthermore, in *Lloyd and London Police* (1999), Ceyssens states,

> In order to establish a charge of deceit it is necessary to show that an officer wilfully or negligently makes a false, misleading or inaccurate statement pertaining to official duties. As was noted in McCoy and Fort Frances Police (1969), 1 O.P.R. 16 (O.P.C.) . . . to properly convict an officer under this provision it is necessary to [prove] an "intention to deceive." (p. 6-88)

For deceit, there would appear to be a mental element required of intent to deceive to support a conviction. Professional standards investigators and chiefs of police should be guided by these decisions in determining whether there is misconduct in the case of an investigation into the misconduct of deceit.

SUSPENSIONS

Police officers in Ontario may be suspended with or without pay. These provisions are found in section 89 of the *Police Services Act.* Police officers may be suspended if they are under investigation or charged with any federal or provincial offence or misconduct as defined in section 80 (ss. 89(1–2), PSA). Generally speaking, in cases of misconduct, there is supporting evidence to support that misconduct may have occurred. The suspensions are valid until lifted by the chief of police or until the final disposition of the charges or misconducts against the officer (s. 89(3–4), PSA). Conditions can be placed on the officers during suspension, such as having to report in to their office, not using any of their powers as a police officer, or not using or wearing any police-issued identification or equipment (s. 89 (5), PSA). Police officers in Ontario can be suspended without pay only when they are convicted of an offence and receive a term of imprisonment. This suspension without pay can continue even if the conviction is under appeal (s. 89(6), PSA).

LO⁶ THE HEARING PROCESS

THE STANDARD

The standard for holding a hearing into misconduct by a police officer in Ontario is **reasonable grounds**. Subsection 76(9) of the *Police Services Act* states,

> Subject to subsection (10), if at the conclusion of the investigation and on review of the written report submitted to him or her the chief of police believes on reasonable grounds that the police officer's conduct constitutes misconduct as defined in section 80 or unsatisfactory work performance, he or she shall hold a hearing into the matter.

The OIPRD (2010) has defined reasonable grounds as "facts or circumstances of a case that would lead an ordinary and cautious person to believe that misconduct has occurred. This belief must be more than just suspicion of misconduct and must be based on factual evidence" (p. 29). This is the standard to determine misconduct; if reasonable grounds do not exist, the complaint will be classified as unsubstantiated.

deceit: To lie, mislead, or falsify information for personal gain, to avoid discipline, or to harm another person.

reasonable grounds: Facts-based evidence that would lead an average person to believe that an officer has breached the code of conduct or engaged in unsatisfactory work performance. This belief must be beyond reasonable suspicion to substantiate the complaint.

The standard of reasonable grounds was one of the recommendations Justice Patrick Lesage (2005) made in changing the police discipline process in Ontario and is reflected in the *Independent Police Review Act, 2007*, which received royal assent on May 17, 2007 (most of the sections only came into effect on October 19, 2009).

SIX-MONTH TIME LIMIT

For internal complaints, if six months have elapsed since the day described in subsection 83(18), no notice of hearing can be served unless the board, in the case of a municipal police officer, or the commissioner, in the case of a member of the OPP, is of the opinion that it was reasonable, under the circumstances, to delay serving the notice of hearing (s. 83(17), PSA). Regarding an internal complaint, the time limit starts "on which the facts on which the complaint is based first came to the attention of the chief of police or board, as the case may be" (s. 83(18)). In *Dhinsa v. Hamilton Police Service* (unreported, 2007), retired Superintendent Robert Fitches ruled that the police service took eight days too long in serving the subject officer with a notice of hearing, and the service had ample time to get an extension from the police services board. Fitches quashed all the misconducts against the officer. This judgment is consistent with other judgments delivered by the OCPC where the commission has ruled that the time limit starts when there is supporting evidence that misconduct may have occurred (*Brannagan v. Peel Regional Police*, 2003; *Gough v. Peel Regional Police*, 2003).

THE HEARING OFFICER

In Ontario, a chief of police may delegate powers and duties to a police officer or a former police officer of the rank of inspector or higher, a judge or retired judge, or such other person as may be prescribed to conduct a hearing of misconduct (s. 94(1), PSA). The standard to conduct a hearing is reasonable grounds that an officer's conduct constitutes misconduct as defined in section 80 or unsatisfactory work performance (s. 29, O. Reg. 268/10). This is conditional on the completion of an investigation into the alleged misconduct of the officer

and on review of a written report submitted to the chief. This was reaffirmed in an unreported judgment (*Oliver v. South Simcoe Police Service*, 2010) where the adjudicator, Superintendent Neil Tweedy (retired), stated that an investigation must be completed and a report submitted to the chief as an essential requirement according to the legislation. He went on to say, "Proper 'Notice of Investigation' did not occur pursuant to the Act, and a decision to charge the officer was announced before the completion of the investigation and the chief's review of the written report provided him" (para. 510). The officer was subsequently found not guilty of all misconducts of unsatisfactory work performance, deceit, neglect of duty, and insubordination.

THE DEFENCE

The defence representation for the officer alleged to have committed misconduct may be a person authorized under the *Law Society Act* (s. 83 (4), PSA; s. 1, 10, SPPA).

THE PROSECUTION

The prosecution must be designated by the chief of police (s. 82(1), PSA). This is done in writing, and a copy of the designation is filed as an exhibit at the start of the disciplinary hearing. The prosecution may be an officer equal in rank or higher from the same police service authorized under the *Law Society Act* (s. 82(1), PSA) or a police officer equal in rank or higher from another police service with the approval of the chief of police (s. 82(2)).

HEARING PROCEDURES

Procedural requirements are found throughout the *Police Services Act* (ss. 82–87, and s. 94) and the *Statutory Powers Procedure Act*.

STANDARD OF PROOF

The standard of proof to make a finding of guilt against a police officer in Ontario who has been charged with misconduct or unsatisfactory work performance as

DECODING POLICE TERMS

Clear and convincing evidence: "weighty, cogent and reliable evidence upon which a trier of fact, acting with care and caution, can come to the fair and reasonable conclusion that the officer is guilty of misconduct" (*Allan v. Munro*, 1994, p. 664).

FIGURE 8.11

Mr. Justice Patrick Lesage, author of the Report on the Police Complaints System in Ontario.

defined in section 84 of the *Police Services Act* is **clear and convincing evidence**.

The clear and convincing evidence standard is higher than the standard of a balance of probabilities but lower than beyond a reasonable doubt (RCMP External Review Committee, 1991, p. 33). In his 2005 report on the public complaints system in Ontario, Justice Patrick Lesage (shown in Figure 8.11) supported the clear and convincing evidence standard:

> I am of the view that the "clear and convincing evidence" standard should not be replaced with a "balance of probabilities" standard. The "clear and convincing evidence" standard is not a standard that is referred to in Ontario statutes other than in the PSA, but it has been accepted as the relevant standard in the misconduct hearings of many professional bodies. (p. 77)

RESIGNATIONS

When a police officer resigns or retires from a police service and is still under charge for misconduct, the disciplinary hearing tribunal loses jurisdiction (s. 90(1), PSA) unless the officer is hired by another police service within five years (s. 90(3)). In a 2007 appeal by a public complainant to the Ontario Civilian Commission on Police Services (now the OCPC), which resulted in a finding of not guilty against a police officer who was charged with the misconduct of breach of confidence, the commission ruled it had no jurisdiction to hear the appeal since the officer retired prior to the appeal being heard (*Ray and Cole and OPP*, 2007). As found in the *Holder* decision, the commission did not have jurisdiction over persons who were not members of a police service. It was the status of parties at the time an appeal was heard that determined jurisdiction, not their status on the date that the decision being appealed from was rendered. Once Sergeant Ray retired, he ceased to be a police officer.

SENTENCING DISPOSITIONS

Police officers can receive punishment ranging from reprimand to loss of pay or days off, to demotion or dismissal (s. 85, PSA). Where the prosecution is seeking a demotion or dismissal, the officer shall be served with notice (s. 85(4)).

If the misconduct is not deemed to be serious in an internal investigation, informal discipline without a hearing is available if the officer consents (s. 76(10)). Informal discipline punishment varies but can include a reprimand, treatment, counselling, training, or attendance of mandatory programs (s. 85(7)). Other punishments may include suspension without pay for up to 30 days (240 hours) (85(1)(d)), forfeiture of up to 3 days pay (24 hours) (85(1)(e)), forfeiture of up to 20 days off (160 hours) (85(1)(f)), or a combination of these (85(1)(g)). The chief of police must give the subject officer written notice of any penalty with reasons (s. 85(8)). Informal resolution is discussed in detail earlier in this chapter.

Appellate authorities have made it clear that an officer can be dismissed for a single misconduct (*Venables*, 2008). The courts have also made it clear that an officer may be dismissed to rid the employer of an unfit employee. In *Burnham* (1987), the Supreme Court of Canada quoted Justice Morden, in an Ontario Court of Appeal decision, where he said, "The basic object of dismissing an employee is not to punish him or her in the usual sense of this word (to deter or reform or, possibly, to exact some form of modern retribution) but rather, to rid the employer of the burden of an employee who has shown that he or she is not fit to remain an employee" (p. 589).

SENTENCING PRINCIPLES

Sound principles for sentencing have been outlined in numerous judgments and appeals in police disciplinary hearings. These principles start out with the

clear and convincing evidence: The courts have held clear and convincing evidence to be "weighty, cogent and reliable evidence upon which a trier of fact, acting with care and caution, can come to the fair and reasonable conclusion that the officer is guilty of misconduct" (*Allan v. Munro*, 1994, p. 664). In *Lloyd and the London Police Service*, 1999 May 20, the Commission stated in clarifying the clear and convincing evidence standard, "An analysis to justify the conclusion is not enough. It is not the conclusion that must be clear and cogent but rather the evidence that leads to the conclusion (*I.F.K. v. College of Physicians and Surgeons*, (Unreported, B.C. C.A., March 13,1998), para. 42)" (OCCPS 99-04, p. 9).

presumption that the hearing is an employer and employee matter, and where misconduct is proven on clear and convincing evidence, the sentencing of the officer will be in accordance with the penalties available to the hearing officer and guided by case law.

When an officer is convicted on clear and convincing evidence, the adjudicator must consider the following factors: "the nature and seriousness of the misconduct; the ability to reform or rehabilitate the officer; and the damage to the reputation of the police service if the officer was to remain on the police service" (*Williams*, 1995, p. 14). Other mitigating and aggravating factors include

- employment history and experience;
- recognition of the seriousness of the transgression;
- handicap or other relevant personal circumstances;
- the need for deterrence;
- management's approach to the matter; and
- consistency of the penalty with other disciplinary decisions. (*Nelles v. Colbourg Police Service*, 2007, p. 12)

In *Galassi v. Hamilton Police Service* (2003), the adjudicator used the following criteria, which have been cited in other cases:

- public interest;
- seriousness of the misconduct;
- recognition of the seriousness of the misconduct;
- employment history;
- need for deterrence;
- ability to reform or rehabilitate the police officer;
- damage to the reputation of the police force;
- handicap and other relevant personal circumstances;
- effect on police officer and police officer's family;
- management approach to misconduct in questions;
- consistency of disposition;
- financial loss resulting from unpaid interim administrative suspension; and
- effect of publicity. (p. 34)

APPEALS

A police officer convicted of misconduct or unsatisfactory work performance as a result of internal discipline may appeal the conviction and/or sentence to the OCPC (s. 87, PSA). Under the amendments to the *Police Services Act* that came into effect October 19, 2009, a police officer, other than a chief of police or deputy chief of police, cannot appeal to the Divisional Court. Judicial review is still available under certain conditions if legal requirements are met. A chief of police cannot appeal the decision of a hearing officer (adjudicator) appointed by the chief of police involving an acquittal or sentence of a police officer.

If, in the absence of an explicit appeal right, the chief were granted standing to review his decision or, as in this case, the decision of a police officer he has delegated to hold the hearing on his behalf, it could erode confidence—on the part of police generally, those subject to discipline proceedings, and the public at large—in the independence and fairness of the discipline process. The PSA reflects principles of fairness and natural justice in that it does not allow the chief, who has control of virtually all aspects of the discipline process, to seek to overturn a decision he does not like by a hearing officer he appointed. (*Watson v. Peel Police Service*, 2007, para. 30)

Sentencing matters from a hearing officer's disposition have been appealed to the Ontario Court of Appeal (*OPP v. Favretto*, 2004). In the case of *Favretto*, leave to appeal to the Supreme Court of Canada was dismissed with costs against the OPP (Supreme Court of Canada, 2005).

If a person wants to introduce fresh evidence, the requirements of *Palmer v. The Queen* (1980) must be met. On the issue of introduction of fresh evidence, the commission has been guided by the four-part test set out by the Supreme Court of Canada in *R. v. Palmer* (1980) at page 775:

(1) The evidence should generally not be admitted if, by due diligence, it could have been adduced at trial provided that this general principle will not be applied as strictly in criminal cases as in civil cases (due diligence);

(2) The evidence must be relevant in the sense that it bears upon a decisive or potentially decisive issue in the trial (relevance);

(3) The evidence must be credible in the sense that it is reasonably capable of belief (credibility); and

(4) It must be such, that if believed, it could reasonably, when taken with the other evidence adduced at trial, be expected to have affected the result (potential to alter the original result). (quoted in *Purbrick and the OPP*, 2011, p. 5)

CHAPTER SUMMARY

This chapter is by no means an exhaustive look at police discipline and the *Code of Conduct* under the *Police Services Act*. The reader should have an appreciation of Part V of the *Police Services Act* and Ontario Regulation 268/10 as they relate to internal complaints and investigations into allegations of police misconduct. In addition, Ontario Regulation 263/09, as it relates to the resolution of local complaints, under some circumstances may lead to an internal complaint. This chapter outlined the inapplicability of section 11 of the *Charter* in police discipline matters, the four purposes of discipline, and the four principles of the common law duty of procedural fairness. The police disciplinary hearing process was briefly outlined, including the standards to conduct a hearing and make a finding of guilt. The *Code of Conduct* was discussed, along with the sentencing principles in accordance with case law. Police officers must realize that they have chosen a career where the courts have stated on numerous occasions that police officers will be held to a higher standard than members of the general public.

LO¹ State the legislation that governs police officers and police services in Ontario.

The *Police Services Act* and its regulations govern police officers and police services in Ontario. The code of conduct for police officers is found in Ontario Regulation 268/10.

LO² Define discipline and state the four purposes of discipline.

Discipline "is what happens when one breaks the rules. Discipline is used to impose order or control over someone" (RCMP External Review Committee, 1991, p. 2). The four purposes of discipline are to

1. Protect the employer's interest in maintaining integrity and discipline in the police workplace.
2. Protect the rights of police officers suspected of misconduct.
3. Ensure a high standard of conduct within the police constabulary, and
4. Ensure the interests of the public are protected whether or not they register a formal complaint. (Ceyssens, 2005, p. 5-44)

LO³ State the four principles of the common law duty of procedural fairness.

The four principles are

1. A formal notice must be served advising of the proposed action.
2. Reasons must be provided.

3. The affected party must be provided with a meaningful opportunity to make representation before the decision is made.
4. The decision must be made in good faith. (Ceyssens, 2005, p. 5-23)

LO⁴ Describe the investigative process for allegations of police misconduct, including tunnel vision, and the impact of the *Canadian Charter of Rights and Freedoms*.

Investigators in professional standards investigating internal complaints must keep an open mind and not fall into the trap of tunnel vision. Tunnel vision is having a "narrow focus on a particular investigative or prosecutorial theory, so as to unreasonably colour the evaluation of information received and one's conduct in response to that information" (Kaufman, 1998, p. 26). Police officers must remember that police discipline matters are for the most part administrative in nature, involving the police service and officer. Section 11 of the *Charter* has not played a role in police discipline as the courts have taken the position, especially as it relates to double jeopardy or impartial hearings, that police discipline involves an employer–employee relationship.

LO⁵ Describe the code of conduct offences and unsatisfactory work performance under Ontario Regulation 268/10 and the *Police Services Act*.

Unsatisfactory work performance is described in sections 28 and 29 of Ontario Regulation 268/10 along with the Code of Conduct described in detail in the Schedule of the Regulation. Examples of how appellant authorities have interpreted the law and procedures for police discipline are outlined in the chapter.

LO⁶ Explain the disciplinary hearing process, including the standard for holding a hearing, the standard of proof for conviction, and sentencing principles for assessing penalty during disposition.

Reasonable grounds is the standard for holding a hearing. The standard for conviction is clear and convincing evidence. The principles for sentencing are outlined in a number of cases referenced in this chapter.

The Public Complaints System

LEARNING OUTCOMES

After reading this chapter, you will be able to:

LO1 State the four principles underlying the public complaints system as outlined in the terms of reference of the Lesage report.

LO2 State and explain the four principles of independent, effective, and efficient civilian oversight of the public complaints system.

LO3 State who may file a public complaint against the police, and to what the complaint may relate to.

LO4 State the steps and requirements for a member of the public to file a Part V public complaint under the Ontario *Police Services Act*.

LO5 Explain the informal discipline process under Part V of the *Police Services Act*.

LO6 State the steps and requirements for a member of the public to file a local complaint, and define the alternative dispute resolution process.

> *All parties agreed that a fair, effective and transparent complaints system was essential for maintaining the integrity of the policing profession.*
>
> —*The Honourable Patrick J. Lesage (2005, p. 35)*

In this chapter we will discuss the legislation that governs public complaints against the police in Ontario. We will identify the principles of the terms of reference within the Lesage report, along with the principles of effective civilian oversight of public complaints against the police. The role of the Office of the Independent Police Review Director (OIPRD) in dealing with Part V of the *Police Services Act* (PSA) complaints will be examined, as will the local complaint resolution process, including the alternative dispute resolution process. This chapter will also examine who can file a public complaint and how it is filed under Part V of the PSA, as well as how a complaint is filed locally. The informal resolution process will be described.

THE PUBLIC COMPLAINTS SYSTEM IN ONTARIO

THE LESAGE REPORT

This chapter deals with the public complaints system in Ontario as outlined in Part V of the Ontario *Police Services Act* and Ontario Regulation 263/09, which deals with local complaints. The Office of the Independent Police Review Director (OIPRD) is discussed in detail in Chapter 12 but is also referenced throughout this chapter. In June 2004, the Ontario government requested Justice Patrick Lesage (see Figure 9.1) to review the system of public complaints against police in Ontario and make recommendations. The province established terms of reference for Justice Lesage to consider in writing his report. The resulting document was the *Report on the Police Complaints System in Ontario* (2005), referred to as the Lesage report.

The terms of reference served as a framework for Justice Lesage in reviewing the existing public complaints model in the PSA and making recommendations to develop a new system that would be "fair, effective and transparent" (Lesage, 2005, p. 3) for the public and police. The current public complaints system in Ontario is primarily based on Lesage's recommendations, and the Lesage report (see Figure 9.2) is the foundation of the *Independent Police Review Act, 2007*, which became effective on October 19, 2009, and is now incorporated within the PSA.

John Woods/The Canadian Press

FIGURE 9.1
The Honourable Patrick Lesage, Q.C., author of the 2005 *Report on the Police Complaints System in Ontario.*

LO1 TERMS OF REFERENCE PRINCIPLES IN THE LESAGE REPORT

The Lesage report (2005) is premised on the following four principles, set out in the terms of reference:

1. the police are accountable to an independent civilian authority;
2. the complaints process must be fair, effective, and transparent;

REPORT ON THE POLICE COMPLAINTS SYSTEM IN ONTARIO

THE HONOURABLE PATRICK J. LESAGE, Q.C.

April 22, 2005

FIGURE 9.2

The Lesage report (2005). Justice Lesage took a balanced approach in hearing submissions from various parties before writing his report and making recommendations. This report led to the creation of the OIPRD, the rewriting of Part V of the *Police Services Act*, and the establishment of Ontario Regulation 263/09, which are all discussed in this chapter.

3. the resolution of public complaints must have public confidence and trust, and support from the police community; and

4. the province is ultimately responsible for ensuring accountability of the police in matters of law enforcement and public trust (Figure 9.3).

WHAT DOES A SOUND PUBLIC COMPLAINTS SYSTEM LOOK LIKE?

In the *Police Investigating Police*, a report by the Commission for Public Complaints Against the RCMP (2009), the first finding was that there clearly

FIGURE 9.3

Like all police officers, the RCMP are accountable to the public.

is a role for civilian involvement and oversight in a public complaints system, but the challenge is what an effective and efficient system would look like. The Supreme Court of Canada has recognized the reality that the very nature of police work involves interaction between the police and the public, which may lead to frivolous and vexatious complaints as well as good faith complaints (*R. v. McNeil*, 2009). As such, a public complaints system must balance the rights of the police with the rights of public complainants *but* with independent civilian oversight. In his book *Police Powers in England and Wales*, Professor Leonard Leigh describes the principles behind an ideal public complaints system:

> It must be efficient and administered with integrity. It must be fair and just both to the police and the public. It must provide machinery which is theoretically, and as far as possible practically accessible to the public at large. It must be structured in such a way as to conduce to public confidence in its integrity. This does not necessarily mean that it must respond to the dictates of some pure form of participatory democracy. It does mean the procedure cannot be left wholly in the hands of the police alone. (pp. 284–285)

In a speech to the Canadian Association for Civilian Oversight of Law Enforcement, the Honourable Justice Sidney Linden (see Figure 9.4), Ontario's first public complaints commissioner, took the position that an effective public complaints system is part of police customer service. The complaint process provides police with constructive feedback while instilling public confidence and trust in the police, all critical for effective law enforcement. An effective public complaints system balances the rights of the police to procedural fairness and safeguards with a process that provides the public with easy and informed access to a system that is viewed as independent, transparent, and accountable to civilian oversight. The key words in any effective public complaints system involving complaints against the police are *independent*, *transparent*, and *accountable*, with independent *civilian involvement* and *oversight*. This is a recurring theme throughout the literature (Linden, 2009).

The Lesage report led to the implementation of the OIPRD. As part of its mandate, the OIPRD is responsible for providing "effective oversight of public complaints, promoting accountability of police services across Ontario and increasing public confidence in the complaints system" (OIPRD, 2011b,

FIGURE 9.4

Justice Sidney B. Linden speaking at the 2009 Canadian Association for Civilian Oversight of Law Enforcement Conference as the keynote speaker on "Independent Oversight: Past, Present, Future." Justice Linden was the first police complaints commissioner for Metropolitan Toronto and chairman of the Police Complaints Board. In his presentation, Justice Linden reflected on the beginnings of oversight in Canada and where he thinks it should be heading.

p. 5). In the first OIPRD annual report, Gerry McNeilly (Figure 9.5) stated,

> While Mr. LeSage was carrying out research for his 2005 report, he found an overwhelming consensus among the groups he met that police officers are no more likely to engage in misconduct than any other group of professionals. In fact, most praised the work of the men and women who are willing to protect and serve their communities.
>
> Nevertheless, concerns were raised about the legitimacy and integrity of investigations of complaints against police being carried out by the same police service as the

FIGURE 9.5

The first Independent Police Review Director, Gerry McNeilly.

subject of the complaints. There was also agreement that Ontario's system for dealing with police complaints needed improvement and oversight....

… The ideal system would combine the benefits of police involvement with the independence of civilian oversight. (OIPRD, 2010, p. 3)

LO² PRINCIPLES OF AN EFFECTIVE PUBLIC COMPLAINTS SYSTEM

The Lesage report emphasized the need for an effective and efficient public complaints system in Ontario with independent oversight to ensure accountability and integrity of the police profession. This public complaints system had to be easily accessible to the general public which included public awareness.

The Lesage report led to the creation of Bill 103, the *Independent Police Review Act, 2007*. This Bill amended the *Police Services Act*. The most significant amendments were the repeal of the former Part V, and the addition of Part II.I of the PSA. Part II.1 (sections 26.1 to 26.9) established the Independent Police Review Director (s. 26.1 (1), PSA) who cannot be a police officer or former police officer (s. 26.1 (2), PSA). The legislation allows for the creation of regional offices (s. 26.1 (7), PSA) and any employees, who are appointed under the *Public Service Act of Ontario, 2006* cannot be a current serving police officer (s. 26.1 (5), PSA). The Office of the Independent Police Review Director assumed its responsibilities on October 19, 2009. One of the primary functions of the Independent Police Review

Director is to manage public complaints made to the Director under Part V and the regulations (s. 26.2, PSA). In addition, the chief of police shall designate a senior officer as defined in s. 114 of the PSA to serve as a liaison officer to the Director (s. 26.3). This part also allows for the appointment of investigators (s. 26.5, PSA) to carry out investigations under Part V and the regulations. There are additional powers under Part II.I including search and seizure authorities. Part V of the PSA permits the OIPRD to either refer the complaint back to the police service or, it may, retain the complaint for the purpose of investigation. The OIPRD *Rules of Procedure* provide a list of considerations to determine whether to refer or retain the complaint for investigation (2009, Rule 6.1).

Justice Lesage in his report speaks to a public complaints system that is accountable, independent, accessible, and has integrity. The OIPRD has adopted the principles of accountability, integrity, independence and accessibility. For more information please refer to their website: https://www.oiprd.on.ca/cms/

Part V of the *Police Services Act* is discussed within this chapter.

LO3 WHO CAN MAKE A PUBLIC COMPLAINT AND ABOUT WHAT?

One of the goals of the OIPRD was to make the public complaint system accessible to the public. The OIPRD has an excellent website and complaint forms to ensure that the process is readily available to the public.

The OIPRD website details the process for making a complaint. One of the goals of the OIPRD was to make the public complaint system accessible to the public. The OIPRD has an excellent website and complaint forms and the process is readily available to the public.

WHO CAN MAKE A COMPLAINT?

Any member of the public, either personally or through an agent, can make a complaint to the OIPRD about the policies or services offered by a police service or about the conduct of a police officer (ss. 58(1) & (3), PSA). Police officer is defined in section 2 of the PSA. In order to make a complaint, the complainant must be one or more of the following:

- a person who is directly affected;
- a witness who was present at the time and place of the misconduct;
- a person in a personal relationship with the person who is directly affected and suffered loss, damage, distress, danger, or inconvenience owing to the misconduct; or
- a person who in the opinion of the OIPRD has knowledge of the conduct or who has compelling evidence of misconduct as defined in s. 80, PSA, or unsatisfactory work performance, and that evidence would be admissible in a court proceeding (ss. 60(5) & (6), PSA).

If the OIPRD decides not to deal with the complaint, then the complainant and the chief of police of the subject police service are notified with reasons. The chief of police must notify the subject officer of the substance of the complaint and reasons why the OIPRD did not proceed with the complaint (ss. 60(7) & (8), PSA).

There is also a category of persons under subsection 58(2) of the PSA who cannot make a complaint to the OIPRD, including the Solicitor General (Minister of the MCSCS), an employee of the Ontario Civilian Police Commission or of the OIPRD, members or auxiliary members of the subject police force, and members or employees of the police services board of the subject police force.

WHAT CAN A COMPLAINT BE ABOUT?

A member of the public can complain to the OIPRD about the policies or services of a police service or the behaviour of a police officer (s. 58(1), PSA). The OIPRD can investigate systemic issues resulting from public complaints.

TIME LIMITATIONS OF COMPLAINTS

The OIPRD may decide not to deal with a complaint if it is given more than six months after the facts on which it is based occurred, unless the complaint involves a minor or a person with a disability, the complainant is or was the subject of a criminal charge with respect to the complaint, and it is in the *public interest* to proceed (s. 60(2), PSA). The "kettling" incident at the Toronto G20, pictured in Figure 9.6, is one case where the public interest was at issue.

Eldar Curovic

FIGURE 9.6
A crowd being "kettled" during the G20 protest in Toronto.

Vexatious, Frivolous, or Bad Faith Complaints

The OIPRD may refuse to deal with a public complaint if the OIPRD deems the complaint to be vexatious, frivolous, or made in bad faith; if it is better to deal with the complaint under another law; or it is not in the public interest to deal with the complaint (s. 60(4), PSA). The terms *vexatious*, *frivolous*, and *made in bad faith* are explained in detail in the OIPRD's 2010–2011 annual report (2011b, p. 17).

Resignations/Retirements

If a police officer resigns or retires after a complaint is lodged but before it is disposed of, no further action can take place against the police officer unless he or she is employed by another police service within five years of the resignation or retirement. The OIPRD must be notified promptly of any resignation or retirement (s. 90, PSA).

LO4 STEPS IN A PART V PSA PUBLIC COMPLAINT PROCESS

A member of the public who is not excluded under the legislation may make a public complaint against the policies or services of a police service, or the conduct of a police officer. The process to do this is explained in detail in the public information handout *Talk to Us: Step-by-Step—How to Make a Complaint against the Police* (OIPRD, 2011g). This information is readily available in any police station or detachment and can also be found on the OIPRD website. The complaint must be made in its entirety in a signed OIPRD form (OIPRD, 2011c; see Appendix A).

Anonymous complaints are not accepted. The complaint may be made in person at any police service or e-filed, mailed, or faxed to the OIPRD. Inquiries by telephone are permitted, but the complaint must be filed in writing and signed. Complaints made at the police service must be forwarded to the OIPRD within three business days, and no notice is given to the subject officer until the OIPRD approves it. The OIPRD will provide feedback to the complaint within two business days of receiving it (OIPRD, 2009, rule 4). The OIPRD will decide whether to retain the complaint or refer it. A complaint may be withdrawn by the complainant in accordance with the rules at any time during the process, including the hearing (OIPRD, 2009, rule 10).

After the complaint is received and processed, and unless the complaint fits an exception, it will be investigated. In the case of a complaint on the officer's conduct, the subject officer will receive notice unless the chief of police or OIPRD decides otherwise (s. 62, PSA). When the investigation is finished and is reviewed by the chief of police, the complaint

informal resolution: A process for informally resolving less serious complaints against police without a hearing with the consent of the respondent officer, and in the case of a public complaint, with the consent of the complainant subject to review by the OIPRD.

is either substantiated or unsubstantiated based on reasonable grounds. The OIPRD has defined reasonable grounds as "facts or circumstances of a case that would lead an ordinary and cautious person to believe that misconduct has occurred. This belief must be more than just suspicion of misconduct and must be based on factual evidence" (p. 29).

Once the chief of police receives and reviews the report of the investigation into misconduct and determines on reasonable grounds that there is misconduct, as defined in section 80 of the PSA or unsatisfactory work performance, a hearing must take place. If the officer is found guilty on "clear and convincing evidence," the officer will be subject to a penalty in accordance with section 85, PSA.

The officer and complainant may appeal the decision of the hearing officer to the Ontario Civilian Police Commission (OCPC) (s. 87, PSA) within 30 days of receiving notice of the decision of the adjudicator. After the OCPC hears the appeal, it may confirm, vary, or revoke the decision of the hearing officer; substitute its own decision; or order a new hearing (s. 87(8), PSA).

LO5 INFORMAL COMPLAINT RESOLUTION

In cases where the conduct or unsatisfactory work performance is not serious, **informal resolution** is available if all the parties consent and the OIPRD approves it (ss. 66(6) & 93(2), PSA). This can happen under section 66 or 93 of the *Police Services Act*. Subsection 66(4) of the act states,

> If at the conclusion of the investigation and on review of the written report submitted to him or her the chief of police is of the

opinion that there was misconduct or unsatisfactory work performance but that it was not of a serious nature, the chief of police may resolve the matter informally without holding a hearing, if the police officer and the complainant consent to the proposed resolution.

Under section 66, the chief of police may discipline the respondent officer without a hearing if the officer consents. If the officer does not consent, the chief of police must hold a hearing. The OIPRD must be notified of any penalty in the case of informal resolution, and any documentation that is placed in the officer's file shall be expunged in two years provided that the officer has no other negative documentation related to misconduct (ss. 66(10)–(12), PSA).

A complainant may always ask for a review by the OIPRD if he or she is dissatisfied with how the complaint was handled by the police service. A complainant cannot appeal a decision made by the OIPRD (OIPRD, 2011g).

The informal complaint resolution process is also available under s. 93 of the *Police Services Act*. Section 93 states,

> If at any time during an investigation under this Part into a complaint about the conduct of a police officer other than a chief of police or deputy chief of police the conduct appears to be obviously conduct that is not of a serious nature, the chief of police of the police force to which the complaint relates may resolve the matter informally, if the police officer and the complainant, if any, consent to the proposed resolution. (s. 93(1), PSA)

This allows the police service with the approval of the OIPRD (s. 93(2)) to attempt an informal resolution between the complainant and the respondent officer with their consent where "the conduct appears to be obviously conduct that is not of a serious nature" (s. 93 (1) (3), PSA. The key word here is *obviously*. This can be done within

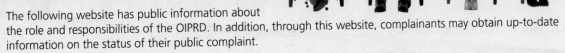
the police service with or without the assistance of third parties. The consent can be withdrawn within 12 business days of the consent being given by either the respondent officer or the complainant by notifying the chief of police and the OIPRD (s. 93(5), PSA). Any statements made during this process are not admissible in future civil proceedings, including PSA hearings, without the consent of that person (s. 96(6)).

An example of an outstanding voluntary alternative dispute resolution program (VADRP) consistent with section 93 of the *Police Services Act* is offered through the Ottawa Police Service (see Figure 9.7). Excellent background information on the program is provided on the Ottawa Police Service website (http://ottawapolice.ca/en/ServingOttawa/SectionsAndUnits/ProfessionalStandardsSection/VADRP.aspx), including what the program is, the strengths of the program, and possible outcomes. One of the strengths of the VADRP is that it "provides a system of alternate dispute resolution to the Ottawa Police Service in its handling of public complaints against members, as well as internal personnel issues. In addition, it offers members of the public and of the police service, the opportunity for a timely, effective, private, and voluntary resolution of a complaint" (Ottawa Police Service, 2010, para. 2).

LO⁶ LOCAL COMPLAINT RESOLUTION

This issue was addressed in the Lesage report (2005) and was one of Justice Lesage's recommendations. Recommendation 12 outlines the process that the police would follow in a complaint of a less serious nature. As a result of this recommendation, Ontario Regulation 263/09 was created to deal with complaints made in person that are deemed to be less serious and can be resolved between the police service and complainant outside the scope of Part V of the PSA. The nature of the complaint has to meet the criteria referenced in this chapter and Ontario Regulation 263/09.

Many aspects of recommendation 12 are consistent with the previous legislation. Ontario Regulation 263/09, *Public Complaints Local Complaints*, governs the local resolution complaints process and is not part of the formal public complaint system, nor is the OIPRD actively involved, although it provides an oversight function. Professor Leonard Leigh, who has been quoted in a number of Supreme Court of Canada cases, states in his book *Police Powers in England and Wales* (1985),

> Informal resolution is an endeavour to filter these cases out of the system. A case is considered suitable for informal resolution when the complainant gives his consent to its being so dealt with and where the chief officer is satisfied that the conduct of, even if proved, would not justify a criminal or disciplinary charge.
>
> If the chief officer determines the matter is suitable for informal resolution he must seek to resolve informally, usually through the medium of an officer appointed from his force to do so. (p. 270)

Courtesy of Ottawa Police Service

FIGURE 9.7
Members of the Ottawa Police Service's Voluntary Alternative Dispute Resolution Program (VADRP).

POLICING ONLINE

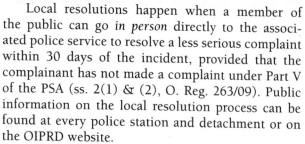

To read recommendation 12 of the Lesage report, go to

http://www.attorneygeneral.jus.gov.on.ca/english/about/pubs/LeSage/en-fullreport.pdf

Local resolutions happen when a member of the public can go *in person* directly to the associated police service to resolve a less serious complaint within 30 days of the incident, provided that the complainant has not made a complaint under Part V of the PSA (ss. 2(1) & (2), O. Reg. 263/09). Public information on the local resolution process can be found at every police station and detachment or on the OIPRD website.

Complainants must be advised that they can make a complaint under Part V of the PSA and they will be given a copy of *Talk to Us: Step-by-Step—How to Make a Complaint against the Police*, issued by the OIPRD. Public education print materials are provided in every police service in a location easily visible to the public. Complainants will be advised that the nature of the complaint cannot be serious; otherwise, the complaint must be made under Part V of the PSA (clauses 3(a) & (c), O. Reg. 263/09).

The chief of police or a delegate of the police service (s. 9, O. Reg. 263/09) must review the complaint to ensure the complainant has not made a complaint under Part V; if he or she has, the chief of police cannot accept or deal with the complaint (ss. 3(1) & (2), O. Reg. 263/09). The chief of police must ensure that the matter is *less serious*, and if it is serious, will ask the complainant to make a complaint under Part V and explain the process (ss. 3(3) & (4), O. Reg. 263/09). There may be occasions when the chief of police believes it is not in the public interest to proceed with a local complaint and may deal with the complaint as a Part V complaint (para. 3 (4) 3, O. Reg. 263/09). When in doubt, the chief of police may consult the OIPRD (s. 3(5), O. Reg. 263/09). Complaints against the chief of police or the deputy chief of police are not eligible for the local complaint process (para. 3 (4) 2, O. Reg. 263/09).

Under section 3 the type of conduct that would be acceptable to be dealt with by way of local resolution includes complaints that involve the handling of personal property (other than money or a firearm) not consistent with s. 132 (1), PSA (s. 80 (1) (h), PSA). In addition if the police officer uses profane, abusive or insulting language to a member of the police service or public or is otherwise uncivil to a member of the public; acts in a disorderly manner that is likely to bring discredit to the police service; or conspires, neglects or omits promptly and diligently to perform a duty; fails to work in accordance with orders; fails to report a matter; or omits to make any necessary entry in a record; or abets or is knowingly an accessory to any of this preceding conduct (O. Reg. 268/10, s. 2 (1) (a) (i), (iv), (v), and (xi); s. 2 (1) (c) (i), (iii), (vi), and (viii); and s. 3). This conduct as well as improperly dressed or untidy in appearance has been referred to as less serious conduct. If there is any issue in determining whether conduct is less serious, then the Independent Police Review Director can be consulted.

POLICING ONLINE

For more information on the local resolution processes through the OIPRD, refer to the document *Talk to Us: Dealing with Your Complaint by Local Resolution* (OIPRD, 2011e) found at

https://www.oiprd.on.ca/CMS/oiprd/media/image-Main/PDF/OIPRD-DealingWithComplaint_Eng.pdf

Less serious complaints may include:

- Personal property, other than money or a firearm;

- The use of profane language;

- Acting in a disorderly manner;

- Neglect of duty;

- Failure to work in accordance with orders;

- Failure to report a matter;

- Omitting to make any necessary entry in a record;

- Improper dress or appearance; or

- Conspiring and abetting the misconduct. (OIPRD, 2010, p. 18)

- Note: Must examine the facts of the complaint on a case-by-case basis.

One of the issues that Justice Lesage addressed was to ensure there was still oversight of the local complaint process. If a chief of police refuses to deal with a local complaint, the chief needs to provide notice to the complainant and the OIPRD, and if the complaint is against an officer, to him or her as well (s. 3(6), O. Reg. 263/09). In the event that the nature of the complaint does fit the local complaint process, and the complainant refuses to proceed under Part V of the PSA, the chief of police generates an internal complaint (s. 3(7), O. Reg. 263/09).

Local complaint resolution, with independent civilian oversight to avoid the potential of abuse within the system, was advocated for by a number of groups who made presentations to Justice Lesage and is outlined in his report. Ontario Regulation 263/09 outlines the process for the chief of police to follow when attempting to resolve a local complaint. If the local complaint is about the conduct of a police officer, after speaking with the complainant the chief of police will discuss the complaint with the officer and then follow up with the complainant. The chief of police may attempt to get the complainant and subject officer together, and if need be facilitate an apology by the officer to the complainant or in absence of this, with the consent of the complainant, officer, and the OIPRD, refer the officer and complainant to the **alternative dispute resolution (ADR) process** (ss. 4(1)–(4), O. Reg. 263/09). The OIPRD defines the alternative dispute resolution process as including "mediation, conciliation, negotiation or any other means of facilitating the resolution of issues in dispute" (s. 4(1), O. Reg. 263/09).

The person who facilitates the ADR process cannot be an employee of any police service, and all oral and written communication made during the process is "without prejudice" to both the complainant and the officer (s. 4(5), O. Reg. 263/09). Any resolution of a local complaint must be confirmed in writing by the complainant, the chief of police, and, if applicable, the subject officer (s. 5, O. Reg. 263/09). These resolutions must be reported to the OIPRD with 15 days after the end of each fiscal quarter (s. 8(3), O. Reg. 263/09). If the local complaint is about a policy or service, the chief of police notifies the police services board. The ADR process is only defined within the local complaint process, and if at any time during the ADR process there is evidence that the complaint should have been processed under Part V of the PSA, the chief of police must cease the process and advise the complainant to proceed under Part V. If this is the case, the chief of police shall provide reasons in writing to the complainant, the OIPRD, and, if applicable, the subject officer. Once again, if the complainant refuses to pursue the complainant under Part V, the chief of police must make an internal complaint (ss. 4(6)–(11), O. Reg. 263/09).

All local complaints must be documented in forms provided by the OIPRD and signed by the complainant and the chief of police, including the nature of the complaint, the resolution being sought, and the steps taken during the process. The form must be signed by the complainant, and after the chief of police makes a record of the matter, no further steps are taken (s. 6, O. Reg. 263/09). Local complaints must be resolved within 30 days unless the OIPRD approves an extension of up to another 30 days as agreed by the complainant, the chief of police, and, if applicable, the subject officer. As with all aspects

> **alternative dispute resolution (ADR) process:** Any process approved by the OIPRD that allows an independent third party to resolve a public complaint that is less serious between a member of the public and a police officer.

of the local complaint process, the complaint must always fit the criteria under the regulation, and the duties of the chief of police under the regulation must be completed. If at any time the complainant is intimidated or coerced, or the complaint is not resolved within 30 days unless there is an extension, the complainant may make a complaint under Part V (s. 7, O. Reg. 263/09).

The OIPRD must receive a copy of the local complaint form within seven days of it being completed and signed or not later than five days if the chief of police commences an internal complaint. The OIPRD may request any information from the chief of police concerning a local complaint (s. 8, O. Reg. 263/09).

Members of the public have a right to a review of any complaint made by them to the OIPRD where the chief of police or commissioner has classified the complaint as unsubstantiated or less serious. The member of the public will be required to fill out a Request for Review form, which can be obtained at any police station or detachment, or through the OIPRD (OIPRD, 2011f).

CHAPTER SUMMARY

This chapter outlined the principles in the terms of reference in the 2005 Lesage report. Emphasis was placed the principles of independent civilian police oversight, which led to the creation of the OIPRD. The chapter described who can file a public complaint and under what circumstances, and the steps the complainant must take. Part V complaints under the PSA were discussed in depth, as well as local complaints under Ontario Regulation 263/09. Informal resolution was described, along with the options available to the complainant and the respondent officer. The local resolution process was examined, including the function of the alternative dispute resolution process.

LO¹ State the four principles underlying the public complaints system as outlined in the terms of reference of the Lesage report.

The Lesage report (2005) on a police complaints system is premised on the following four principles:

- the police are accountable to an independent civilian authority;
- the complaints process must be fair, effective, and transparent;
- the resolution of public complaints must have public confidence and trust, and support from the police community; and
- the province is ultimately responsible for ensuring accountability of the police in matters of law enforcement and public trust.

LO² State and explain the four principles of independent, effective, and efficient civilian oversight of the public complaints system.

The Lesage report emphasized the need for an effective and efficient public complaints system in Ontario with independent oversight to ensure accountability and integrity of the police profession. This public complaints system had to be easily accessible to the general public which included public awareness.

The OIPRD has identified and is committed to the following the principles of independent, effective, and efficient civilian oversight of the public complaints system in Ontario ensuring accountability, integrity, independence, and accessibility.

LO³ State who may file a public complaint against the police, and to what the complaint may relate to.

Any member of the public, either personally or through an agent, can make a complaint to the OIPRD about the policies or services offered by a police service or about the conduct of a police officer (ss. 58(1) & (3), PSA). In order to make a complaint, the complainant must be one or more of the following:

- a person who is directly affected;
- a witness who was present at the time and place of the misconduct;
- a person in a personal relationship with the person who is directly affected and suffered loss, damage, damage, distress, danger or inconvenience owing to the misconduct; or
- a person, who in the opinion of the OIPRD has knowledge of the conduct or who has compelling evidence of misconduct as defined in s. 80, PSA, or unsatisfactory work performance, and that evidence would be admissible in a court proceeding. (ss. 60(5) & (6), PSA)

A member of the public can complain to the OIPRD about the policies or services of a police service or the behaviour of a police officer (subs. 58 (1), PSA).

LO⁴ State the steps and requirements for a member of the public to file a Part V public complaint under the *Ontario Police Services Act*.

Defined persons under the PSA may make a public complaint to the OIPRD about the policies or services of a police service or the behaviour of a police officer in a prescribed form. Anonymous complaints are not accepted. This complaint may be made in person at any police service or e-filed, mailed, or faxed to the OIPRD. Inquiries by telephone are permitted, but the complaint must be filed in writing and signed. Complaints made at the police service must be forwarded to the OIPRD within three business days, and no notice shall be given to the subject officer until the OIPRD approves it. The OIPRD will provide feedback to the complaint within two business days of receiving it (OIPRD, 2009, rule 4). The OIPRD will decide whether to retain the complaint or refer it. A complaint may be withdrawn by the complainant in accordance with the rules any time during the process, including the hearing provided certain requirements are met (OIPRD, 2009, rule 10).

LO⁵ Explain the informal discipline process under Part V of the *Police Services Act*.

In cases where the chief of police finds the conduct or unsatisfactory work performance is not serious, informal resolution is available if the police officer and complainant consent, and in the case of a public complaint, the OIPRD approves it (s. 66 or

s. 93, PSA). Under s. 68 (4) OIPRD may deem the misconduct or unsatisfactory work performance less serious when sending the report to the chief of police. Under sections 66 and 68 of the PSA, the chief of police may discipline the officer without a hearing if the police officer consents. Either the officer or the complainant may withdraw their consent within 12 business days (s. 66 (8), 68 (7), PSA). If the police officer does not consent, the chief of police must hold a hearing. The OIPRD must be notified of any penalty in the case of informal resolution, and any documentation that is placed in the officer's file will be expunged within two years, provided that the officer has no other negative documentation related to misconduct (ss. 66(10)–(12), 68 (7), PSA).

Under section 93, the police service, with the approval of the OIPRD, may attempt an informal resolution between the complainant and the respondent officer with their consent if the conduct appears to be *obviously* less serious. This can be done within the police service with or without the assistance of third parties. The consent can be withdrawn within 12 business days by either the respondent officer or the complainant by notifying the chief of police and the OIPRD. Any statements made during this process are not admissible in future civil proceedings without the consent of that person.

LO6 State the steps and requirements for a member of the public to file a local complaint, and define the alternative dispute resolution process.

Ontario Regulation 263/09 was created to deal complaints made in person by a complainant that are deemed to be less serious and can be resolved between the police service and complainant outside the scope of Part V of the PSA. The nature of the complaint has to meet the criteria referenced in this chapter and Ontario Regulation 263/09. If the local complaint is about the conduct of a police officer, after speaking with the complainant the chief of police will discuss the complaint with the officer and then follow up with the complainant. The chief of police may attempt to get the complainant and subject officer together, and if need be facilitate an apology by the officer to the complainant. In the absence of an apology, with the consent of the complainant, the officer, and the OIPRD, the chief may refer the officer and complainant to the alternative dispute resolution (ADR) process. ADR can be defined as any process approved by the OIPRD that allows an independent third party to resolve a public complaint that is less serious between a member of the public and a police officer.

4

Policing Governance and Oversight

INDEPENDEN

MATTERS REL

This part of the text includes a review of the civilian authorities with administrative and oversight power over the actions of police officers. This part also reviews the policies and procedures affecting policing today.

CHAPTER 10: Civilian Governance

CHAPTER 11: Policing Policies and Procedures

CHAPTER 12: Civilian Oversight

Civilian Governance

LEARNING OUTCOMES

After reading this chapter, you will be able to:

LO1 Define civilian governance for police services and identify the differences between civilian governance and police oversight bodies.

LO2 Briefly describe the role of the Solicitor General as it relates to governance in policing.

LO3 Describe civilian governance in policing as it relates to the relationship between the police chief and civilian authority.

LO4 Briefly discuss the types of police services boards and their roles, functions, and responsibilities in accordance with the *Police Services Act* and its regulations.

LO5 Briefly discuss the code of conduct as it relates to members of police services boards.

> *The subject of governance may be the most important issue examined by this Inquiry. A liberal democracy such as Canada is founded on the rule of law and a system of responsible government. Two principles are fundamental to policing in a democratic society. The first is that police who enforce our laws are ultimately responsible to civilian authorities. The second is that the police must be independent in all operational matters.* *

—The Honourable Mr. Justice Wallace T. Oppal (1994a, p. 6)

There is a considerable amount of literature on the subject of civilian governance of policing in Canada, including observations and recommendations gleaned from public inquiries into allegations of police misconduct, such as the McDonald Commission, the APEC Inquiry, the Marshall Commission, the Arar Commission (see Figure 10.1), and the Ipperwash Inquiry (see Figures 10.2 and 10.3). These inquiries also determined whether there was any political interference in police operations. The Honourable Mr. Justice Wallace Oppal (Commission of Inquiry into Policing in British Columbia, 1994) stated that "the subject of governance may be the most important issue examined by this Inquiry" (1994b, p. v).

A brief background on Maher Arar is provided by Justice Dennis O'Connor from the public inquiry into

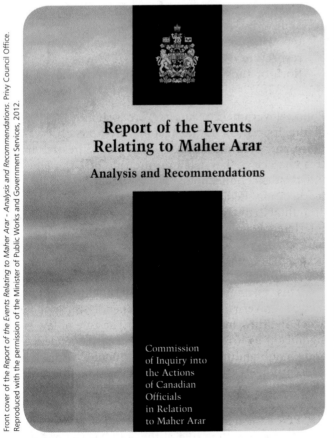

FIGURE 10.1
The Arar Commission report.

FIGURE 10.2
Sam George, with artwork created by his brother, Dudley George. Dudley George was shot and killed in 1995 when police fired on unarmed native protestors occupying Ipperwash Park. The inquiry into the events at Ipperwash led to the release of the Ipperwash Inquiry report in 2007.

---

*Oppal, W. T. (1994). *Closing the Gap: Policing and the community–The report:* V1. Commission of Inquiry: Policing in British Columbia. Victoria, Canada: Attorney General, B.C., p. v. Copyright © Province of British Columbia. All rights reserved. Reprinted with permission of the Province of British Columbia. www.ipp.gov.bc.ca.

REPORT OF THE

IPPERWASH

INQUIRY

Ontario

VOLUME 1   Investigation and Findings

VOLUME 2   Policy Analysis

VOLUME 2   Inquiry Process

VOLUME 4   Executive Summary

The Honourable Sidney B. Linden, Commissioner

FIGURE 10.3
The Report of the Ipperwash Inquiry.

the actions of Canadian officials relating to the treatment of Maher Arar in 2002 and 2003 by American and Syrian officials.

> Maher Arar is a Canadian citizen. He is married and has two children. He has a Bachelor of Engineering in Computers from McGill University and a Master's degree in Telecommunications from the University of Quebec's *Institut national de la recherche scientifique*.
>
> On September 26, 2002, while passing through John F. Kennedy International Airport in New York, Mr. Arar was arrested and subsequently detained by American officials for 12 days. He was then removed against his will to Syria, the country of his birth, where he was imprisoned for nearly a year. While in Syria, Mr. Arar was interrogated, tortured and held in degrading and inhumane conditions. He returned to Canada after his release on October 5, 2003. (Commission of Inquiry into the Actions of

Canadian Officials in Relation to Maher Arar, 2006, p. 9)

The inquiry subsequently cleared Mr. Arar of any wrongdoing. He was never charged in Canada, the United States, or Syria. The Canadian government made an apology and financial settlement to Mr. Arar. Justice O'Connor made 23 recommendations in his 2006 report, including recommendations pertaining to oversight of national security investigations and information sharing. Emphasis on this oversight goes beyond central coordination of national security investigations through RCMP headquarters, as supported by the following comment in the report:

> The foundations for centralized oversight of national security investigations are found in ministerial directions issued in November 2003. One of those directions provides that it is the responsibility of the Commissioner to ensure that all national security investigations are centrally coordinated at RCMP Headquarters in order to "enhance the Commissioner's operational accountability" and in turn "enhance ministerial accountability, by facilitating the Commissioner's reporting to the Minister," especially with respect to "high profile RCMP investigations or those that give rise to controversy. (p. 328)

Police–government relations were a significant part of the Ipperwash Inquiry. Some of these observations and recommendations will be addressed in this chapter as they relate to the rule of law, police independence, and police accountability. The hallmark of any democracy is a policing model that is accountable to civilian authority but free of political interference. Police services boards and governments have struggled in the past to find a delicate balance between accountability and independence (Roach, 2007, 2011).

This chapter will address the definitions of civilian governance, police independence, police accountability, and the rule of law. The rule of law is significant as it relates to both police independence and accountability. The mandate, structure, and roles and responsibilities of police services boards will also be discussed. There will be limited discussion of the role of the Ontario Civilian Police Commission (OCPC) as it relates to the oversight of police services boards, and the role of the Solicitor General as it relates to policies and accountability of police services in Ontario.

LO¹ DIFFERENCES BETWEEN CIVILIAN OVERSIGHT AND CIVILIAN GOVERNANCE

Civilian oversight of police, which is discussed in Chapter 12, deals with independent bodies that oversee police conduct and governance matters, including the OCPC, the Office of the Independent Police Review Director (OIPRD), and the Special Investigations Unit (SIU). There is some discussion in this chapter on the role of the OCPC and the OIPRD in the oversight of municipal police services boards under the *Police Services Act* and its regulations.

Although the chief of police and the police services board have a role in the police discipline process, it is important to make a clear distinction between civilian governance (sometimes referred to as police governance) and civilian oversight (sometimes referred to as police oversight). According to Murphy and McKenna (2007), "Police governance is more closely aligned with the approaches taken to the overall guidance and direction of a police service, including the formation of organizational strategic goals and objectives" (p. 37). In Ontario, this governance is dictated through the *Police Services Act* and its regulations. Other authorities have also identified the differences between civilian governance and civilian oversight. Synyshyn (2007) describes governance as

> a degree of power over an organization, while reviewing or investigating complaints does not. In effect, governing bodies are connected to and therefore a part of an organization. Their role also demands that they associate with the organization in such a way that they can objectively criticize and evaluate its performance. (p. 3)

Civilian (or police) oversight in Ontario relates to the independent arm's-length civilian agencies responsible to the Ministry of Community Safety and Correctional Services (MCSCS), such as the OCPC, or the Ministry of the Attorney General, as in the case of the OIPRD, relating to public complaints against the conduct of police officers and the policies of or services provided by a police service (Figure 10.4). Civilian oversight also includes the SIU, which examines police conduct that leads to the serious injury or death of a civilian, or an allegation of sexual assault against a police officer (see Chapter 12). Section 113 of the *Police Services Act* requires that the SIU and the unit conduct investigations "into the circumstances of serious injuries and deaths that may have resulted

FIGURE 10.4
An aerial photograph taken during the kettling incident at Queen Street and Spadina Avenue in Toronto, which was roundly condemned in the 2012 OIPRD report *Policing the Right to Protest: G20 Systemic Review Report.*

Eldar Curovic

from criminal offences committed by police officers" (s. 113(5)) and that the results of these investigations are reported to the Attorney General (s. 113(8)). Ontario Regulation 267/10 outlines the responsibilities that police officers have during an SIU investigation (Figure 10.5).

It is important to understand definitions under section 2 of the *Police Services Act* as they play a key role in many decisions involving the OCPC and the courts, and will be used throughout this book. In some cases, the decisions of the commission or the courts have led to the creation of regulations under the *Police Services Act* (*Ottawa-Carleton Police Services Board v. Ontario [Civilian Commission on Police Services]*, 2000, 2001).

GOVERNANCE BODIES

There are two forms of policing governance models in Canada. The first model, sometimes referred to as police governance, deals with the RCMP and provincial police services, while the second model, sometimes referred to as civilian governance, deals with regional and municipal police services. The second model, for the most part, takes the form of police services boards.

In the first model, the RCMP (Figure 10.6) and provincial police services are accountable to the government minister responsible for policing. In the case of the RCMP, this is the Minister of Public Safety and Emergency Preparedness, and for the OPP

Police Services Act - O. Reg. 267/10 http://www.e-laws.gov.on.ca/html/regs/english/elaws_regs_1...

Ontario

ServiceOntario
e-Laws

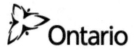

Français

Police Services Act

ONTARIO REGULATION 267/10

CONDUCT AND DUTIES OF POLICE OFFICERS RESPECTING INVESTIGATIONS BY THE SPECIAL INVESTIGATIONS UNIT

Consolidation Period: From August 1, 2011 to the e-Laws currency date.

Last amendment: O. Reg. 283/11.

This is the English version of a bilingual regulation.

Definitions and interpretation

1. (1) In this Regulation,

"SIU" means the special investigations unit established under section 113 of the Act; ("UES")

"subject officer" means a police officer whose conduct appears, in the opinion of the SIU director, to have caused the death or serious injury under investigation; ("agent impliqué")

"witness officer" means a police officer who, in the opinion of the SIU director, is involved in the incident under investigation but is not a subject officer. ("agent témoin") O. Reg. 267/10, s. 1 (1).

(2) The SIU director may designate an SIU investigator to act in his or her place and to have all the powers and duties of the SIU director under this Regulation and, if the SIU director appoints a designate, any reference to the SIU director in this Regulation, excluding this subsection, means the SIU director or his or her designate. O. Reg. 267/10, s. 1 (2).

(3) For the purposes of this Regulation, a person appointed as a police officer under the *Interprovincial Policing Act, 2009* is deemed to be,

(a) if the person was so appointed by a member of the Ontario Provincial Police, a member of that police force;

(b) if the person was so appointed by a member of a municipal police force, a member of that police force; or

1 of 5 05/09/12 11:35 AM

FIGURE 10.5
Ontario Regulation 267/10.

FIGURE 10.6
The regimental badge of the RCMP.

(Figure 10.7), it is the Minister of Community Safety and Correctional Services (formerly the Solicitor General). The *RCMP Act* provides that "the Governor in Council may appoint an officer, to be known as the Commissioner of the Royal Canadian Mounted Police, who, under the direction of the Minister, has

the control and management of the Force and all matters connected therewith" (*RCMP Act*, s. 5(1)). This wording for the RCMP commissioner is similar to that for the commissioner of the OPP. The *Police Services Act* states, "There shall be a Commissioner of the Ontario Provincial Police who shall be appointed by the Lieutenant Governor in Council" (s. 17(1)), and "Subject to the Solicitor General's direction, the Commissioner has the general control and administration of the Ontario Provincial Police and the employees connected with it" (s. 17(2)). Although the first model is subject to police governance to the extent that the commissioner of the OPP is "subject to the Solicitor General's direction," many Ontario communities that choose to have their policing done by the OPP have the option of forming their own police services board (PSA, s. 10). This is discussed in detail in this chapter.

In a letter to members of the OPP dated December 7, 2011, OPP Commissioner Chris D. Lewis stated, "As the overall leader of this organization, I am responsible to be accountable to government; the people we serve; to our municipal leaders and our Police Services Boards; and to the men and women of the OPP" (Figure 10.8).

FIGURE 10.8
Commissioner Chris D. Lewis, OPP.

FIGURE 10.7
The shoulder flash of the OPP.

THE RCMP AND PROVINCIAL POLICE MODEL: POLICE GOVERNANCE

When discussing the subjects of police independence and accountability of the RCMP to the federal government, Justice Hughes (see Figure 10.9) proposed the following five principles:

- When the RCMP are performing law enforcement functions (investigation, arrest and prosecution) they are entirely independent of the federal government and answerable only to the law.
- When the RCMP are performing their other functions, they are not entirely independent but are accountable to the federal government through the Solicitor General of Canada or such other branch of government as Parliament may authorize.
- In all situations, the RCMP are accountable to the law and the courts. Even when performing functions that are subject to government direction,

officers are required by the *RCMP Act* to respect and uphold the law at all times.

- The RCMP are solely responsible for weighing security requirements against the Charter rights of citizens. Their conduct will violate the Charter if they give inadequate weight to Charter rights. The fact that they may have been following the directions of political masters will be no defence if they fail to do that.
- An RCMP member acts inappropriately if he or she submits to government direction that is contrary to law. Not even the Solicitor General may direct the RCMP to unjustifiably infringe Charter rights, as such directions would be unlawful. (Commission for Public Complaints Against the RCMP, 2001, s. 31.3.2)

LO² THE ROLE OF THE SOLICITOR GENERAL OF ONTARIO

While the legislation refers to the Solicitor General, the ministry responsible for police services in Ontario is now called the Ministry of Community Safety and Correctional Services (MCSCS; Figure 10.10). The ministry was created in 2002 when the Solicitor General of Ontario and Ministry of Correctional Services were amalgamated. The duties and responsibilities of the Solicitor General:

(a) monitor police forces to ensure that adequate and effective police services are provided at the municipal and provincial levels;

(b) monitor boards and police forces to ensure that they comply with prescribed standards of service;

(c) REPEALED: 1995, c. 4, s. 4 (1).

(d) develop and promote programs to enhance professional police practices, standards and training;

(e) conduct a system of inspection and review of police forces across Ontario;

(f) assist in the co-ordination of police services;

(g) consult with and advise boards, community policing advisory committees, municipal chiefs of police, employers of special constables and associations on matters relating to police and police services;

(h) develop, maintain and manage programs and statistical records and conduct research studies in respect of police services and related matters;

FIGURE 10.9
The Honourable Edward (Ted) Hughes.

FIGURE 10.10
The Honourable Madeleine Meilleur, Minister of Community Safety and Correctional Services.

(i) provide to boards, community policing advisory committees and municipal chiefs of police, information and advice respecting the management and operation of police forces, techniques in handling special problems and other information calculated to assist;

(j) issue directives and guidelines respecting policy matters;

(k) develop and promote programs for community-oriented police services; and

(l) operate the Ontario Police College.
   (s. 3 (2), PSA)

And while there may be no civilian governance between the Solicitor General of Ontario and the OPP, OPP Commissioner Tom O'Grady (since retired) made it clear during the Ipperwash Inquiry that had a government minister directed him on police operational matters, he would not have followed the directions (Linden, 2007a). Justice Linden went on to say,

The relationship between the Solicitor General and the police is very carefully circumscribed in relation to the line between policy and operational matters. The Solicitor General can impose policy that would affect the operation of the force, but cannot influence operational matters and has no direct contact with police officers concerning operational matters. [He] agreed that if the proper protocol for communication between the Solicitor General and the police were overridden, particularly in the area of police operations, it could give rise to the perception or reality of political interference.* (pp. 124 & 172)

Given the similar wording of section 5 of the *RCMP Act* and section 17 of the Ontario *Police Services Act*, one could argue that Justice Hughes's five principles for RCMP independence and accountability would also be applicable to the OPP and other provincial police forces in Canada. The literature emphasizes that in any successful police governance model, the roles, functions, and responsibilities of the police and the governing oversight bodies (Solicitor General or police services boards) must be clear and well defined, with sound policies in the place. This can be best accomplished where roles, functions, and responsibilities are codified in legislation (Plumptre, 2007).

> **civilian governance:**
> For municipal and regional policing, an internal but arm's-length civilian body of municipal elected and appointed individuals and provincial appointees, whose mandate is derived from the statutes and regulations to ensure accountability of police services while maintaining their independence in accordance with the rule of law.

CIVILIAN GOVERNANCE

There are numerous definitions of **civilian governance**, sometimes referred to as police governance. The key words in the definition of civilian governance are *civilian*, *governance*, *independence*, *accountability*, and *the rule of law*.

KEY TERMS IN CIVILIAN GOVERNANCE

Civilian

Civilians are people who are not members of a police service. Who participates in civilian governance of police services in Ontario is dictated by the *Police Services Act*. The legislation states that people such as judges, justices of the peace, police officers, and criminal lawyers cannot be members of a police services board (s. 27(13)). Confidence and public trust

*Linden, S. B. (The Honourable) (2007). *The Ipperwash Inquiry. Volume 1*. Ministry of the Attorney General. Toronto, Canada. Queen's Printer. P. 124 and 172. © Queen's Printer for Ontario, 2007. Reproduced with permission.

FIGURE 10.11

The Honourable Wallace Oppal.

in governance of policing are premised on civilian involvement in both governance and oversight.

In June 1992, the attorney general of British Columbia requested the Honourable Mr. Justice Wallace Oppal (see Figure 10.11) to conduct the Commission of Inquiry into Policing in British Columbia. Justice Oppal examined different aspects of policing in British Columbia, with a focus on governance as being critical to ensure accountability and independence of the police. He stated, "Thus in a system of responsible government, the police are ultimately accountable to civilian authority"* (1994b, p. B-3).

Governance

The word *governance* "is derived from the Latin, *gubernare,* to steer" (Armstrong & Francis, 2008, p. 47). Armstrong and Francis define *governance* as "the processes by which organisations are directed, controlled and held to account. It encompasses authority, accountability, stewardship, leadership, the direction and control exercised in the organization" (2008, p. 45). According to Halpenny, governance "relates to accountability" and the issues relating to governance "can be formulated in many different ways but are commonly brought into focus through the use of the concept of 'police independence'" (2010, p. 11). Darren Caul, a former police board member, states that "absent a legal orientation, police governance is oriented to the ideals of protecting police independence from state intrusion while ensuring police accountability" (2009, p. 21).

In Canada, the courts and boards of inquiry have provided guidance in these areas, but it is notable that many of the recommendations from inquiries on these issues have never been implemented. Ontario would appear to

be the closest to legislating political independence with respect to police services boards and municipal policing, as legislation within the *Police Services Act* (s. 31 (4)) and Ontario Regulation 421/97 (s. 2) prohibit board member's interference in the day-to-day operations of a police force. However, there is no similar explicit wording for the Minister of Community Safety and Correctional Services in Ontario, as was identified by the Honourable Sidney Linden during the Ipperwash Inquiry (2007b, pp. 313–314). There was even discussion during the Ipperwash Inquiry about forming a provincial police services board, but given the complexities of policing the entire province with its many individual communities, this was never made a specific recommendation.

The Independent Grocers Alliance (IGA) grocery franchise has a pledge that begins with "the strength of democracy rests in the community; the strength of a community rests in its local institutions. As the community grows, so grows the nation." Although this quote about institutions probably refers to grocery stores, it is also applicable to police services. Darren Caul states, "Although the police are a major nexus between civil society and the state, democracy is not possible unless the police behave democratically" (2009, p. 14). This notion is supported by Justice Oppal:

> The role of a board is very important in the governance of police. The board is the employer of the police and collectively represents the community at large…. Police boards must be aware of their community's needs and priorities in the areas of public safety and policing. They should and must hold the police chief accountable for policing in their communities. They must critically assess the performance of both the chief constable and the department.† (1994b, pp. vi–vii)

LO3 POLICE INDEPENDENCE, ACCOUNTABILITY, AND RULE OF LAW

Police Independence

Police independence generally means that the police are able to conduct their day-to-day operations without political interference. Various public inquiries have been conducted that alleged political interference into the conduct of the police by politicians or government (the Ipperwash Inquiry, APEC Inquiry, McDonald Commission, and Marshall Commission).

FIGURE 10.12
The Honourable Sidney Linden.

The Honourable Sidney Linden, commissioner of the Ipperwash Inquiry (see Figure 10.12), stated, "It is not appropriate for the government to enter the law enforcement domain of the police. Law enforcement properly falls within the responsibility of the police. To maintain police independence, the government cannot direct when and how to enforce the law"* (2007c, p. 44). Police independence must be balanced with the need for police to be accountable to their governing authorities and operate within the policies and procedures established by police services boards, who are enabled through legislative authorities.

In *R. v. Campbell* (1999), the Supreme Court of Canada adopted what is commonly known as the Blackburn doctrine, an often-quoted passage written by Lord Denning (Figure 10.13) that refers to police independence from government interference in conducting criminal investigations. The Supreme Court stated,

> While for certain purposes the Commissioner of the RCMP reports to the Solicitor General,

FIGURE 10.13
The Right Honourable Lord Denning (1899–1999).

the Commissioner is not to be considered a servant or agent of the government while engaged in a criminal investigation. The Commissioner is not subject to political direction. Like every other police officer similarly engaged, he is answerable to the law and, no doubt, to his conscience. (para. 33)

In describing the principle of police independence from government, the Blackburn doctrine is often quoted in relation to the commissioner of police in *R. v. Metropolitan Police Comr., Ex parte Blackburn* (1968 at p. 769), and repeated by Justice Binnie, SCC, in *R. v. Campbell*.

> I have no hesitation, however, in holding that, like every constable in the land, he [the Commissioner of Police] should be, and is, independent of the executive. He is not subject to the orders of the Secretary of State, save that under the Police Act 1964 the Secretary of State can call on him to give a report, or to retire in the interests of efficiency. I hold it to be the duty of the Commissioner of Police, as it is of every chief constable, to enforce the law of the land. He must take steps so to post his men that crimes may be detected; and that honest citizens may go about their affairs in peace. He must decide whether or not suspected persons are to be prosecuted; and, if need be, bring the prosecution or see that it is brought; but in all these things he is not the servant of anyone, save of the law itself. No Minister of the Crown can tell him that he must, or must not, keep observation on this place or that; or that he must, or must not, prosecute this man or that one. Nor can any police authority tell him so. The responsibility for law enforcement lies on him. He is answerable to the law and to the law alone. (1999, para. 33)

As such, communication by police services boards should take place only with the chief of the police service or, in the case of municipal policing contracts, with the OPP detachment commanders. Regarding OPP matters, the Solicitor General (Minister of the MCSMS), probably through a deputy minister, must communicate only with the commissioner or his or her designate. These views have been reinforced in the inquiries discussed in this chapter.

Police Accountability

True civilian governance cannot exist without accountability. Government at all levels must ensure

---

*Linden, S. B. (The Honourable) (2007). *The Ipperwash Inquiry. Volume 4*. Ministry of the Attorney General. Toronto, Canada. Queen's Printer. P. 44. © Queen's Printer for Ontario, 2007. Reproduced with permission.

accountability of the police while respecting independence. This is particularly so in a democratic society where police must balance their role with their legal responsibilities of safeguarding the rights of all citizens. The principle of accountability in policing is the foundation of sound policing and ideal governance to ensure transparency and public confidence in both the police and those responsible for overseeing them (Armstrong & Francis, 2008; Caul, 2009).

Rule of Law

The preamble to the *Canadian Charter of Rights and Freedoms* (see Figure 10.14) states, "Whereas Canada is founded upon principles that recognize the supremacy of God and the rule of law." Justice Oppal defined the rule of law as being that "governments must exercise their powers according to law and citizens must not be exposed to arbitrary acts"* (1994b, B-2). Justice Oppal went on to say,

A liberal democracy such as Canada is founded on the rule of law and a system of responsible government. Two principles are fundamental to policing in a democratic society. The first is that police who enforce our laws are ultimately responsible to civilian authorities. The second is that the police must be independent in all operational matters. They must, upon reasonable grounds, be free to investigate anyone without any political interference or any fear of political interference.† (p. 6)

The rule of law has also been addressed by the Supreme Court of Canada, as cited in an Ontario case where the court stated,

Constitutionalism and the rule of law are cornerstones of the Constitution and reflect our country's commitment to an orderly and civil society in which all are bound by the enduring rules, principles, and values of our Constitution as the supreme source of law and authority. In the *Secession Reference* at p. 258, the Supreme Court outlined three essential elements of the rule of law. First, the law is supreme over both governments and private persons: "[t]here is…one law for all." Second, the creation and maintenance of a positive legal order is the

FIGURE 10.14
The *Canadian Charter of Rights and Freedoms*.

*Oppal, W. T. (1994). *Closing the Gap: Policing and the community–The report: V1*. Commission of Inquiry: Policing in British Columbia. Victoria, Canada: Attorney General, B.C., B-2. Copyright © Province of British Columbia. All rights reserved. Reprinted with permission of the Province of British Columbia. www.ipp.gov.bc.ca.
†Oppal, W. T. (1994). *Closing the Gap: Policing and the community–The report: V1*. Commission of Inquiry: Policing in British Columbia. Victoria, Canada: Attorney General, B.C., p. 6. Copyright © Province of British Columbia. All rights reserved. Reprinted with permission of the Province of British Columbia. www.ipp.gov.bc.ca.

normative basis for civil society. The third feature is that the exercise of public power must be based on a legal rule that governs the relationship between the state and the individual. (*Lalonde v. Ontario (Commission de restructuration des services de santé)*, 2001, para. 108)

The police and governments, especially, must take caution in not giving the rule of law some flexibility in how police, ultimately through the courts, enforce the law and use their discretion. Justice Linden addressed this during the Ipperwash Inquiry in referencing the Ontario Court of Appeal decision in *Henco Industries Ltd. v. Haudenosaune Six Nations Confederacy Council* (2006), which dealt with the First Nations occupation of property in Caledonia where ownership was in dispute (see Figure 10.15):

> But the rule of law has many dimensions, or in the words of the Supreme Court of Canada is "highly textured." One dimension is certainly that focused on by the motions judge: the court's exercise of its contempt power to vindicate the court's authority and ultimately to uphold the rule of law. The rule of law requires a justice system that can ensure orders of the court are enforced and the process of the court is respected.

> Other dimensions of the rule of law, however, have a significant role in this dispute. These other dimensions include respect for minority rights, reconciliation of Aboriginal and non-Aboriginal interests through negotiations, fair procedural safeguards for those subject to

criminal proceedings, respect for Crown and police discretion, respect of the separation of the executive, legislative and judicial branches of government and respect for Crown property rights.* (2007b, pp. 38–39)

In another contempt proceeding (*R. v. Peel Regional Police Service, Chief of Police,* 2000), Justice Hill cited the Peel Regional police chief and police services board for contempt for failing to provide adequate and effective police services in that prisoners were not being delivered to the court in a timely fashion, resulting in untimely delays. Justice Hill stated that this case was about "the rule of law" (para. 2). As a result of this contempt citation, additional police personnel were hired and the court received an apology. In the end, Justice Hill did not order a contempt of court trial (para. 142).

WHAT IS GOOD GOVERNANCE?

In examining the key terms for civilian governance, defining good civilian governance in policing is not easy, given the number of governance models. Mel Gill explains,

> Good governance…is about Vision (planning for the future), Destination (setting goals and providing a general "road map"), Resources (securing the resources necessary to achieve the goals or reach the destination), Monitoring (periodically ensuring that the organizational vehicle is well-maintained and progressing, within legal limits, toward its destination) and Accountability (ensuring efficient use of resources; reporting progress and detours to stakeholders). (cited in Ministry of Public Safety and Solicitor General, 2003, p. 13)

Gill makes it clear that "assessment of board performance and organizational effectiveness is essential to demonstrating accountability and generating public trust" (cited in Lalonde & Kean, 2003, p. 144). Boards must be assessed on both their end product and the processes used to achieve the end product. Some police boards on occasion have been described as dysfunctional, while others have been described as effective. It is only through an annual critical assessment and evaluation of a board's performance that board efficiency and effectiveness can be objectively identified. Armstrong and Francis (2008) define evaluation as a "process of systematically collecting useful information to decisions and judgements against criteria" (p. 50). This criterion, also referred to as benchmarks, in Ontario is found in the *Police Services Act* and its regulations.

Colin Mcconnell / GetStock.com

FIGURE 10.15

In early 2006, the First Nations community demonstrated and took control over property in Caledonia over dispute of a land claim. The land ownership issue remains in dispute.

*Linden, S. B. (The Honourable) (2007). *The Ipperwash Inquiry. Volume 2.* Ministry of the Attorney General. Toronto, Canada. Queen's Printer. P. 38-39. © Queen's Printer for Ontario, 2007. Reproduced with permission.

LO⁴ THE ROLE OF POLICE SERVICES BOARDS

Responsibilities of municipal and regional police services boards are defined in section 31 of the *Police Services Act*. For the OPP, civilian/police governance varies depending on the level of policing service provided, but ultimately the commissioner of the OPP is accountable to the Solicitor General (Minister of the MCSCS). Regardless of the civilian/police governance model, the OPP commissioner maintains independence in the day-to-day operations of the police service. Responsibilities of the OPP are defined in section 19 of the *Police Services Act*.

Balancing Police Independence with Police Accountability

"In any democratic society based on the rule of law and responsible government, it is fundamental that police independence be balanced with accountability"* (Oppal, 1994b, p. xxv). Whenever the police and the public interact, especially in public demonstrations where physical altercations result in serious bodily harm or death, where there are serious allegations of violating constitutional rights, or in cases of what are perceived to be politically motivated investigations, the issue of government interference or meddling is raised. For the most part, it seems clear in municipal policing, at least in Ontario, that police enjoy independence with respect to operational matters, and governments direct and create policy consistent with the *Police Services Act* and its regulations (Thomas, 2007). This has been commented on in many of the inquiries identified in this chapter. Perhaps one of the best descriptions of what civilian governance should be was provided by Justice Linden during the Ipperwash Inquiry:

> The relationship between the police and government is a delicate balance. Many things can go wrong if the balance is upset or tipped too far in one direction.
>
> On the one hand, the police will have too much "independence" if they are not subject to legitimate direction from democratically elected authorities. Nor should the police be "independent" of requirements to explain and justify their actions. Tipping the balance too far in favour of police independence, therefore, could result in the police effectively becoming a law unto themselves.
>
> On the other hand, the balance can be tipped too far in favour of government intervention or

authority. Governments should not be allowed to influence specific law enforcement decisions or specific operational decisions of the police....

In short, it is equally dangerous for governments to become either too involved in policing or not involved enough. Yet the police/government debate is not simply about preventing police from becoming a law unto themselves or inappropriate government influence. It is also about ensuring public accountability and transparency for police and government decision-making.† (Linden, 2007b, p. 304)

Providing Police Services in Ontario

Municipalities in Ontario must provide adequate and effective police services (s. 4, PSA) either through their own police services or through services contracted with the OPP, in what is commonly referred to as a section 5.1 PSA contract. The provisions of this type of contract are found in Ontario Regulation 420/97. Although there is no provision for a police services board under this regulation, the act does provide the option for one or more municipalities served by the same OPP detachment to establish a community policing advisory committee. The role of the community policing advisory committee includes advising the OPP detachment commander about policing priorities and objectives, but, as already noted, this role does not include directing day-to-day policing operations (s. 5(6), PSA). The term of office for members of the community policing advisory committee cannot exceed the term of office of the municipal council that appointed the member (s. 5.1(7), PSA). A member of the community policing advisory committee may serve until a successor is selected and can be reappointed (s. 5.1(8), PSA).

Every municipality that maintains a police service must have a police services board or a joint police services board (s. 27), unless policing is provided by the OPP (s. 5.1) or two or more councils, on approval by the commission, amalgamate their police forces (s. 6). Policing also may be provided by another police services board in a neighbouring municipality (s. 6.1). In this case, the municipality that receives this option of policing "may select a person to advise the other municipality's board with respect to objectives and priorities for police services" (s. 6.1(2)). The term of office for this advisor cannot exceed the term of office of the municipal council that appointed the advisor (s. 6.1(3), PSA). The advisor may serve until a successor is selected and can be reappointed (s. 6.1(4), PSA).

---

*Oppal, W. T. (1994). *Closing the Gap: Policing and the community–The report: VI*. Commission of Inquiry: Policing in British Columbia. Victoria, Canada: Attorney General, B.C., p. xxv. Copyright © Province of British Columbia. All rights reserved. Reprinted with permission of the Province of British Columbia. www.ipp.gov.bc.ca.
†Linden, S. B. (The Honourable) (2007). *The Ipperwash Inquiry. Volume 2*. Ministry of the Attorney General. Toronto, Canada. Queen's Printer. P. 304. © Queen's Printer for Ontario, 2007. Reproduced with permission.

FIGURE 10.16
The Peel Police Services Board crest.

An example of a joint police board is the Regional Municipality of Peel Police Services Board (Figure 10.16). This board is responsible for policing in Brampton and Mississauga under section 31 of the *Police Services Act* and for policing in the Town of Caledon and under section 10. The functions and responsibilities of a section 10 PSA board include participating in the selection of the OPP detachment commander; determining policing priorities and objectives, including establishing local policies with the detachment commander; monitoring the performance of the detachment commander; and receiving reports on secondary employment activities. In addition, the board reviews the detachment commander's administration of Part V PSA public complaints and receives regular reports on the results of public complaints (s. 10(9), PSA).

The PSA addresses exceptions to policing agreements, but these are beyond the scope of this chapter.

THE MANDATE OF POLICE SERVICES BOARDS

Unless otherwise specified, municipalities in Ontario must provide adequate and effective police services that include the core services of crime prevention, law enforcement, assistance to victims of crime, public order maintenance, and emergency response (ss. 4(1) & (2), PSA). The mandate for police services boards to operate in Ontario is found in the Ontario *Police Services Act* and the regulations.

The courts have also provided direction where boards have challenged the OCPC, to which they are accountable (*Ottawa-Carleton Regional Police Services Board v. Ontario [Civilian Commission on Police Services]*, 2000, 2001; *Wallaceburg Police Services Board v. Ontario Civilian Commission on Police Services*, 1997), or where police services boards have failed to provide adequate and effective police services (*R. v. Peel Regional Police Service, Chief of Police*, 2000). As has been discussed in detail in this chapter, the courts have also provided guidance on issues of police governance, especially as it relates to police services being accountable but independent (*R. v. Campbell*, 1999).

LO5 CONDUCT OF POLICE SERVICES BOARDS

Police services boards are governed by their own code of conduct (O. Reg.421/97, *Members of Police Services Boards—Code of Conduct*) and their own code of ethics (the Canadian Association of Chiefs of Police Ethical Framework). The duties of a police services board are outlined in the *Police Services Act* and its related regulations and depend on what type of board exists and the police services provided.

Police services boards are held accountable by the OCPC and the courts. There have been cases where the boards have challenged the OCPC and the courts have ruled in favour of the board. In one case, a regional police services board refused to follow the direction of the commission to send a recently appointed inspector to the Ontario Police College for initial training. The board challenged the commission's position on this pending a judicial review by the Ontario Divisional Court. The commission then ordered a section 25 hearing into the conduct of the board, which in essence suspended the board members' authority to continue in their capacity as board members. The board sought interim relief to allow it to continue its functions. The Divisional Court by way of judicial review ruled in favour of the board and stated, "The Board did not disobey the Commission. The decision of the Commission to investigate the members with the consequence that they would be unable to carry out their duties on the Board constituted an inappropriate exercise of statutory power" (*Ottawa-Carleton Regional Police Services Board v. Ontario Civilian Commission on Police Services*, 2000, p. 1).

In a subsequent hearing, the court ruled in favour of the Ottawa-Carleton Regional Police Services Board, stating there was no regulation under the *Police Services Act* regarding recruit training. The court stated,

> The inspector's failure to take basic recruiting did not offend the Police Services Act or its regulations. The Commission read into the Act

a requirement that did not exist. The appropriate standard of review to be applied by this Court to the direction issued by the respondent is one of correctness. It may well be desirable to amend the regulations to prescribe basic recruit training. However until now it has not been done. It is our conclusion that the respondent (the Commission), in interpreting the initial period of training as it did, read into the statute a requirement that simply was not there and thereby erred in law. (2001, p. 1, paras. 25 & 26)

There is now a regulation in place (O. Reg. 36/02, *Courses of Training for Members of Police Forces*) regarding initial training for police officers hired by police services. This is a classic example of how a regulation is established and why definitions—in this case, the definition of *prescribed*—are so important. This regulation now requires every municipal police officer to complete the basic recruit training at the Ontario Police College (OPC; see Figure 10.17) within six months of the officer's appointment unless exempted by the OPC director.

In another decision (*Ontario Civilian Commission on Police Services v. Wallaceburg Police Services Board*, 1997), the Ontario Divisional Court ruled against a police services board. In this case the board laid off three employees for budgetary reasons. The commission ruled that these layoffs constituted a reduction in the size of the police service and directed the board to rehire the employees. The board refused and the commission started misconduct proceedings under section 25 of the *Police Services Act*. The members of the board were found guilty of misconduct and ordered removed from the board. They appealed by way of judicial review to the Ontario Divisional Court on the grounds that

Ontario Police College, http://www.opconline.ca/images /opcfull.jpg. © Queen's Printer for Ontario, 2001. Reproduced with permission.

FIGURE 10.17
The Ontario Police College, Aylmer, Ontario.

the board was denied procedural fairness and natural justice. The court dismissed the appeal, upholding the commission's decision. The Divisional Court stated that

Clearly the Commission had the authority to make a finding of misconduct with respect to the Board's failure to comply with the Commission's directive under section 9(2) of the *Police Services Act* to reinstate its employees. There was no impropriety of the notice of hearing or denial of natural justice with respect to the hearing. The Board was not denied an opportunity to present its case before the Commission and there was no error in the Commission's finding. (1997, p. 1)

In accordance with section 32 (PSA), every member of a police services board must take an oath or affirmation of office that is prescribed within section 1, Ontario

DECODING POLICE TERMS

Oath of office for police services board member:
I solemnly swear (affirm) that I will be loyal to Her Majesty the Queen and to Canada, and that I will uphold the Constitution of Canada and that I will, to the best of my ability, discharge my duties as a member of the *(insert name of municipality)* Police Services Board faithfully, impartially and according to the *Police Services Act,* any other Act, and any regulation, rule or by-law.

So help me God. *(Omit this line in an affirmation.)*

or

I solemnly swear (affirm) that I will be loyal to Canada, and that I will uphold the Constitution of Canada and that I will, to the best of my ability, discharge my duties as a member of the *(insert name of municipality)* Police Services Board faithfully, impartially and according to the *Police Services Act,* any other Act, and any regulation, rule or by-law.

So help me God. *(Omit this line in an affirmation.)*
(O. Reg. 421/97, s. 7)

Regulation 268/10. The code of conduct for police services board members requires them to take an oath of office to "discharge their duties loyally, faithfully, impartially and according to the Act, any other Act and any regulation, rule or by-law, as provided in their oath or affirmation of office" (O. Reg. 421/97, s. 7).

Section 31: Responsibilities of Boards

A board is responsible for providing adequate and effective police services in the municipality. This includes appointing members of a municipal police service; setting policing priorities and objectives with the chief; establishing policies in accordance with the PSA and its regulations, including the release of personal information of certain members of the public; and hiring the chief and deputy chief, establishing their collective agreements, and evaluating their performance. Other responsibilities include receiving reports on secondary employment of members of the police service, creating legal indemnification guidelines, and creating policies for public complaints consistent with the PSA and its regulations as well as the rules established by the OIPRD, including steps for reviewing public complaints (ss. 31(2) & (3), PSA).

Members of police services boards are also governed by the code of conduct set out in Ontario Regulation 421/97. Although board members may give orders and directions to the chief of police, they are prohibited from giving orders to other members of the police force, and, as already noted, the board cannot direct the chief with respect to the daily operations of the police service (ss. 31(3) & (4), PSA; s. 2, O. Reg. 421/97). A member of a police services board that interferes with the day-to-day operations of a police service is subject to investigation, and where the misconduct is substantiated, subject to a hearing and discipline if the alleged misconduct is proven (*Aspden and the Ontario Civilian Commission on Police Services*, 2007).

The Canadian Association of Police Boards (CAPB) provides guidance and training for members of police services boards through their website and annual conferences. The CAPB has also created a best practices framework for members of police services boards (CAPB, 2005). Police services boards can be sued (*Hill v. Hamilton-Wentworth Regional Police Services Board*, 2007; *Jane Doe v. Metropolitan Toronto (Municipality) Commissioners of Police*, 1990). Police services boards also play a role in police discipline involving its chief of police and, if applicable, its deputy chiefs of police under the *Police Services Act*, and with probationary constables (*Nicholson v. Haldimand-Norfolk Regional Board of Commissioners of Police; Proctor v. Sarnia Board of Commissioners of Police*). Boards also have responsibilities under the *Police Services Act* to the OIPRD.

As we've pointed out throughout this chapter, police services boards must be careful not to blur the boundary between direction and operational interference or control (Sossin, 2007). Having said this, nothing stops a police services board from conducting inquiries of their own where it is in the public interest to review existing policies or create new ones (Toronto Police Services Board, 2010).

CHAPTER SUMMARY

This chapter has emphasized the importance of governance in policing. The fact that there have been five inquiries or commissions and a number of studies and publications on the topic reinforces the importance of governance in policing. Police accountability and police independence in accordance with the rule of law have been discussed in detail. The Supreme Court of Canada reaffirmed the importance of police accountability and independence in *R. v. Campbell*, a case that has been cited in many of the inquires that focused on police–government relations. As Justice Oppal stated in his inquiry into policing in British Columbia, "The subject of governance may be the most important issue examined by this Inquiry" (1994b, p. v).

LO1 **Define civilian governance for police services and identify the differences between civilian governance and police oversight bodies.**

Civilian governance for municipal and regional policing is defined as an internal but arm's-length civilian body of municipal elected and appointed individuals and provincial appointees whose mandate, as set out in the statutes and regulations, is to ensure accountability of police services while maintaining their independence in accordance with the rule of law. According to Murphy and McKenna, "Police governance is more closely aligned with the approaches taken to the overall guidance and direction of a police service, including the formation of organizational strategic goals and objectives" (2007, p. 37). In Ontario, government matters are dictated by the *Police Services Act* and its regulations. Civilian (or police) oversight, at least in Ontario, relates to independent, arm's-length civilian agencies responsible to the Ministry of Community Safety and Correctional Services, such as the OCPC or the Ministry of the Attorney General, as in the case of the OIPRD or the SIU.

LO2 **Briefly describe the role of the Solicitor General as it relates to governance in policing.**

While the legislation makes reference to the Solicitor General, the Ministry of Community Safety and Correctional Services, created through the amalgamation of the Ministry of the Solicitor General and Ministry of Correctional Services, is responsible for police services boards in Ontario. The duties and responsibilities of the Solicitor General are outlined in detail in section 3(2) of the PSA.

LO3 **Describe civilian governance in policing as it relates to the relationship between the police chief and civilian authority.**

Civilian governance in policing can be best described as the balancing act of police services being fully accountable to civilian government while being independent in operational matters and accountable to the rule of law. Police independence generally means the police being able to conduct their day-to-day operations without political interference. True civilian governance cannot exist without accountability. Government at all levels must ensure accountability of the police while respecting independence. The principle of accountability in policing is the foundation of sound policing, and ideal governance ensures transparency and public confidence, in both the police and those responsible for overseeing them. The preamble to the *Canadian Charter of Rights and Freedoms* states, "Whereas Canada is founded upon principles that recognize the supremacy of God and the rule of law." Justice Oppal defined the rule of law as being that "governments must exercise their powers according to law and citizens must not be exposed to arbitrary acts" (1994b, p. B-2).

LO4 **Briefly discuss the types of police services boards and their roles, functions, and responsibilities in accordance with the Police Services Act and its regulations.**

Responsibilities of municipal and regional police services boards are defined in section 31 of the *Police Services Act*. A board is responsible for providing adequate and effective police services in the municipality. This includes appointing members of a municipal police service; setting policing priorities and objectives with the chief; establishing policies in accordance with the PSA and its regulations, including the release of personal information of certain members of the public; and hiring the chief and deputy chief, establishing their collective agreements, and evaluating their performance. Other responsibilities include receiving reports on secondary employment of members of the police service, creating legal indemnification guidelines, and creating policies for public complaints consistent with the PSA and its regulations, as well as with the rules established by the OIPRD, including steps for reviewing public complaints.

Unless otherwise specified, municipalities in Ontario must provide adequate and effective police services, which include the core services of crime prevention, law enforcement, assistance to victims of crime, public order maintenance, and emergency response. The mandate for police services boards to operate in Ontario is found in the Ontario *Police Services Act* and the regulations.

LO⁵ Briefly discuss the code of conduct as it relates to members of police services boards.

Police services boards are governed by their own code of conduct (O. Reg.421/97, *Members of Police Services Boards—Code of Conduct*) and their own code of ethics (the Canadian Association of Chiefs of Police Ethical Framework). The duties of a police services board are outlined in the *Police Services Act* and its related regulations and depend on what type of police services board exists and the police services provided. Police services boards are held accountable by the OCPC and the courts.

Policing Policies and Procedures

LEARNING OUTCOMES

After reading this chapter, you will be able to:

LO1 Explain what adequate and effective police services must include at the minimum in accordance with the Ontario *Police Services Act*.

LO2 List and explain the three primary objectives of the *Adequacy and Effectiveness of Police Services* regulation.

LO3 Describe the primary functions of the *Policing Standards Manual (2000)* as it relates to the *Adequacy and Effectiveness of Police Services* regulation.

LO4 Explain the responsibilities under section 31 of police services boards as they relate to the *Adequacy and Effectiveness of Police Services* regulation.

LO5 Describe the primary requirements that police services' business plans must address in accordance with the *Adequacy and Effectiveness of Police Services* regulation.

> *Systemic failure is not new to policing.*
>
> —*Justice Archie Campbell (1996)*

Police services in Ontario are legislated to provide adequate and effective police services in accordance with the *Police Services Act* (PSA) and its regulations. Subsection 4(1) of the PSA states, "Every municipality to which this subsection applies shall provide adequate and effective police services in accordance with its needs." The Minister of Community Safety and Correctional Services (MCSCS; referred to as the Solicitor General in the PSA) is responsible for the oversight of police services, and where applicable, police services boards in Ontario. The duties and powers of the minister include ensuring that "adequate and effective police services are provided" and standards are met in accordance with the PSA.

As outlined in Chapter 10, the MCSCS and police services boards cannot interfere in the day-to-day operational decisions of the Chief of Police or Commissioner of the OPP.

LO¹ HISTORY OF ADEQUACY AND EFFECTIVENESS OF POLICE SERVICES REGULATION

In 1997, the Ontario *Police Services Act* was amended to include recommendations made in the *Report of the Who Does What Panel* (1996). Some of the recommendations in this report included that "municipalities should deliver adequate and effective police services; municipal councils should have greater say in police budgets; and the province of Ontario should set standards on adequate and effective police services" (Ministry of the Solicitor General and Correctional Services [MSGCS], 1999a, p. 3). The *Police Services Act* specifies that "adequate and effective police services must include, at a minimum, crime prevention,

DECODING POLICE TERMS

Duties and powers:

3. (2) The Solicitor General shall,
   (a) monitor police forces to ensure that adequate and effective police services are provided at the municipal and provincial levels;
   (b) monitor boards and police forces to ensure that they comply with prescribed standards of service;
   (c) REPEALED: 1995, c. 4, s. 4 (1).
   (d) develop and promote programs to enhance professional police practices, standards and training;
   (e) conduct a system of inspection and review of police forces across Ontario;
   (f) assist in the co-ordination of police services;
   (g) consult with and advise boards, community policing advisory committees, municipal

chiefs of police, employers of special constables and associations on matters relating to police and police services;
   (h) develop, maintain and manage programs and statistical records and conduct research studies in respect of police services and related matters;
   (i) provide to boards, community policing advisory committees and municipal chiefs of police information and advice respecting the management and operation of police forces, techniques in handling special problems and other information calculated to assist;
   (j) issue directives and guidelines respecting policy matters;
   (k) develop and promote programs for community-oriented police services; and
   (l) operate the Ontario Police College. (Police Services Act, c. P-15, s. 3(2))

FIGURE 11.1
Police officers must perform various tasks as required in emergency situations, as demonstrated at the 2010 G20 summit in Toronto.

law enforcement, assistance to victims of crime, public order maintenance, and emergency response" (Figure 11.1). In addition, municipalities must also provide "all the infrastructure and administration necessary for providing such services, including vehicles, boats, equipment, communication devices, buildings and supplies" (ss. 4(2) & (3), 135(1), PSA).

As a result of the *Report of the Who Does What Panel* (1996) and in furtherance of the PSA, the MCSCS formed the Adequacy Standards Steering Committee, which included key stakeholders from the Ontario Association of Chiefs of Police (OACP), Police Association of Ontario (PAO), Ontario Association of Police Service Boards (OAPSB), Ontario Senior Police Officers' Police Association (OSOPA), Ontario Provincial Police (OPP), Ontario Provincial Police Association (OPPA), and Association of Municipalities of Ontario (AMO). This committee, working with representatives of the MCSCS, formed the basis of a regulation that was introduced early in 1999 to specify minimum policing requirements related to "critical provincial interest in policing" (MSGCS, 1999a, p. 4). This critical policing interest is often referred to as public policy and public safety issues in policing, which are raised with government as

a result of reports such as the *Report of the Who Does What Panel,* commissions or public inquiries, inquests, court cases, investigations, and public interest groups. For instance, Justice Archie Campbell's *Bernardo Investigation Review* report (1996) led to the creation of Ontario Regulation 550/96, *Violent Crime Linkage Analysis System Reports,* which was passed into legislation on February 15, 1997, and Ontario Regulation 354/04, *Major Case Management,* which became law on January 1, 2005. Police services have developed policies and procedures that incorporate these regulations, as well as the minimum requirements outlined in the Ontario Regulation 3/99, *Adequacy and Effectiveness of Police Services.*

LO² THE ADEQUACY AND EFFECTIVENESS OF POLICE SERVICES REGULATION

Ontario Regulation 3/99, *Adequacy and Effectiveness of Police Services,* was introduced in January 1999. Section 37 of the regulation provided police services with a two-year window to meet the requirements of the regulation by January 1, 2001. This window included four phases: information and education, self-assessment, planning, and implementation. The ministry provided supports and guidelines to assist police services in fulfilling their obligations (MSGCS, 1999a). On January 1, 2001, the regulation was proclaimed into law.

The objectives of the regulation were to

- Identify core policing functions and flexible service delivery options including the cost-effective delivery of specialized police services
- Focus on functional activities, organizational structure and management systems by establishing provincial standards that are outcome oriented and not process-based

DECODING POLICE TERMS

Critical provincial interest in policing:

Significant issues of:

- Public safety;

- Police officer safety;

- The administration of justice; and

- Police accountability. (MSGCS, 1999a, p. 4)

- Emphasize the importance of police business planning and police accountability to police services boards and the Minister. (MSGCS, 1999c, p. 7)

LO³ POLICING STANDARDS MANUAL (2000)

The intent of the adequacy regulation was to ensure that the citizens of Ontario received consistent, efficient, and cost-effective core policing services, taking into account the size, location, and diversity of the community. The overall emphasis of the adequacy regulation is on what police services should do, not how they should do it (MSGCS, 1999c). The "how" of what police services do is usually addressed in standard operating procedures (SOPs). The regulation specifies minimum police services to be provided, including the size of some specialized units and the minimum training requirements, in some cases referred to as "ministry-accredited training" or minimum "ministry-approved competency-based requirements" (MSGCS, 1999b, p. 6). Of interest is *who* can provide ministry-accredited training. According to the *Guide to Questions and Answers on the Adequacy Standards Regulation* developed by the MSGCS, "Training can be provided by any learning institution, including police-in-service training, and public and private sector learning institutions (e.g., community colleges), where courses meet the standards established by the Ontario Police College" (1999a, p. 20). Refer to Figure 11.2 for a picture of police officers in training. Police services boards and the OPP are required to develop policies and procedures based on MCSCS

Courtesy of the London Police Service

FIGURE 11.2
Police officers are required to complete the Basic Constable Training course at the Ontario Police College and annual in-service training sessions at their respective police services.

guidelines. The original set of guidelines was referred to as the *Policing Standards Manual* (2000) (Ministry of the Solicitor General, 2000). See Box 11.1 for the preamble in the *Policing Standards Manual* (2000).

The ministry developed a self-assessment tool for police services to use in implementing the adequacy regulation. This self-assessment tool was in the form of a matrix that addressed the following:

- Analysis of core functions/service delivery requirements
- Police Services Board analysis of policy requirements
- Chief of Police analysis of procedure and process requirements. (MSGCS, 1999e, p. 1)

BOX 11.1

POLICING STANDARDS MANUAL (2000) PREAMBLE

This Manual, and the guidelines contained within, is one of the mechanisms by which the Solicitor General meets the statutory requirements set out in section 3(2) of the Ontario *Police Services Act*. In particular, the guidelines:

- set out the Ministry's position in relation to policy matters;

- provide information and advice respecting the management and operation of police services;

- provide recommendations for local policies, procedures and programs;

- promote coordination in the delivery of police services;

- promote the delivery of community-oriented police services; and

- promote professional police practices, standards and training.

Source: Reprinted from the Ministry of Community Safety and Correctional Services, (2000a, February). *Policing standards manual (2000)*. Toronto, Canada: Queen's Printer. Retrieved February 21, 2012, from http://www.ontla.on.ca/library/repository/ser/10256510//200107.pdf, preamble

LO4 THE RESPONSIBILITIES OF POLICE SERVICES BOARDS

This subject is discussed in detail in Chapter 10. There are primarily two types of police services boards under the PSA; section 31 (municipal) police services boards, and section 10 (OPP contracts with municipalities) police services boards. This chapter will focus primarily on section 31 police services board responsibilities as they relate to the adequacy and effectiveness regulations, the corresponding policing standards, other regulations that affect board responsibilities and functions, and relevant sections of the PSA.

What is clear in the legislation is that a police services board has a number of responsibilities, including establishing "policies for the effective management of the police force" (31(1)(c), PSA) and establishing "guidelines for dealing with complaints under Part V" (cl. 31(1)(i), PSA) that are consistent with the legislation and OIPRD rules of procedure (s. 31(1.1), PSA). The board has additional responsibilities consistent with subsection 61(2), PSA (police services or policies of the police service), and section 63, PSA, dealing with its obligation to review a complaint related to a policy or service.

An ideal framework in addressing a police services board's obligations under the legislation can be broken down into four areas:

- governance and administration related to the police services board;
- the relationship between the police services board and the Chief of Police;
- the role of the Chief of Police in relation to the police services board (see Figure 11.3); and

FIGURE 11.3
Police chiefs are required to work closely with police services boards to understand the needs of the community.

- policies and procedures within MCSCS policing standards (Ottawa Police Services Board, 2011).

GOVERNANCE AND ADMINISTRATION

The board's governance and administration responsibilities relate to their own functions, including setting job descriptions, qualifications, pay and benefits, and training; forming internal committees; establishing a working protocol with council; carrying out negotiations; providing legal services; creating media communications; performing community outreach; dealing with complaints; and fulfilling the board's responsibilities to the Ontario Civilian Police Commission (OCPC), OIPRD, and MCSCS. Police services board members must take board training prescribed by the OCPC and must be fully apprised of Ontario Regulation 421/97, *Members of Police Service Boards—Code of Conduct.*

LO5 THE RELATIONSHIP WITH THE CHIEF OF POLICE

The board's relationship with the Chief of Police includes reporting relationships, the chief's obligations to the board under the PSA and its regulations, and the board's obligations to the Chief of Police under the PSA and its regulations, especially the board's obligation to not direct "the Chief of Police with respect to specific operational decisions or with respect to the day-to-day operation of the police force" (s. 31(3), PSA; s, 2, O. Reg. 421/97). However, the board "may give orders and directions to the Chief of Police, but not to other members of the police force, and no individual member of the board shall give orders or directions to any member of the police force" (s. 31(4), PSA). A board also has a responsibility to establish an effective performance management system to monitor and evaluate its Chief of Police (cl. 31(1)(e), PSA), establish by-laws for the effective management of the police service (s. 31(6), PSA), and implement a quality assurance process to ensure the delivery of adequate and effective police services in accordance with the PSA and its regulations (s. 35, Ont. Reg. 3/99). A board has responsibility, as well, regarding the public complaints and overall conduct of its Chief of Police, and where applicable the deputy chiefs of police. The Chief of Police and the board work collectively to prepare a business plan for its police service at least once every three years; the business plan must address at minimum the five primary requirements outlined in section 30 of Ontario Regulation 3/99 (see Box 11.2).

THE RESPONSIBILITIES OF THE CHIEF OF POLICE TO THE POLICE SERVICES BOARD

The Chief of Police has a number of obligations to the police services board, including following the orders and direction of the board (provided that they do not amount to the board giving direction to the day-to-day operations of the police service); working closely with the board on all policy and complaint issues; preparing an annual report; establishing internal policies and procedures with the board for the effective management of the police service; working closely with the public and media (see Figure 11.4); and working with oversight agencies such as the OCPC, OIPRD, and Special Investigations Unit (SIU). The Chief of Police is also responsible for the overall professionalism, including discipline, of the police service. Together, the Chief of Police and the police services board are responsible for policing issues within their community that reflect the declaration principles reflected in section 1 of the PSA, which are discussed later in this chapter.

ESTABLISHING POLICIES AND PROCEDURES: MCSCS POLICING STANDARDS

In January 1999, the Ministry of the Solicitor General developed an overall strategy for police services to meet the minimum requirements of the *Adequacy and Effectiveness of Police Services* regulation to respond to the six core areas of policing (MSGCS, 1999d). In 2000, the Ministry of the Solicitor General issued the *Policing Standards Manual (2000)* with guidelines for the board and police service to meet their obligations under the regulation, the PSA, and other related regulations.

The MCSCS has continued to update existing standards and create new standards in keeping with the ministry's critical provincial interest in policing, primarily through all chiefs memoranda (which includes the OPP commissioner). In addition, the MCSCS establishes new regulations requiring minimum police response, such as regulations for the Violent Crime Linkage Analysis System (ViCLAS) and major case management (MCM). MCM will be discussed further in this chapter.

Police services boards establish policies and procedures based on the ministry's standards and regulations, recommendations from other agencies such

Louie Palu/The Globe and Mail/The Canadian Press

FIGURE 11.4
Toronto Police Chief Bill Blair speaking to the media following the G20 summit.

as the OIPRD, public inquiries, inquests, or board reviews of possible systemic issues. These policies and procedures form part of the direction to the Chief of Police from the board, consistent with the legislation.

THE ROLE OF THE ONTARIO CIVILIAN POLICE COMMISSION (OCPC)

The issues surrounding adequate and effective police services and infrastructure quite often come to the surface in section 40 hearings by the OCPC into the reduction or abolition of a police service. The OCPC is "an independent oversight agency committed to serving the public by ensuring that adequate and effective policing services are provided to the community in a fair and accountable manner under the Ontario *Police Services Act*" (OCPC, 2012, para. 1). The following cases are but two examples of the role the commission plays in ensuring adequate and effective police services, including the minimum number of personnel required to police and the minimum requirements of police facilities.

Section 40 Hearings: Reduction or Abolition of Police Force

Subsection 40(1) states, "A board may terminate the employment of a member of the police force for the purpose of abolishing the police force or reducing its size if the Commission consents and if the abolition or reduction does not contravene this Act." Over the years, a number of police services have been abolished under this section of the *Police Services Act* and replaced with the OPP by virtue of a section 10 or section 5.1 contract under the act. Some examples of this are described below.

Kenora Police Service: Application for Consent to Abolition In its decision regarding the disbandment of the Kenora Police Service, the OCCPS explained its reasoning:

The role of the Commission under s. 40 was two-fold: to ensure the adequacy and effectiveness of policing under the alternate service delivery model, and to ensure that severance arrangements were in place for any members who were subject to termination.

The first role related to issues of community safety and provincial standards, while the second required the Commission to assess

whether employees who were adversely affected by a change in delivery of policing services were being treated fairly. Section 4 of the *PSA* prescribed certain indicia of adequacy and effectiveness. One of these was staffing. The application for consent to abolishment was granted, subject to conditions which included:

- the addition of five constables
- completion of renovations to the City [police] facility.* (OCCPS, 2008, p. 3)

Goderich Police Service: Consent to Abolition In an application to the OCPC to disband the Goderich Police Service, the commission initially ruled against the application, primarily owing to its concerns on inadequate police facilities.

On October 27, 1997 we provided a written decision. We concluded that the proposal was satisfactory from the prospective of staffing, supervision, communications, dispatching and equipment.

However, we were not satisfied with the aspect of the proposal dealing with accommodation. Specifically, the plan was to close the existing police facility in the town core and move the staff several kilometers away—to the OPP Detachment located on Highway #21.

We had concerns about the capacity of the existing detachment facility to satisfactorily accommodate the additional staff. We did not believe that a community the size and location of Goderich could be adequately policed without a visible local presence in the form of a police office.† (OCPC, 1997b, pp. 1–2)

In ruling against the original application for disbandment, the commission stated,

The nature of this scheme is self-evident. It is to ensure that no municipal police force is abolished unless arrangements are in place which will satisfactorily meet the policing needs of the community in question. Any new arrangement must provide for appropriate staff, equipment and facilities to ensure adequate and effective policing. (OCCPS, 1997a, p. 3)

In a subsequent submission to the commission, the board proposed a storefront location with adequate office

---

*Ontario Civilian Police Commission, *OCCPS Disbandment Decision DSB #08-02, Kenora Police Service: Application for Consent to Abolishment*, December 18, 2008, online at: http://www.ocpc.ca/files/BH042009K903P6242311S647FU278S.pdf. © Queen's Printer for Ontario, 2008. Reproduced with permission.
†Ontario Civilian Police Commission, *Ontario Civilian Commission on Police Service: In the Matter of an Application by the Town of Goderich for consent to the abolition of the Goderich Police Service*, December 19, 1997, online at http://www.ocpc.ca/files/MD0N2003V802A4137211D515QQ232P.pdf. © Queen's Printer for Ontario, 1997. Reproduced with permission.

space, secure storage, access to police system communications, and parking. As a result, the commission approved the application for disbandment. Police services may also contract with each other to provide specialized services such as tactical teams, containment teams, dog services, diving services, and so on (s. 7, PSA).

Systemic Failure

Systemic failure is not new to policing. The term was used on a number of occasions by the late Justice Archie Campbell in his 1996 review of the Paul Bernardo investigation (see Figure 11.5), often referred to as the Campbell report. The words have also been associated with investigative bias, confirmatory bias, noble cause corruption, and tunnel vision in the context of investigations that have gone wrong. For policing, especially as it relates to policies and procedures, and to providing adequate and effective police services, there are lessons learned through inquiries, commissions, inquests, and court cases. For instance, at the time of the Campbell report in 1996, the adequacy regulation did not exist.

FIGURE 11.5

The Campbell report cited systemic failure in the Paul Bernardo murder investigation and recommended that procedures and standards be created to reduce such shortcomings.

On other occasions, policies and procedures have been in place but not followed. And in other situations, such as the G20 summit, the OIPRD does a systemic review (s. 57, PSA) as a result of public complaints for the purpose of making recommendations for police services who find themselves facing future similar events.

> **systemic failure:**
> Failing to have a system in place to address or respond to specific investigative (operational or administrative) issues, or having a system in place to address or respond to specific investigative issues but failing to apply or enforce it.

In one police jurisdiction, the police services board was cited with contempt for failing to provide adequate security protection in accordance with section 137 of the PSA (*R. v. Peel Regional Police Service, Chief of Police*, 2000). Specifically, the board failed to provide adequate police services within the court building pertaining to security. In the end, the court did not issue a contempt trial order, but the police services board hired seven additional court security officers and apologized to the court.

SECRECY AND CONFIDENTIALITY

As discussed in Chapter 3, police officers take an oath of secrecy when they start employment with their respective police services (see Box 11.3 for the wording of the oath). As members of a police service, officers are bound by the provisions of the *Police Services Act* and its regulations.

Police officers' conduct is subject to the *Code of Conduct* (O. Reg. 268/10) and the *Police Services Act*. Officers are subject to a higher standard of conduct, which includes not disclosing any information to unauthorized persons or obtaining confidential information for their own purposes. Many police services have internal policies that restrict the use of the Canadian Police Information Centre (CPIC). An example of wording in such polices is "CPIC queries shall not be conducted for the sole purpose of

---

BOX 11.3

OATH OF SECRECY

I solemnly swear (affirm) that I will not disclose any information obtained by me in the course of my duties as *(insert name of office)*, except as I may be authorized or required by law.

So help me God. (Omit this line in an affirmation.) (Ont. Reg. 268/10, s. 4)

Source: Ontario Regulation 268/10. Retrieved October 21, 2011, from http://www.e-laws.gov.on.ca/html/regs/english/elaws_regs_100268_e.htm s. 4

satisfying a Member's personal interest in any individual. All queries shall be for specific, authorized, work related activities. The use of any other purpose is prohibited" (*Mallen and Hamilton Police Service*, 2011, p. 2). In this case, an officer was convicted of insubordination for using the CPIC for personal reasons. In sentencing this officer, the hearing officer stated, "Breaches of confidentiality involving CPIC abuse are considered serious misconduct by both police management and civilian oversight, as the conduct offends not only the Service's contract with the RCMP, but also violates individual privacy rights" (*Mallen*, 2011, p. 3).

In another police discipline case, an officer pled guilty to discreditable conduct for improper use of the police service's Record Management System (RMS) for personal use. In assessing penalty, the hearing officer stated, "Police officers have access to a tremendous amount of data systems for the sole purpose of public safety and law enforcement. The systems are not to be accessed for personal use. I find his actions serious and will consider this as an aggravating circumstance in my decision" (*Healey and Ontario Provincial Police*, 2011, p. 4).

Police officers have been dismissed for misuse of their office to obtain information for their own use and the repetitive abuse of the CPIC and the police service's RMS. The OCPC, in dismissing an appeal of dismissal by a police officer, stated,

> The Commission has ruled in the past that the personal use of CPIC constitutes major misconduct. The use of CPIC must be solely reserved for official police work and must never be used for personal reasons. Fundamental to the successful functioning of the CPIC system is a strong sense of trust; trust that the system is there to help police officers in pursuit of their official duties and trust that no police officer will purposely or willfully misuse the system. (*Coon and Toronto Police Service*, 2003, p. 13)

In one of the most serious cases involving breach of confidence, a police officer was dismissed for sharing CPIC and RMS information and operational matters, including "his disclosure of the Tactical Unit raid to the Informant" (*Barlow and Ottawa Police Service*, 2011, para. 68). In dismissing this officer's appeal of his dismissal, the OCPC reiterated that dismissal "is reserved for those cases in which conduct is so disreputable that the police officer is no longer of any use to the service or it would cause irreparable damage" (para. 75). What is clear from the discipline cases is that breach of confidentiality, whether through misuse of the CPIC

or RMS disclosure of confidential information, is considered very serious and may result in dismissal. The purpose of the CPIC is discussed in detail later in this chapter.

POLICIES AND PROCEDURES IN LAW ENFORCEMENT

Law enforcement agencies operate in a paramilitary manner, where policies and procedures advise members how to handle occurrences and how to follow both administrative and operational procedures. Law enforcement is the primary policing function, and this includes the enforcement of municipal, provincial, and federal laws. While police officers perform their duties they are required to follow protocol, which could include such requirements as wearing hats, having a clean and pressed uniform, completing reports, and maintaining confidentiality and secrecy. The code of conduct (see Figure 11.6) speaks to the consequences of police officers failing to perform their duties, breaching their oath of office by misusing or abusing their authority, having improper appearance, and breaching confidentiality.

USE OF FORCE

Police officers are trained and qualified to use force to apprehend criminals or to protect life or property.

> The *Criminal Code of Canada*, other legislation and case law address the use of force by police and other authorized persons. The *Equipment and Use of Force Regulation* (R.R.O. 1990,

FIGURE 11.6
Police officers must adhere to a code of conduct.

Reg. 926), under the *Police Services Act*, sets out requirements in relation to the use of force including use of approved weapons, training and reporting, as well as use/technical specifications for handguns. (MCSCS, 2010, para. 1)

There are many regulations pertaining to all police functions, and none are more important than the ones affecting police officer's use-of-force options. As described in Box 11.4, the use of Tasers, otherwise referred to as conducted energy weapons (CEWs), is controversial (see Figure 11.7). Members of the public have died following the deployment of CEWs, which is not to say that the use of the CEWs caused the deaths, but rather that following their deployment,

FIGURE 11.7
Police officers are sometimes required to use conducted energy weapons.

death was one of the outcomes. In 2008, the Ministry of Community Safety and Correctional Services conducted a review of the policies and procedures involving CEWs (MCSCS, 2009). Refer to Box 11.4 for the purposes of the study.

The study concluded that CEWs are an effective less lethal option, and their use should be continued by police officers in Ontario. The report recommended that the Minister of Community Safety and Correctional Services endorse their use along with the following guidelines:

- establish standardized training for users and trainers;
- implement policy and procedures to guide police services in the deployment of CEWs and accountability of their use;
- establish who is authorized in a police service to use CEWs;
- establish when CEWs may be used in consultation with the Ontario Use of Force model;
- document and record the use of CEWs on the Use of Force Report; and
- educate the public on the risks and benefits of CEWs.

TRAFFIC SAFETY

Traffic safety is a major component of all police services, and the safe operation of motor vehicles through selective traffic enforcement strategies projects a positive community image, as seen in

---

BOX 11.4

USE-OF-FORCE OPTIONS

In 2008, the Minister of Community Safety and Correctional Services directed ministry staff to undertake a review of conducted energy weapons (CEWs) with its policing partners.

The objectives of the review were to:

- Identify policies and procedures in place by Ontario police services regarding the use of CEWs;

- Identify training that has been provided to police service members regarding CEWs;

- Collect CEW use statistics to recognize trends; and

- Provide a foundation for discussion with police partners on operational and policy issues in relation to training, guidelines, deployment, etc.

Source: Reprinted from Ministry of Community Safety and Correctional Services. (2009, December 7). *Review of conducted energy weapon use in Ontario: Report of the Policing Standards Advisory Committee.* Toronto, ON: Author, p. 2. Retrieved from http://www.mcscs.jus.gov.on.ca/stellent/groups/public/@mcscs/@www/@com/documents/webasset/ec081155.pdf

FIGURE 11.8
Police officer directing traffic.

FIGURE 11.9
Police officers at a major crime scene.

Figure 11.8. Each police service has policies and procedures to guide police officers on how to conduct investigations and evidence-gathering activities. Police officers who fail to adhere to those polices and procedures face may disciplinary action from their police service. For example, the Ministry of Transportation Ontario requires collision reports to be filed with the ministry within 10 days. Most police services mandate that each report must be filed internally within 5 days to allow for corrections and processing. If a police officer mistakenly leaves a report unfinished or unfiled, that officer would be liable for progressive discipline under the *Police Services Act*.

CRIME INVESTIGATION AND CRIME PREVENTION

Crime investigation and crime prevention are also major components of all police services, and here, again, officers need to adhere to many internal and external policies and procedures. For example, all police services investigating certain types of serious crime, such as homicides (Figure 11.9), sexual assaults, and abductions, are required to use the Major Case Management (MCM) system, including the computer software system called Powercase.

MCM is useful in helping police identify common links in crimes committed in different locations—crimes that might have been committed by the same person. These are termed *multi-jurisdictional crimes*, as they occur in locations that are policed by different police services. In the past, these types of investigations have been problematic, as police services worked in isolation. Information concerning crimes was considered confidential and

was kept "in house" rather than shared with other police services.

According to the Ministry of Community Safety and Correctional Services,

MCM helps police solve major cases by:

- Providing an efficient way to keep track of, sort and analyse huge amounts of information about a crime: police notes, witness statements, door-to-door leads, names, locations, vehicles and phone numbers are examples of the types of information police collect
- Streamlining investigations
- Making it possible for police to see connections between cases so they can reduce the risk that serial offenders will avoid being caught
- Preventing crime and reducing the number of potential victims by catching offenders sooner.* (2012, para. 5)

Box 11.5 describes some cases in which police used MCM to solve serious crimes, including the murder of Holly Jones in 2003 (see Figure 11.10).

Following Mr. Justice Archie Campbell's review of the Bernardo investigation (1996), all municipal police services and the OPP have had access to the MCM system. The rules and regulations regarding use of the system are stringently monitored, and over the last 10 years there has been compliance with the procedures.

The *Police Services Act* has a regulation governing the minimum investigative and case management standards: the *Major Case Management* (Ont. Reg. 354/04). Subsection 1 of this regulation

*Source: "Policing Services: Major Case Management" (2009) http://www.mcscs.jus.gov.on.ca/english/police_serv/MajorCaseManagement/mcm.html. © Queen's Printer for Ontario, 2009. Reproduced with permission.

BOX 11.5

BENEFITS OF MAJOR CASE MANAGEMENT PRINCIPLES

Here are examples of high profile cases where police used Major Case Management:

- In the Holly Jones murder, MCM helped the Toronto Police Service manage the large amount of information they built up during their investigation.

- During the two SARS outbreaks, MCM helped police and medical authorities manage the large amount of information they needed to track.

- The Ontario Provincial Police used MCM for their investigation into the circumstances and handling of the E-coli bacteria outbreak.

- Toronto Police Service and Peel Regional Police Service jointly used MCM to work together in solving the Cecilia Zhang murder.

- One of Canada's worst mass murders involved eight biker gang members found dead west of St. Thomas. The Ontario Provincial Police used MCM in the complex investigation that led to the arrest of eight people, six charged with first degree murder and two charged as accessories after the fact.

Source: "Policing Services: Major Case Management" (2009) http://www.mcscs.jus.gov.on.ca/english/police_serv/MajorCaseManagement/mcm.html. © Queen's Printer for Ontario, 2009. Reproduced with permission.

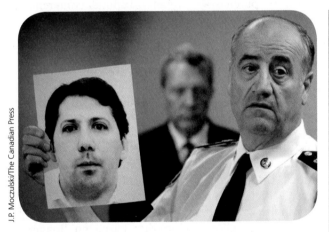

J.P. Moczulski/The Canadian Press

FIGURE 11.10
Chief Fantino addressing the media regarding the Holly Jones murder case.

states, "Every board shall establish policies with respect to major cases in accordance with the Ontario Major Case Management Manual."

TECHNOLOGY

Technology is significantly changing society at a rapid rate, and policing is not immune to these effects, as there are many pending technical improvements required for service delivery, crime detection, criminal and traffic investigation, and crime prevention. The police have to detect crimes that evolve as technology is evolving—for example, the Internet-based crimes of fraud, child pornography, bullying, stalking, and criminal harassment. However, police services are funded by the public purse, and this funding is significantly less than those funds available to organized crime.

THE CANADIAN POLICE INFORMATION CENTRE

The Canadian Police Information Centre (CPIC) database, created in 1972 and located in RCMP headquarters in Ottawa (RCMP, 2012b), provides "information [that] can be viewed by some government departments and agencies and more than 80,000 law enforcement officers from across the country. Records are added and purged over time. In 2007, the database was accessed an average 392,792 times each day" ("How CPIC Works," 2008, para. 4).

The use of CPIC is governed by a strict CPIC policy and reference manual. Police officers sometimes get themselves in trouble by conducting unauthorized CPIC inquiries, such as record checks on friends, neighbours, or associates. These checks would not be in the course of the officers' duties and would therefore be deemed unauthorized. Police officers who fail to adhere to CPIC polices and

POLICING IN ONTARIO: SIX PRINCIPLES

Ontario is the first province in Canada to have a declaration of principles written into its statutes. With these principles, Ontario's police are committed to:

1. Ensuring the safety and security of all people and property in Ontario.

2. Safeguarding the fundamental rights guaranteed by the *Canadian Charter of Rights and Freedoms* and the *Ontario Human Rights Code*.

3. Working closely with the communities they serve.

4. Respecting victims of crime and working to understand their needs.

5. Being sensitive to the diverse, multiracial and multicultural character of Ontario society.

6. Ensuring that police services are representative of the communities they serve. (s. 1, PSA)

Source: "Policing Services: Policing in Ontario" (2011) http://www.mcscs.jus.gov.on.ca/english/police_serv/about.html. © Queen's Printer for Ontario, 2011. Reproduced with permission.

procedures face disciplinary action from their police service.

These core activities and principles provide an outline for police services to follow, such as the outline in Box 11.6. When police services hire individuals as police officers, all of these guidelines must be considered. Most police services in Ontario strive to ensure that they are representative of the communities they serve. Recruiting strategies are aimed at recruiting members of visible minorities, women, people with language skills, and those who have diverse backgrounds.

All applicants must successfully complete the Applicant Testing Service tests, and all must meet the standard set by the province.

FINANCIAL POLICIES

Financial resources for police services are limited and are used prudently and effectively, as monitored through ongoing analysis and monthly reports. All police services have policies and procedures for such financial issues as budgeting and auditing, financial reporting, purchasing, property disposal, conferences and seminars, expense claims, and donations and sponsorships (Peterborough Police Service, 2012).

Police services operate within a corporate structure, and police services boards must approve policing budgets. Financial policies are in place to ensure approval processes are followed and the right people with the right financial authority are able to approve expenses before the money is spent. While these financial policies generally do not directly affect frontline police officers during the course of their duties, the police budget certainly does. All buildings, vehicles, uniforms, computers, radios, in-car terminals, weapons, and equipment are affected by budgeting decisions, which are based on financial policies and procedures.

CHAPTER SUMMARY

This chapter has addressed a few examples of policies and procedures that are mandated by the *Police Services Act*, the adequacy regulation, and other regulations under the PSA. Many police services boards, such as the Ottawa Police Services Board (2011), have their policies and procedures posted on their websites. Police services boards' policies and procedures should not be confused with standard operating procedures, which are specific to police operations. Police officers are governed by a code of conduct (O. Reg. 268/10, Schedule), and any breach of confidentiality, especially as it relates to misuse of the CPIC, is considered to be a serious breach of the discipline code.

LO¹ Explain what adequate and effective police services must include at the minimum in accordance with the Ontario *Police Services Act*.

The PSA specifies that adequate and effective police services must include, at a minimum, crime prevention, law enforcement, assistance to victims of crime, public order maintenance, and emergency response. In addition, municipalities must provide for all the infrastructure and administration necessary for providing such services, including vehicles, boats, equipment, communication devices, buildings, and supplies.

LO² List and explain the three primary objectives of the *Adequacy and Effectiveness of Police Services* regulation.

The intent of the adequacy regulation was to ensure that the citizens of Ontario received consistent, efficient, and cost-effective core policing services, taking into account the size, location, and diversity of the community. The overall emphasis on the adequacy regulation is on what police services should do, not how they should do it. The objectives of the *Adequacy and Effectiveness of Police Services* regulation were to

> identify core policing functions and flexible service delivery options including the cost-effective delivery of specialized police services; focus on functional activities, organizational structure and management systems by establishing provincial standards that are outcome oriented and not process-based; [and] emphasize the importance of police business planning and police accountability to police services boards and the Minister. (MCGCS, 1999c, p. 7)

LO³ Describe the primary functions of the *Policing Standards Manual (2000)* as it relates to the *Adequacy and Effectiveness of Police Services* regulation.

This manual, and the guidelines it contains, is one of the mechanisms by which the Solicitor General meets the statutory requirements set out in section 3(2) of the PSA. In particular, the guidelines "set out the Ministry's position in relation to policy matters; provide information and advice respecting the management and operation of police services; provide recommendations for local policies, procedures and programs; promote coordination in the delivery of police services; promote the delivery of community-oriented police services; and promote professional police practices, standards and training" (Ministry of the Solicitor General, 2000, p. 1).

LO⁴ Explain the responsibilities under section 31 of police services boards as they relate to the *Adequacy and Effectiveness of Police Services* regulation.

Police services boards have a number of responsibilities, including establishing policies for the effective management of the police force; establishing guidelines for dealing with complaints that are consistent with the legislation; and dealing with its obligation to review a complaint related to a policy or service.

LO⁵ Describe the primary requirements that police services' business plans must address in accordance with the *Adequacy and Effectiveness of Police Services* regulation.

A police service's business plan must address five primary requirements: "objectives, core business and functions of the police service in responding to providing adequate and effective police services; listing performance objectives relating to identified policing needs as outlined in subsection 30 (2) of the Adequacy Regulation; information technology; resource planning; and police facilities" (s. 30, Ont. Reg. 3/99).

Civilian Oversight

LEARNING OUTCOMES

After reading this chapter, you will be able to:

LO1 Summarize the responsibilities of oversight agencies.

LO2 Describe the mandate of the Office of the Independent Police Review Director.

LO3 Define the function of the Ontario Civilian Police Commission.

LO4 Explain the role of the Special Investigations Unit.

LO5 Describe the RCMP independent external investigation process.

> *When civilians are seriously injured at the hands of police, it is critical that the results of the consequent criminal and administrative investigations are exposed to public view—to ensure confidence not only in police oversight, but in policing itself. That was the intent behind the creation of the SIU.*
>
> —*André Marin (2008)*

Policing is a difficult job. Often police officers are put in situations not of their making; they often have to react to other people's actions. Policing is frequently unpredictable, and that is part of what draws people to the job—no two days are ever the same. This unpredictability is often alternated with many long hours spent following organizational policies and procedures, which usually involves a high quantity of paperwork. When police officers find themselves in those "jackpot" situations, they inevitably rely on the training they received in use-of-force techniques, police service policies, and procedures, as well as their common sense. Decisions are made in seconds and are often reviewed by Monday morning quarterbacks following the events. Sometimes those split-second decisions would have been different if the officer had had time to develop a plan, but most times the decisions are the right ones.

LO¹ RESPONSIBILITIES OF OVERSIGHT AGENCIES

In Ontario there are three main oversight bodies that review the actions of police officers: the Office of the Independent Police Review Director (OIPRD), the Ontario Civilian Police Commission (OCPC), and the Special Investigations Unit (SIU). Additionally, other agencies, such as the Ontario Ombudsman's office, provide special reviews on police actions, such as the actions during the G20 in Toronto (Figure 12.1). All of these agencies have varying mandates and powers, and the reports they generate are interesting reading to those who are invested in the policing profession; the real issue is the implementation of changes that often take place following these reports. When highly controversial incidents occur, **government inquiries** sometimes take place, and those inquiries also make recommendations for change.

It is fair to say that historically the attitude towards the reception of oversight was one of resentment and even active resistance by both police leaders and front line officers. With some that continues to be the case, but, overall it is also fair to say that such oversight is now generally accepted with a far higher degree

government inquiries:
An investigation by the government into an issue of public concern. It can take the form of a determination, examination, hearing, inquiry, investigation, review, or other activity.

© ZUMA Wire Service / Alamy

FIGURE 12.1
Police officers using force in Toronto at the G20 summit. What other options do the police have?

of cooperation and recognized as a necessary part of police professionalism and the maintenance of community confidence. (Tinsley, 2009, "Introductory Remarks," para. 3)

Police services have generally agreed to follow the procedures associated with reporting contentious incidents to the appropriate authorities within the prescribed time limits. However, there are always cases where someone was negligent and did not follow the reporting process, and when this happens it reflects poorly on the police service involved.

WHY HAVE OVERSIGHT AGENCIES?

Do police agencies really need oversight bodies to review their actions? In a word, yes. "As an institution, **oversight agencies** are an independent, hopefully credible body, to which the individual citizen may make complaint if they feel that they have been offended by the acts of the police, who are agents of the state exercising extraordinary powers" (Tinsley, 2009, "The Purpose of Independent Oversight," para. 2). Other forms of oversight include the growing number of **civil actions** launched against the police and the associated media coverage of those incidents (see Figures 12.2 and 12.3). The OIPRD, the OCPC, the SIU, special inquiries, independent investigations, and internal investigations all work to provide oversight of the policing profession.

Oversight of the policing function is important for many reasons. Miller (2002) states, "The potential for oversight to enhance the legitimacy of the police in the eyes of the public and its consistency with democratic principles are also important" (p. 18). If review processes are timely and transparent, the reputation of policing organizations will be enhanced. The Canadian Association for Civilian Oversight of Law Enforcement (CACOLE; 2011) describes the goals of these oversight bodies: "Although agency size, statutory authority and responsibilities vary from province to province, civilian oversight agencies share a common goal: a positive relationship between the public and the police" (para. 1).

In this chapter we will discuss the functions, mandates, and processes of the following civilian oversight bodies:

oversight agencies: Organizations that have the authority to provide some form of civilian oversight of policing agencies.

civil actions: Legal procedures that invoke the use of civil law and procedures for one individual or company to take another individual or company to court to resolve a dispute.

FIGURE 12.2
Toronto police crowd control officers engage protestors.

- the Office of the Independent Police Review Director,
- the Ontario Civilian Police Commission, and
- the Special Investigations Unit.

FIGURE 12.3
The media play a role in civilian oversight.

LO² THE OFFICE OF THE INDEPENDENT POLICE REVIEW DIRECTOR

The Office of the Independent Police Review Director (OIPRD) was created in October 2009. The OIPRD is designed to be an **arm's-length agency** of the Ontario Ministry of the Attorney General. According to the OIPRD, the organizational goal is to "provide an objective, impartial office to accept, process and oversee the investigation of public complaints against Ontario's police" (OIPRD, 2011d, p. 2). "The Independent Police Review Act, 2007, sets out the powers and responsibilities of the OIPRD and the police under the new public complaints system" (OIPRD, 2011h). The act gives the OIPRD responsibility for making sure that the public complaints system is working for everyone. The OIPRD also provides outreach and education to communities and police to ensure an understanding of the complaints system in Ontario (OIPRD, 2011h).

On its website, the OIPRD outlines its role in the complaints process:

- The OIPRD will review all complaints received to determine whether the complaint is about policy, service or conduct.
- The Director will have discretion to deal with complaints beyond the current deadline of six months, but must consider,
- Is the complainant a minor or under a disability?
- Was the complainant charged criminally in relation to the complaint?
- Is it in the public interest to deal with the complaint?
- The OIPRD will not be involved in any internally lodged "chief's complaint." (OIPRD, 2011a, para. 1)

According to the *Police Services Act*, the OIPRD's oversight role commences with an initial complaint by a member of the public and concludes when an investigation has been completed. Police leaders are responsible for discipline of police officers and for holding *Police Services Act* hearings (OIPRD, 2011a). The OIPRD also performs an audit function to ensure that the complaints system is being administered effectively. Finally, the OIPRD also conducts systemic reviews, and has recently completed the G20 systemic review.

> **arm's-length agency:** An agency of government accountable to the people through the legislature. In Ontario, examples include the LCBO, Hydro One, Ontario Power Generation, and the Ontario Human Rights Commission.

THE FUNCTION OF THE OIPRD

The OIPRD makes sure that public complaints against the police in Ontario are dealt with in a manner that is transparent, while complying with standards and procedures designed to effectively manage the process. Both the OIPRD and the police follow the same standards and procedures to make sure there is a consistent public complaints system throughout Ontario (OIPRD 2011d).

When the OIPRD receives complaints about policy or service, those complaints are sent to the service in question for investigation. Following an investigation by the police service, a report is generated and the results of the investigation are shared with those involved, including the OIPRD.

When the OIPRD investigates a conduct complaint, a report is completed and sent to the chief, the respondent officer, and the complainant. This report outlines whether the complaint was unsubstantiated or there was found to be misconduct (OIPRD 2011a).

This sharing of information demonstrates the transparency of the process, as both the complainant and the police officer involved are given copies of the reports, along with updates on the progress of the investigation. This adds credibility to the process and allows all involved parties to be informed of the state of the investigation.

When the police service investigates a complaint, a report is sent to the OIPRD, the respondent officer, and the complainant. Where there are reasonable grounds for a claim of misconduct or unsatisfactory work performance,

POLICING ONLINE

The results of disciplinary hearings can be found at the OIRPD website:

https://www.oiprd.on.ca/CMS/Investigations/Results-of-disciplinary-hearings.aspx

a hearing may be convened. However, if the conduct is not of a serious nature, the matter may be resolved informally. The officer and complainant have a 12-day cooling off period to withdraw consent after informal resolution agreements (OIPRD, 2011a).

Often less serious matters can be resolved informally after the complainant and the involved police officer have time to consider their options. Both parties have to agree to an informal resolution, which sometimes involves an apology. This resolution is often more meaningful and provides both parties with a lasting outcome. As mentioned above, the act also allows both parties to withdraw consent within 12 days if they decide that they were unhappy with the informal resolution outcome.

LO³ THE ONTARIO CIVILIAN POLICE COMMISSION

THE FUNCTION OF THE OCPC

The OCPC has specific authority to hold different types of hearings to ensure compliance with the Ontario *Police Services Act*. The commission holds hearings related to police services boards and municipal councils. The commission also approves the restructuring of municipal police services. This could include the disbandment of a police service or the joining of one or more police services to form a new organization. When reviewing restructuring of police services, the commission rules on whether or not prescribed standards of police services are being met (OCPC, 2011b).

The commission also determines, among other things, whether or not a disabled member of a police service has been accommodated as required under the **Ontario Human Rights Code**. In addition, the commission has oversight over disputes about membership in municipal police bargaining units, such as the Ontario Provincial Police Association (OCPC, 2011b).

THE MANDATE OF THE OCPC

"The Commission is responsible for ensuring that adequate and effective police services are provided throughout Ontario" (OCPC, 2011a, para. 2). All police services in Ontario must meet **adequacy standards,** and to do so they must provide, or have a contract to provide, police services in their area.

Either a member of the public who makes a complaint about a police officer or a police officer found guilty of an offence under the *Police Services Act* may appeal to the commission in writing within 30 days of receiving notice. "After hearing the appeal, the Commission may: confirm, vary or revoke the decision of the hearing officer; substitute its own decision; or where the complaint is related to events occurring after October 19, 2009, it may also order a new hearing" (OCPC, 2011b, p. 7).

LO⁴ THE SPECIAL INVESTIGATIONS UNIT

"In 1990, Ontario became and has remained the only province in Canada to have an independent civilian oversight body responsible for carrying out criminal investigations involving police" (Marin, 2008, p. 11). Prior to 1990, it was the police service themselves who investigated occurrences involving police officers. There was often a perception that these investigations were not impartial, as a result of the police investigating the police. In 1990, the SIU was created as an arm's-length agency of the government

DECODING POLICE TERMS

Adequate and effective police services must include, at a minimum, all of the following police services:

1. Crime prevention.

2. Law enforcement.

3. Assistance to victims of crime.

4. Public order maintenance.

5. Emergency response. (PSA, 1990, s. 2)

Source: Section 2 *Police Services Act*. Retrieved from http://www.e-laws.gov.on.ca/html/statutes/english/elaws_statutes_90p15_e.htm

FIGURE 12.4

The Special Investigations Unit logo.

(SIU, 2011a; Figure 12.4). Box 12.1 describes a case that the SIU successfully concluded following a thorough investigation, which led to exoneration of the officers. Since this time Alberta and Nova Scotia have civilian oversight agencies, and British Columbia is in the process of establishing a civilian oversight agency as well.

THE FUNCTION OF THE SIU

The SIU conducts investigations into police activity where someone has been seriously injured, alleges sexual assault, or has died. The Honourable John Osler provides a definition of serious injury.

"Serious injuries" shall include those that are likely to interfere with the health or comfort of the victim and are more than merely transient or trifling in nature and will include serious injury resulting from sexual assault. "Serious Injury" shall initially be presumed when the victim is admitted to hospital, suffers a fracture to a limb, rib or vertebrae or to the skull, suffers burns to a major portion of the body or loses any portion of the body or suffers loss of vision or hearing, or alleges sexual assault. Where a prolonged delay is likely before the seriousness of the injury can be assessed, the Unit should be notified so that it can monitor the situation and decide on the extent of its involvement.* (SIU, 2011b, p. 10)

The Honourable Patrick J. LeSage recommended that this definition be "codified through legislation" in his 2011 review of the SIU and police relations. This definition of serious injury is meant to ensure that the SIU is contacted when the Unit's statutory jurisdiction is engaged. When police services fail to notify the SIU of injury, their decision is often influenced by their interpretation of this definition.

THE MANDATE OF THE SIU

The Special Investigations Unit is designed to give the public confidence that the police will be held accountable when there are serious injuries, sexual assault allegations, or deaths resulting from the actions of the

---

BOX 12.1

SIU CASE STUDY: INVESTIGATION RESULTS IN EXONERATION OF OTTAWA POLICE OFFICERS

On April 22, 2009, Ottawa Police Service officers pursued a vehicle on Highway 417 as they had information that the driver of the vehicle was a suspect in a shooting. There was an interaction, and the driver, a 43-year-old Montreal resident, sustained firearm injuries and later died.

The SIU investigation determined that on this date, the vehicle was stopped at Highway 417 and Walkley Road. The driver got out of the car carrying a revolver, and pointed it at two of the officers, including the subject officer. As a result, the subject officer discharged his pistol in the direction of the man from inside his cruiser. One of the projectiles struck the man. Almost simultaneously, the man shot himself in the left temple area of his head with the revolver. He was taken to hospital where he succumbed to his injuries two days later. According to the pathologist, the self-inflicted wound, and not the wound inflicted by the officer, was the fatal one.

---

*Special Investigations Unit 2009-2010 Annual Report (2011), found on the website of the Special Investigations Unit at http://www.siu.on.ca/pdfs/siu_annual_2009-2010 .pdf, p. 10. © Queen's Printer for Ontario, 2011. Reproduced with permission.

police (SIU, 2011b). Box 12.2 provides an example of the case of a firearm death, in which it was determined that the death was self-inflicted and there was no criminal liability related to the police actions. This independent investigation was an important step for all involved in this incident, including the family of the deceased. It is important for them to know that the police did not cause the death of their loved one.

Table 12.1 shows the type of cases the SIU investigated from April 2009 to March 2010. As is demonstrated by the types of serious occurrences listed, the mandate of the SIU requires skilled personnel to conduct investigations and make findings.

All SIU investigators are civilians, including some who are former police officers. According to the SIU, "By the end of 2009–10, of the Unit's investigators stationed at the head office, eight were of non-policing background while six investigators had a policing background"* (2011b, p. 11).

"While some proposed that to be truly independent the SIU should be composed entirely of civilians, others suggested that skilled police criminal investigators were necessary to ensure the competence of a police oversight body" (Marin, 2008, p. 92). When the SIU was first launched, the credibility and skills of the investigators were questioned by serving police officers and sometimes by the public. "Ministry officials also expressed the view that the SIU could not investigate potential homicides without having experienced homicide investigators on its team" (Marin, 2008, p. 95). Over the last 20 years, the knowledge, skills, and abilities of the members of the SIU have been developed to equal those of trained police officers.

All members of police services are required to cooperate with the SIU during investigations. Police officers who are involved in an SIU investigation are designated as either a witness officer or a subject officer.

TABLE 12.1
SIU Occurrences, April 1, 2010–March 31, 2011

Types of Occurrences	No.
Firearm deaths	10
Firearm injuries	12
Custody deaths	30
Custody injuries	163
Other injuries/deaths	1
Vehicle deaths	4
Vehicle injuries	27
Sexual assault complaints	44
Total Occurrences	**291**
Number of cases in which charges were laid	12

Source: *Special Investigations Unit 2010-2011 Annual Report* (2012), found on the website of the Special Investigations Unit at http://www.siu.on.ca/pdfs/final_siu_ar_2010-2011_final_english_hires.pdf, p. 7. © Queen's Printer for Ontario, (2012). Reproduced with permission.

Ontario Regulation 267/10 sets out further duties of police officers during SIU investigations (SIU, 2011b, p. 11). Police services have been known to put up barriers related to SIU investigations, and some police chiefs have been questioned about their lack of cooperation. The SIU has published cases where police services were not forthcoming with information on investigations that clearly fell within the jurisdiction of the SIU.

BOX 12.2

CASE STUDY: INVESTIGATION RESULTS IN NO CRIMINAL LIABILITY BY WATERLOO REGIONAL POLICE

The Waterloo Regional Police Service (WRPS) notified the SIU in October 2009 of the firearm death of a Heidelberg man.

The investigation determined that on the evening of October 13, 2009, WRPS officers attended a residence in Heidelberg after receiving information that a 64-year-old man was threatening to harm himself, and that he had access to firearms. After arriving, the subject officer drew his firearm and took a position behind his police cruiser. He received further information that the man had left the residence and was proceeding to a nearby bush with a long gun. Shortly thereafter, the officer heard a muffled bang, and later received information that the man died of a close range shotgun wound to the head.

Source: *Special Investigations Unit 2009-2010 Annual Report* (2011), found on the website of the Special Investigations Unit at http://www.siu.on.ca/pdfs/siu_annual_2009-2010.pdf, p. 27. © Queen's Printer for Ontario, 2011. Reproduced with permission.

Special Investigations Unit 2009-2010 Annual Report (2011), found on the website of the Special Investigations Unit at http://www.siu.on.ca/pdfs/siu_annual_2009-2010.pdf, p. 11. © Queen's Printer for Ontario, 2011. Reproduced with permission.

THE INVESTIGATIVE PROCESS

According to the SIU, investigations consist of a number of functions, including "examining the scene and securing all physical evidence, monitoring the medical condition of anyone who has been injured, seeking out and securing the cooperation of witnesses, interviewing police witnesses, seizing police equipment for forensic examination, consulting with the coroner if there has been a death, notifying next of kin and keeping the family of the deceased or injured parties informed"* (SIU, 2011b, p. 12). Figure 12.5

FIGURE 12.5
The SIU Reporting and Investigation Process

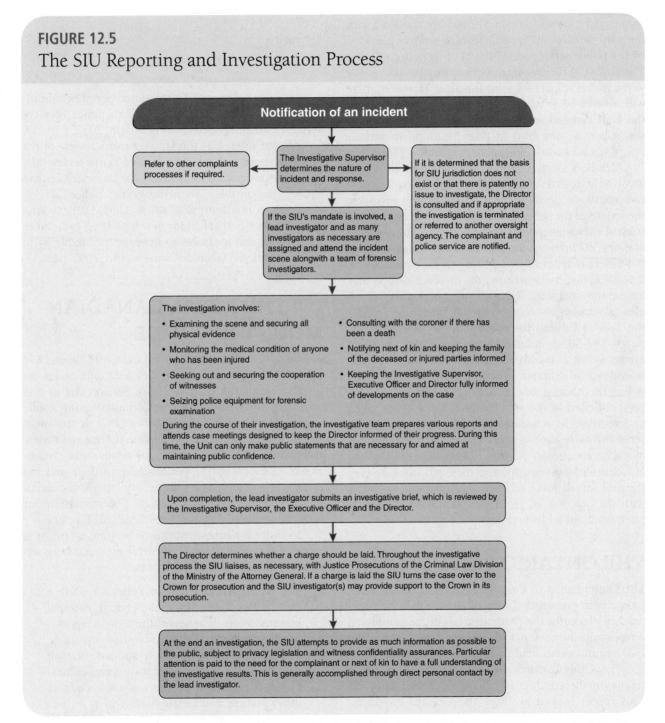

Source: Diagram of SIU Investigative Process (2010) found on the website of the Special Investigations Unit at http://www.siu.on.ca/en/process.php. © Queen's Printer for Ontario, 2010. Reproduced with permission.

Special Investigations Unit 2009-2010 Annual Report (2011), found on the website of the Special Investigations Unit at http://www.siu.on.ca/pdfs/siu_annual_2009-2010.pdf, p. 12. © Queen's Printer for Ontario, 2011. Reproduced with permission.

outlines the investigative process from notification of the incident to informing the public of the results.

Section 11 of Ontario Regulation 267/10 describes parallel police investigations. This section states that police services may conduct parallel investigations while the SIU conducts its investigation into the actions of the police. Chiefs of police are mandated to conduct an internal review where the SIU has been notified with the purpose to review the policies of or services provided by the police service and conduct of its police officers. The skills of SIU investigators have improved over the years, as has respect for their function. However, there will always be friction between police agencies and the Unit charged with investigating situations where the police are involved in cases resulting in serious injury, sexual assault allegations, or death.

Members of the public and families of people involved in cases resulting in serious injury, sexual assault complaints, or death are entitled to answers involving the actions of the police. Investigations need to reveal the truth in a transparent and timely process. "The objective of every SIU investigation is to determine whether there is evidence of criminal wrongdoing on the part of police. It is not to determine whether the involved officers may have committed some lesser offence, such as the breach of a provincial law or professional misconduct under the *Code of Conduct* for police officers"* (SIU, 2011b, p. 6). The SIU is unique in terms of other oversight agencies as it is mandated to determine whether there is evidence of criminal wrongdoing on the part of the police; no other agency has this authority. The SIU has been criticized in the past for the length of time taken to determine the outcome of investigations. It does not serve anyone to have an investigation take many months to reach a conclusion. All stakeholders need to know the outcome of the investigation, as these processes are very stressful for all involved. Not everyone will be happy with the outcome of an investigation, and the SIU is often criticized for its findings.

THE ONTARIO OMBUDSMAN

The Ombudsman of Ontario (Figure 12.6) has been proactive in preparing special reports on police-related matters. Recently, the Ombudsman's office completed a report on the conduct of police officers during the G20 summit event held in Toronto in June of 2010.

The Ombudsman's office has also completed a report on the conduct of police officers in the OPP. This report looked at "how the Ontario Provincial Police deals administratively with operational stress injuries (OSI) among its members, and the Ministry of

FIGURE 12.6
The Ontario Ombudsman logo.

Community Safety and Correctional Services' administrative processes relating to OSI in police services across Ontario" (Ombudsman Ontario, 2012, para. 1).

Also of interest is the Ombudsman's review of the SIU, referenced earlier in this chapter. In this review, "the Special Investigations Unit (SIU), the province's civilian agency responsible for investigating police actions involving serious injury or death, was found to be lacking in teeth; the report called for new legislation to enhance its mandate and measures to improve the credibility of its investigations" (Ombudsman Ontario, 2008, para. 1).

LO5 THE ROYAL CANADIAN MOUNTED POLICE

The Royal Canadian Mounted Police (RCMP; Figure 12.7) is a federal organization that does not come under the jurisdiction of the Ontario *Police Services Act* or any other provincial statute. "The Commission for Public Complaints Against the RCMP (CPC) is an independent body established in 1988 to receive and review complaints about the conduct of regular and civilian RCMP members in the performance of their policing duties. Its mission is to contribute to excellence in policing through civilian review" (Commission for Public Complaints Against the RCMP, 2011, p. 1).

In order for investigations to be transparent, it is often preferred that police agencies get outside expertise to investigate serious offences.

> The RCMP announced, in February 2010, a new policy requiring independent external investigations whenever there is a serious injury or death of an individual involving an RCMP employee, or; it appears that an employee of the RCMP may have contravened a provision of the *Criminal Code* or other statute and the matter is of a serious or sensitive nature. (Commission for Public Complaints Against the RCMP, 2011, p. 4)

**Special Investigations Unit 2009-2010 Annual Report* (2011), found on the website of the Special Investigations Unit at http://www.siu.on.ca/pdfs/siu_annual_2009-2010.pdf, p. 6. © Queen's Printer for Ontario, 2011. Reproduced with permission.

FIGURE 12.7
The RCMP logo.

This criterion is similar to the mandate of the SIU. If an investigation into police actions is required in Ontario, the SIU will conduct it on behalf of the RCMP. In other provinces where a body like the SIU does not exist, an independent external investigation will take place (Commission for Public Complaints Against the RCMP, 2011). Such an arrangement ensures that the SIU is involved in RCMP investigations should an incident happen in Ontario. Similarly, the RCMP may request the OPP or Sûreté du Québec (SQ) to conduct an investigation in other areas should the need arise.

FUTURE TRENDS IN CIVILIAN OVERSIGHT

Outside of Ontario, the issue of civilian oversight remains a priority. In British Columbia, recommendations for civilian oversight are expected following the inquiry into the death of Polish immigrant Robert Dziekanski. In this incident, RCMP officers used a Taser while arresting Mr. Dziekanski; at the conclusion of the arrest, Mr. Dziekanski was deceased (SIU, 2011b). "In the aftermath of this tragedy, public accusations were made of cover-up and police using excessive force" (Marin 2008, p. 6).

In a report submitted to the RCMP in late 2009, the Commission for Public Complaints Against the RCMP "made 23 findings and 16 recommendations aimed at improving RCMP training, policies and procedures. In February 2011, the RCMP accepted 22 of the 23 findings made by the Commission. In addition, the RCMP is in the process of addressing all 16 CPC recommendations" (p. 6). The RCMP is a policing organization in flux—it is moving from a traditional organization to one that is more efficient and effective in this era. The current commissioner, Bob Paulson, is working to meet this objective by focusing on the core functions of the RCMP. Currently, the RCMP is under scrutiny for mainly internal problems, such as sexual harassment allegations, and external problems, such as public complaints.

In Manitoba, as a result of the 2008 Taman Inquiry, chaired by retired Justice Roger Salhany, the government plans to establish an Independent Investigative Unit to conduct investigations into death and serious injury cases at the hands of the police. In this case, an off-duty police officer was responsible for the death of a motorist when he collided with her vehicle while under the influence of alcohol. Quebec is also considering an SIU model for occurrences involving death and imminent death cases as a result of several inquiries that are underway (SIU, 2011b).

When police officers are alleged to be involved in incidents causing death or serious injury, including sexual assaults, there is clearly a need for independent investigations to determine whether any offences took place. This is a trend that is spreading across the country, and Ontario, with its three main oversight bodies, is seen as an example of best practices in this regard. Although other provinces do have some form of civilian oversight of the policing sector, no other province has oversight bodies with the mandate of the SIU or the OIPRD.

CHAPTER SUMMARY

"The nature and role of independent civilian oversight of the police has evolved greatly over the last 30 years and it will continue to evolve" (Tinsley, 2009, "The Future," para. 1). Everyone needs to be held accountable, and many people believe that police officers need to be held to a higher level. Joel Miller stated, "In order to measure and improve on the success of oversight agencies, it is important to evaluate their performance" (2002, p. 19). Keeping viable statistics on the types and quantities of complaints is a good way of understanding the issues. Some police services are proactive and have systems in place to track individual officers; if those officers have more than three complaints in their files they are interviewed and assigned training or other opportunities in order to stop the behaviours that may be causing complaints. With that said, police officers are human beings, and like everyone else, they are subject to the pressures of daily life, which, at times, can lead to poor decisions. When police officers find themselves in challenging situations (see Figure 12.8), they inevitably rely on the training they received in use-of-force techniques, police service policies, and procedures, as well as their common sense. The situation described in Box 12.3 involved a police officer who had recently graduated from Georgian College and had spent around six months on the road. He has credited his training and knowledge as significant factors in his survival and his actions on that fateful day in 2009. The SIU interviewed over 40 witnesses who saw this incident take place and determined that both police officers acted within their rights and

FIGURE 12.8

A Toronto police vehicle set on fire at the G20 summit. How should the police handle this?

© ZUMA Wire Service / Alamy

used lethal force appropriately. The role of the SIU in this case provided the public with an independent review of the facts surrounding these tragic circumstances.

Some police officers do what they can to avoid getting into situations that would require future scrutiny; others get involved in every situation possible and are frequently on the front pages of the newspapers. The majority of officers

BOX 12.3

SIU CASE STUDY: BARRIE MAN SHOT AND KILLED DURING AN INTERACTION WITH THE BARRIE POLICE SERVICE

On July 5, 2009, a 48-year-old Barrie man was shot and killed during an interaction with Barrie Police Service (BPS) officers.

The SIU investigation determined that on that day, a man had been observed acting in an erratic manner. Unknown at the time to the two officers who approached him on Bayfield Street, the man was armed with a knife.

For no apparent reason, he stabbed one of the officers in the throat area, seriously injuring him. The second officer intervened and tackled him to the ground. This officer was also stabbed in the neck area, and he too was seriously injured. However, he managed to extricate himself from the man and create some distance between them. At this time, the first officer discharged his firearm in the man's direction, followed shortly by a number of rounds fired by the second officer.

The individual began walking away from the scene north on Bayfield Street with the knife still in his hand. The second officer pursued him on foot, ordering him numerous times to drop his weapon and get on the ground. The man did not comply and continued to walk north. The officer maneuvered in front of him, and repeated his verbal commands. The man continued toward the officer with the knife raised, prompting the officer to discharge a number of shots. The man was struck and killed. Both officers were taken to a Barrie hospital where they underwent emergency surgery for their life-threatening injuries.

Source: *Special Investigations Unit 2009-2010 Annual Report* (2011), found on the website of the Special Investigations Unit at http://www.siu.on.ca/pdfs/siu_annual_2009-2010.pdf, p. 23. © Queen's Printer for Ontario, 2011. Reproduced with permission.

fall between these two categories. Once you become a police officer you need to take your training seriously—in fact, start taking it seriously while you are in college! If you have a full understanding of what is expected of you and frequently practise use-of-force techniques, while staying in good physical shape, you should find that you will make the right decisions in those sudden "read and react" situations.

LO¹ Summarize the responsibilities of oversight agencies.

"Civilian oversight agencies share a common goal: a positive relationship between the public and the police" (CACOLE, 2011, para. 1).

LO² Describe the mandate of the Office of the Independent Police Review Director.

The OIPRD makes sure that public complaints against the police in Ontario are dealt with in a manner that is transparent, while complying with standards and procedures designed to effectively manage the public complaints process.

LO³ Define the function of the Ontario Civilian Police Commission.

"The Commission is responsible for ensuring that adequate and effective police services are provided throughout Ontario" (OCPC, 2011b, p. 7). All police services in Ontario must meet adequacy standards, and to do so they must provide, or have a contract to provide, police services in their area.

LO⁴ Explain the role of the Special Investigations Unit.

The SIU is designed to give the public confidence that the police will be held accountable when serious injuries, sexual assaults, or death result from the actions of the police.

LO⁵ Describe the RCMP independent external investigation process.

When an incident takes place involving serious injury or death of an individual involving an RCMP employee, an independent external investigation will be conducted.

Appendix A: Ethical Framework*
Adopted by the CAPB Membership August 22, 2003

PREAMBLE

There can be little question that legitimate police powers are derived from the consent of the public. As a result, it is incumbent upon the members of the Canadian Association of Police Boards (CAPB) to safeguard the public trust by acting ethically. Therefore, the primary duty of all CAPB members is to work diligently in support of Canadian democratic values that are enshrined in the Constitution and the Charter of Rights and Freedoms.

To this end, the CAPB endorses the Ethical Framework developed and adopted by the Canadian Association of Chiefs of Police (CACP) to help all police executives foster a professional ethical environment that enables police personnel to act in a manner that is consistent with Canadian democratic values. Further, the CAPB has elected to establish its own Ethical Framework to help all police board members foster a professional ethical environment.

The Ethical Framework highlights the responsibilities of CAPB members to: the public; the Police Chief, police associations and the police organization as a whole; their professional partners; and themselves personally. The Ethical Framework identifies board members' responsibilities and ethical values that are based upon the ethical foundation of justice, rule of law, moral core, human dignity and democratic principles.

Decisions made by CAPB members should be in keeping with the Ethical Framework.

ETHICAL FOUNDATION

The ethical foundation of justice, rule of law, moral core, human dignity and democratic principles forms the context for ethical decision making, which must guide our decisions.

JUSTICE

Fairness, equity and impartiality in the application of the law.

RULE OF LAW

Equality of access to the rights enshrined in the Constitution and the Charter of Rights & Freedoms.

MORAL CORE

The moral imperative to act in a manner that is consistent with what is good, right and just.

HUMAN DIGNITY

Respect for human dignity and the rights of persons.

DEMOCRATIC PRINCIPLES

The balance of individual and personal freedoms with the concept of social order, civic responsibility and the general public good.

Recognition of the legitimate authority of officeholders and the importance of maintaining the public trust.

ETHICAL VALUES

The "rightness" of a decision can be judged on whether it is consistent with these ethical values:

- Empathy
- Honesty
- Courage
- Respect
- Equity
- Transparency
- Integrity
- Trustworthiness

BOARD MEMBER RESPONSIBILITIES

The key relationships for police board members are with the public, their police chief and organization, their police associations, their professional partners, their fellow board members, and themselves personally.

PUBLIC

Responsibilities of CAPB members toward the people they serve and other public officials include:

- Actively advancing the public safety agenda
- Being a wise steward of public resources
- Ensuring the provision of competent and responsive services
- Respecting the legitimate authority of municipal Council and other public office holders
- Being accountable

POLICE CHIEF, ASSOCIATIONS AND THE ORGANIZATION

Responsibilities of CAPB members toward their Chief of Police, police associations, employees of their police service, and the police service as a corporate entity, include:

- Setting and focusing on the strategic priorities
- Fostering a healthy and safe work environment
- Promoting continuous learning and career development
- Fostering professionalism
- Maintaining accountability
- Setting the moral tone
- Respecting the legitimate roles of the Chief of Police and the Associations
- Promoting harmonious and collaborative labour relations

Glossary

A

active listening: Not only hearing the message but also understanding what is being said. p. 56

adequacy standards: A set of standards for police services to operate by. They are found in Ontario Regulation 3/99, *Adequacy and Effectiveness of Police Services*. p. 178

alternative dispute resolution (ADR) process: Any process approved by the OIPRD that allows an independent third party to resolve a public complaint that is less serious between a member of the public and a police officer. p. 137

arm's-length agency: An agency of government accountable to the people through the legislature. In Ontario, examples include the LCBO, Hydro One, Ontario Power Generation, and the Ontario Human Rights Commission. p. 177

B

bobbie: A term used to describe a British police officer. It is based on the founder of British policing, Sir Robert Peel, whose officers were referred to as "Peel's bobbies." p. 3

business plan: A document that addresses the key priorities of a police service and explains who's going to do what by when. p. 74

C

chain of command: A structure whereby instructions and orders are driven down from the top of an organization through each position with authority. Information is provided from a superior to a subordinate. p. 11

chief of police: Also known as the chief constable, the person responsible and accountable for the day-to-day operations of the police service. The chief of police is accountable to the police services board, which, in turn, represents the members of the community they serve. p. 46

civil actions: Legal procedures that invoke the use of civil law and procedures for one individual or company to take another individual or company to court to resolve a dispute. p. 176

civilian governance: For municipal and regional policing, an internal but arm's-length civilian body of municipal elected and appointed individuals and provincial appointees, whose mandate is derived from the statutes and regulations to ensure accountability of police services while maintaining their independence in accordance with the rule of law. p. 149

civilian members: RCMP members who work in non-policing roles such as human resources, forensics, computer programming, and project management, providing support to frontline policing operations. p. 7

clear and convincing evidence: The courts have held clear and convincing evidence to be "weighty, cogent and reliable evidence upon which a trier of fact, acting with care and caution, can come to the fair and reasonable conclusion that the officer is guilty of misconduct" (*Allan v. Munro*, 1994, p. 664). In *Lloyd and the London Police Service*, 1999 May 20, the Commission stated in clarifying the clear and convincing evidence standard, "An analysis to justify the conclusion is not enough. It is not the conclusion that must be clear and cogent but rather the evidence that leads to the conclusion (*I.F.K. v. College of Physicians and Surgeons*, (Unreported, B.C. C.A., March 13, 1998), para. 42)" (OCCPS 99-04, p. 9). p. 125

coach officer: A person who mentors and supervises a new recruit during the probationary period. This person provides direction and evaluates the performance of the recruit. p. 11

communication: A means of sending or receiving information in some sort of medium. p. 55

community consultation: A process of engaging and mobilizing members of the community to work on solutions to areas of mutual concern. p. 76

community policing: A philosophy that emphasizes crime prevention and problem-solving techniques rather than a more traditional reactive approach to policing within a community. A form of policing that is based on the police working with the community to solve problems and provide solutions. Police work and consult with community partners to resolve issues either before or as they arise. p. 49

competency: Any skill, knowledge, ability, motive, behaviour, or attitude essential to successful performance on the job. p. 17

D

deceit: To lie, mislead, or falsify information for personal gain, to avoid discipline, or to harm another person. p. 123

deployed organization: An organization that spans a vast geographical area, with members being posted in areas far from the general headquarters. Examples include the RCMP and the OPP. p. 7

developmental competencies: Specific skills and abilities that can be acquired through training that are preferred by some police services. p. 17

discipline: A response, positive or negative, by an employer to an employee within an organization for failing to follow standards or rules, including governing regulations and laws. p. 115

discretion: An individual's exercise of free will to make choices or judgments that are responsible decisions within the legal boundaries of the law. p. 49

E

essential competencies: The knowledge, skills, and abilities a candidate must exhibit before becoming a police officer. p. 17

ethics in policing: On- and off-duty conduct that is professional and consistent with a police officer's oath of office and code of conduct. p. 103

G

government inquiries: An investigation by the government into an issue of public concern. It can take the form of a determination, examination, hearing, inquiry, investigation, review, or other activity. p. 175

H

haptic communication: A form of nonverbal communication involving the sense of touch. p. 56

I

impersonal communication: An ineffective type of communication that occurs when we treat people as objects, or when we respond to their roles rather than to them as individuals. p. 57

Industrial Revolution: A period of significant change from 1750 to the late 1800s, when the economy of England and Europe transitioned from agriculture to urban factories. Changes took place in agriculture, manufacturing, mining, transportation, and technology and had a major impact on society. p. 3

informal resolution: A process for informally resolving less serious complaints against police without a hearing with the consent of the respondent officer, and in the case of a public complaint, with the consent of the complainant subject to review by the OIPRD. p. 134

International Phonetic Alphabet: A standard form of communicating the alphabet in policing, usually while transmitting over a radio system, which clarifies the letters used when spelling out words so there is no misunderstanding in the correct spelling of a person, place, or thing being checked. p. 66

interpersonal communication: A unique style of communication involving mutual influence and respect. This form of communication is most effective in managing relationships. p. 57

interview stance: A position where a police officer angles his or her body so that the strong side (the side that the pistol is on) is away from the subject. p. 64

K

kinesics: Elements of body language such as posture, stance, gestures, and movements. p. 56

M

mediated interpersonal communication: Communicating with others through a popular media source, such as instant messaging, texting, email, video exchanges, cellphones, Facebook, or Twitter. p. 58

medical requirements: The established vision, hearing, and health standards that a candidate must meet in order to be a police officer. p. 16

minimum requirements in policing: The fundamental requirements set forth by the government as the basic qualifications required to be a police officer. p. 16

municipal policing: Policing organizations that report directly to a municipal police services board (PSB), which reports to a municipal council. These types of police services focus on providing policing to one municipality. p. 9

N

nonverbal communication: The process of sending and receiving wordless messages by way of gestures, body language, touch, facial expression, and eye contact. p. 55

O

oath or affirmation of office: A statement that police officers, special constables, or First Nations constables promise to uphold the Constitution of Canada and, to the best of their ability, complete their duties faithfully, impartially, and according to law. p. 45

oath or affirmation of secrecy: A statement that police officers, auxiliary members of a police force, special constables, or First Nations constables promise to not disclose any information they have gained while performing the lawful duties of their position unless authorized or required by law. p. 45

Ontario Human Rights Code: Provincial legislation designed to give people equal rights and allow them to function without discrimination related to housing, jobs, and services. p. 178

Ontario Police College (OPC): A police training facility in Aylmer, Ontario, operated by the Ontario government. OPC offers training and education for police officers and police services in Ontario. The *Police Services Act* mandates that all police officers in Ontario must complete their initial basic constable training at OPC. p. 46

oversight agencies: Organizations that have the authority to provide some form of civilian oversight of policing agencies. p. 176

P

paralanguage: Speech that also contains nonverbal elements such as pitch, tone, volume, rate, and stress. p. 56

paramilitary organization: An organization that structures its personnel, policies, and procedures along the lines of a military organization. A chain of command is followed as information is passed from the top to the bottom of the organization. Every member must report to a superior rank. p. 5

police challenge: A form of tactical communication used by police officers when they have assessed a situation and selected to draw their firearm to de-escalate a serious bodily harm or death situation. The police challenge is "Police—don't move!" p. 64

police discretion: The judgment police officers use both on the streets and within the administration of a police service. p. 49

police notebook (memo book): A daily journal (recording) of police officers' activity when they are on duty. p. 67

Police Services Act of Ontario (PSA): A provincial statute that regulates and guides all police services and police officers in Ontario. p. 45

police work: Any duty that is conducted by sworn members of a police service that they are legally mandated to perform and that will assist in the regulation and control of society and the maintenance of public order. p. 44

probationary period: When a newly hired police constable is monitored on his or her job performance and suitability for the position of police officer for one year from the date of appointment or on the date he or she completes training at the Ontario Police College. p. 46

problem-oriented policing: A principle of community policing that involves solving specific problems of crime and disorder at their root cause, with the intention of identifying and modifying the particular factors giving rise to each problem within the community. p. 49

professionalism: Ethical and legal behaviour that contributes to the vision, mission, supporting values, goals, and objectives of the organization that employs the professional. p. 99

pseudo-conflict: Conflict triggered by miscommunication. p. 61

public service employees: RCMP members who work in non-policing roles such as administration, communications, and information technology, providing business management support. p. 7

Q

quality service standards: Policies that are followed by employees to meet standards the employer expects. These standards relate to timelines and procedures involved with emails, phone messages, correspondence, etc. p. 74

R

rank structure: An organizational hierarchy designed to provide a clear chain of command related to communication and discipline. p. 10

RCMP Act: A federal statute that regulates and governs the RCMP and their police officers. p. 46

reactionary gap: The distance (space) between the officer and the person(s) he or she is dealing with that will allow the officer to react to the situation if it escalates. p. 64

reactive policing: A type of policing where the police respond to calls for service requiring immediate response. This traditional approach does not focus on preventing crimes from taking place. p. 76

reasonable grounds: Facts-based evidence that would lead an average person to believe that an officer has breached the code of conduct or engaged in unsatisfactory work performance. This belief must be beyond reasonable suspicion to substantiate the complaint. p. 123

regional policing: The amalgamation of small-town Ontario police services in the 1970s to form policing services within each region. Ontario has regional policing in York Region, Niagara Region, Durham Region, Halton Region, Peel Region, and Waterloo Region. p. 8

regular members: RCMP officers responsible for keeping the peace, preventing crime, assisting victims, upholding the law, and working with the communities they serve. p. 6

S

strategic plan: Also called a business plan, a plan required every three years that sets long-term goals, priorities, and initiatives. p. 79

systemic failure: Failing to have a system in place to address or respond to specific investigative (operational or administrative) issues, or having a system in place to address or respond to specific investigative issues but failing to apply or enforce it. p. 167

T

tactical communication: Any communication used by a police officer to resolve a situation. Tactical communication ensures that police officers adhere to a standard and professional approach when communicating with the public in order to prevent conflicts from escalating and ultimately de-escalate the situation. p. 63

traditional policing: A reactive approach to policing that focuses on making arrests after a crime has been committed. This approach limits community consultation and involvement in solutions. The responsibility for problem solving is entirely that of the police service. p. 84

tunnel vision: Having a narrow view of a set of circumstances that is not factually supported by the evidence because of an investigator's or prosecutor's lack of objectivity or failure to be open-minded toward the suspect/accused or the crime that has been alleged or committed. p. 104

U

unfettered discretion: Unrestricted discretion. An unfettered discretion is an opportunity for corruption, discrimination, and an intrusive style of policing. p. 51

V

verbal communication: What is being said and the words that are being used to communicate the message. p. 55

References

Allan v. Munro, Ont. Bd. Inq. 94–32, (1994 July 27). Retrieved from http://www.ocpc.ca/files/6W682003ZP 08EF0689092229831143.pdf

Armstrong, A., & Francis, R. (2008). Assessing ethical governance in a police environment. *Journal of Business Systems, Governance, and Ethics, 3*(3), 45–61.

Aspden and the Ontario Civilian Commission on Police Services. (2007, December 12). OCCPS INQ 07–01. Retrieved from http://www.ocpc.ca/files/5CL820078V12 0L13U21015016Q40H5.pdf

Association of Municipalities Ontario. (2011). Ontario municipal home pages. Retrieved from http://www.amo.on .ca/YLG/ylg/ontario.html

Barlow and Ottawa Police Service (2011, August 15). OCPC Decision: 11–10. Retrieved from http://www.ocpc.ca /files/JW3B2011RP11WF045916Z219MK0203.pdf

Beebe, S., Beebe, S., Redmond, M., & Geerinck, T. (2011). *Interpersonal communication: Relating to others* (5th Canadian ed.). Toronto, ON: Pearson Canada.

Blair, W. (2010). Draft speaking notes: CACP professionalism in policing study. Retrieved from http://www.cacp.ca/media /library/download/988/10-08-23_speaking_notes__2_.pdf

Blake, S. (2001). *Administrative Law in Canada* , 3rd. ed. Markham: Butterworths.

Boniface, G. (August 21, 2001). Ontario Provincial Police media release.

Boyd, L. (2005, Spring). What officers need to know about the PSB. *Beyond the Badge, 158,* p. 8.

Brannagan v. Peel Regional Police. (2003, August 25). OCCPS 03–18. Retrieved from http://www.ocpc.ca/files /J9NV2003R610W2225A10ZH49M454CJ.pdf

Burnham v. Metropolitan Toronto Police, [1987] 2 S.C.R. 572. Retrieved from http://scc.lexum.org /en/1987/1987scr2-572/1987scr2-572.pdf

Campbell, A. (The Honourable). (1996). *Bernardo investigation review: Report of Mr. Justice Archie Campbell, June 1996.* Retrieved from http://www.opconline.ca/depts/omcm /Campbell/Bernardo_Investigation_Review%20PDF.pdf

Canadian Association for Civilian Oversight of Law Enforcement (CACOLE). (2011). Civilian oversight in Canada. Retrieved from http://www.cacole.ca/Links /Canadian%20Links/Civilian%20Oversight%20in%20 Canada%20.htm

Canadian Association of Chiefs of Police (CACP). (2011). CACP Ethical Framework. Retrieved from http://www .cacp.ca/index/aboutus

Canadian Association of Police Boards. (2003). Ethical Framework. Retrieved from http://www.capb.ca /FCKeditor/editor/fileCabinet/Ethical_Framework.pdf

Canadian Association of Police Boards. (2005). *Best practices: A framework for professionalism and success in police board governance*. Ottawa, ON: Author. Retrieved from http://www.capb.ca/FCKeditor/editor /fileCabinet/finalgovernancerpt.pdf

Canadian Charter of Rights and Freedoms, Part I of the *Constitution Act, 1982*, being Schedule B to the *Canada Act 1982* (U.K.), 1982, c. 11. Retrieved from http://laws. justice.gc.ca/eng/Charter/

Carter, L., & Wilson, M. (August 2006). Measuring professionalism of police officers. *The Police Chief , 73*(8), pp. 42–44.

Caul, D. R. (2009). *Municipal police governance in Canada: An examination of the relationship between board structure and police independence* (Master's thesis). Retrieved from http://www.policecouncil.ca/reports /DCaul%20Municipal%20Police%20Governance.pdf

Ceyssens, P. (2005). *Legal aspects of policing*. Salt Spring Island, BC: Earlscourt.

Chan, J. (2004). Using Pierre Bourdieu's framework for understanding police culture. *Droit et Société, 56–47.* Retrieved from http://www.reds.msh-paris.fr /publications/revue/pdf/ds56-57/ds056057-17.pdf

Chartier v. the Queen, [1979] 2 S.C.R. 474. Retrieved from http://scc.lexum.org/en/1979/1979scr2-474 /1979scr2-474.pdf

Colter, W. (1993). *Report of the Niagara Regional Police Force Inquiry.* Toronto, ON: Ontario Ministry of the Attorney General. Retrieved from http://www.archive .org/details/reportofniagarar00roya

Commission for Public Complaints Against the RCMP. (2001, July 31). *APEC—Commission interim report.* Retrieved from http://www.cpc-cpp.gc.ca/prr/rep/phr/apec /apec-31-eng.aspx

Commission for Public Complaints Against the RCMP. (2009, August 11). *Police investigating police: Final public report.* Retrieved from http://www.cpc-cpp.gc.ca/prr/rep/rev/chair-pre/pipR/pip_5-eng.aspx

Commission for Public Complaints Against the RCMP. (2011). *2010–2011 annual report.* Retrieved from http://www.cpc-cpp.gc.ca/prr/anr/2010-2011-eng.aspx

Commission of Inquiry into the Actions of Canadian Officials in Relation to Maher Arar. (2006). *Report of the events relating to Maher Arar: Analysis and recommendations.* Ottawa, ON: Ministry of Public Works and Government Services Canada. Retrieved from http://www.sirc-csars.gc.ca/pdfs/cm_arar_rec-eng.pdf

Constitution Act, 1867 (U.K.), 30 & 31 Vict., c. 3, reprinted in R.S.C. 1985, App. II, No. 5.

Constitution Act, 1982, being Schedule B to the *Canada Act 1982* (U.K.), 1982, c. 11.

Coon and Toronto Police Service. (2003, April 10). OCPC Decision: 03–09. Retrieved from http://www.ocpc.ca/files/T7OU2003B405GD129X153E17825542.pdf

Cory, P. (Justice). (2000). *The inquiry regarding Thomas Sophonow.* Retrieved from http://www.gov.mb.ca/justice/publications/sophonow/index.html

Criminal Code, R.S.C. 1985, c. C-46.

Delattre, E. J. (1989). *Character and cops: Ethics in policing.* Washington, DC: American Enterprise Institute for Public Policy Research.

Dempsey, J., & Forst, L. (2011). *Police* (Instructor Edition). Clifton Park, NY: Delmar Cengage Learning.

Durham Regional Police. (2011). *Durham Regional Police Services 2011–2013 business plan.* Retrieved from http://www.drps.ca/internet_explorer/businessplan.asp

Duxbury, L., & Higgings, C. (2012, March). *Caring for and about those who serve: Work-life conflict and employee well being within Canada's police departments.* Retrieved from http://sprott.carleton.co/wp-content/files/Duxbury-Higgins-Police2012_fullreport.pdf

Elliott, R., & Nicholls, J. (1996). It's good to talk: Lessons in public consultation and feedback. *Police Research Series, Paper 22.* Retrieved from http://library.npia.police.uk/docs/hopolicersold/fprs22.pdf

Evans, D. R., & MacMillan, C. S. (2008). *Ethical reasoning in policing, corrections, and security* (3nd ed.). Toronto, ON: Edmond Montgomery.

Federal/Provincial/Territorial Heads of Prosecution Committee Working Group. (2004). *Report on the prevention of miscarriages of justice.* Retrieved from http://www.justice.gc.ca/eng/dept-min/pub/pmj-pej/pmj-pej.pdf

Ferguson, G. (The Honourable). (2003). *Review and recommendations concerning various aspects of police misconduct: Volume I.* Retrieved from http://www.torontopolice.on.ca/publications/files/reports/ferguson1.pdf

Finn, P., & Tomz, J. (1996, December). Developing a law enforcement stress program for officers and their families. *Issues and Practices in Criminal Justice.* Retrieved from https://www.ncjrs.gov/pdffiles/163175.pdf

Galassi v. Hamilton Police Service. (2003, September 3). OCCPS 03–20. Retrieved from http://www.ocpc.ca/files/G6212003O310U9224S11XA18K1320B.pdf

Geske and Hamilton Police Service. (2003, July 3). OCCPS 03–15. Retrieved from http://www.ocpc.ca/files/O4902003XD10CT228N092V27793938.pdf

Gill, M. (2001). *Governance do's and don'ts: Lessons from case studies on twenty Canadian non-profits.* Ottawa, ON: Institute on Governance.

Gilmartin, K. (2002). *Emotional survival for law enforcement: A guide for officers and their families.* Tucson, AZ: E-S Press.

Gleason, T. (2006, November). Ethics training for police. *The Police Chief, 73*(11). Retrieved from http://www.policechiefmagazine.org/magazine/index.cfm?fuseaction=display&article_id=1054&issue_id=112006

Gough v. Peel Regional Police. (2003, September 18). OCCPS 03–14. Retrieved from http://www.ocpc.ca/files/OGUY2007XZ09C525831026357T303S.pdf

Greenspan, E., Rosenberg, M., & Henein, M. (2012). *2012 Martins annual Criminal Code* (Student Edition). Aurora, ON: Canada Law Book.

Griffiths, C. (2008). *Canadian police work* (2nd ed.). Toronto, ON: Nelson Education.

Halifax Regional Municipality. (2009). HRM's *graffiti management plan.* Retrieved from http://www.halifax.ca/corporate/Graffiti/documents/GraffitiManagementPlanNov10version.pdf

Halpenny, A. (2010). The governance of military police in Canada. *Osgoode Hall Law Journal, 48.* Retrieved from http://ohlj.ca/english/documents/48_1_HALPENNY_changesmade_10_07_14.pdf

Halton Regional Police Service. (2008). Application process. Retrieved from http://www.hrps.on.ca/JoinUs/BeAPoliceOfficer/Pages/HowToApply.aspx

Halton Regional Police Service. (2011). Milton Community Policing Committee. Retrieved from http://haltonpolicingcommittees.ca/who.html

Healey and Ontario Provincial Police. (2011, July 29). OIPRD. Retrieved from https://www.oiprd.on.ca/CMS/oiprd/media/image-Main/PDF/Decision---Complaint-of-J.-HEALEY.pdf

Henco Industries Ltd. v. Haudenosaunee Six Nations Confederacy Council, 2006 CanLII 29083 (O.N. C.A.).

Hill v. Hamilton-Wentworth Regional Police Services Board, [2007] 3 S.C.R. 129.

How CPIC works. (2008, July 19). *Toronto Star*. Retrieved from http://www.thestar.com/specialsections/crime/article/460749—how-cpic-works

Independent Police Review Act, 2007, S.O. 2007, c. 5 - Bill 103. Retrieved from http://www.e-laws.gov.on.ca/html/source/statutes/english/2007/elaws_src_s07005_e.htm

Institute for Law Enforcement Administration (ILEA). (2005). Ethics Train-the-Trainer [Course handout]. Dallas, TX: The Center for American and International Law.

Jane Doe v. Metropolitan Toronto (Municipality) Commissioners of Police (1990), 74 O.R. (2d) 225.

Jones, J. R. (2005). *Reputable conduct: Ethical issues in policing and corrections* (3rd ed.). Scarborough, ON: Prentice Hall.

Josephson, M. (n.d.). *The bell, the book, the candle*. Los Angeles, CA: Josephson Institute of Ethics.

Josephson, M. (2002). *Making ethical decisions: The six pillars of character*. Los Angeles, CA: Josephson Institute of Ethics.

Josephson Institute of Ethics. (2012). Making ethical decisions: The six pillars of character. Retrieved from http://josephsoninstitute.org/MED/MED-2sixpillars.html

Kaufman, F. (Justice). (1998). *Report of the Kaufman Commission on Proceedings Involving*

Guy Paul Morin. Retrieved from http://www.attorneygeneral.jus.gov.on.ca/ english/about/pubs/morin/

Kelling, G. L., & Wilson, J. Q. (1982, March). Broken windows: The police and neighborhood safety. *The Atlantic*. Retrieved from http://www.theatlantic.com/magazine/archive/1982/03/broken-windows/4465/

Lalonde v. Ontario (Commission de restructuration des services de santé), 2001 CanLII 21164 (O.N. C.A.).

Lalonde, M. W., & Kean, D. W. (2003). *Municipal police board governance in British Columbia*. New Westminster, BC: Police Academy, Justice Institute of British Columbia. Retrieved from http://www.pssg.gov.bc.ca/policeservices/shareddocs/policeboards-governancereport.pdf

Leigh, L. H. (1985). *Police powers in England and Wales*. London, England: Butterworths.

Lesage, P. (Justice). (2005, April 22). *Report on the police complaints system in Ontario*. Retrieved from http://www.attorneygeneral.jus.gov.on.ca/english/about/pubs/LeSage/en-fullreport.pdf

Linden, S. B. (The Honourable). (2007a). *The Ipperwash Inquiry. Volume 1: Investigation and findings*. Toronto, ON: Ministry of the Attorney General, Queen's Printer.

Linden, S. B. (The Honourable). (2007b). *The Ipperwash Inquiry. Volume 2: Policy analysis*. Toronto, ON: Ministry of the Attorney General, Queen's Printer.

Linden, S. B. (The Honourable). (2007c). *The Ipperwash Inquiry. Volume 4: Executive summary*. Toronto, ON: Ministry of the Attorney General, Queen's Printer.

Linden, S. B. (The Honourable). (2009, June 8). Presentation to the Canadian Association for Civilian Oversight of Law Enforcement, Ottawa, ON. Retrieved from http://www.cacole.ca/confere-reunion/pastCon/presentations/2009/LindenSpeech.pdf

Lloyd and London Police. (1999, May 20). OCCPS 99–04. Retrieved from http://www.ocpc.ca/files/A9D5200336025210GB13RJ11E435U4.pdf

MacFarlane, B. A. (n.d.). *Wrongful convictions: The effect of tunnel vision and predisposing circumstances in the criminal justice system*. Retrieved from http://www.attorneygeneral.jus.gov.on.ca/inquiries/goudge/policy_research/pdf/Macfarlane_Wrongful-Convictions.pdf

Maguire, S., & Dyke, L. (2011a). *CACP professionalism in policing report: Recommendations*. Retrieved from http://www.cacp.ca/media/library/download/1241/Recommendations.pdf

Maguire, S., & Dyke, L. (2011b). *CACP professionalism in policing research report: Survey results*. Retrieved from http://www.cacp.ca/media/library/download/1242/Survey_Results.pdf

Major Case Management, Ontario Regulation 354/04. Retrieved from http://www.e-laws.gov.on.ca/html/regs/english/elaws_regs_040354_e.htm

Mallen and Hamilton Police Service. (2011, May 13). OIPRD. Retrieved from https://www.oiprd.on.ca/CMS/getattachment/Investigations/Results-of-disciplinary-hearings/mallen-paul.pdf.aspx

Malm, A., Pollard, N., Brantingham, P., Tinsley, P., Plecas, D., Brantingham, P., Cohen, I., & Kinney, B. (2005). *A 30-year analysis of police service delivery and costing*. Abbotsford, BC: Department of Criminology and Criminal Justice, University College of the Fraser Valley, & International Centre for Urban Research Studies. Retrieved from http://www.capb.ca/uploads/files/documents/Police_Costing_Research_Summary_Report.doc

Marin, A. (2008, September). *Ombudsman Report: Investigation into the Special Investigations Unit's operational effectiveness and credibility. "Oversight unseen."* Retrieved from http://www.siu.on.ca/pdfs/marin_report_2008.pdf

Marin, R. J. (The Honourable). (1997). *Policing in Canada: Issues for the 21st century*. Aurora, ON: Canada Law Book.

Martin, D. L. (2001). The police role in wrongful convictions: An international comparative study. In S. D. Westervelt & J. A. Humphrey (Eds.), *Wrongly convicted: Perspectives on failed justice* (pp. 77–98). New Brunswick, NJ:

Rutgers University Press. Retrieved from http://www
.canadiancriminallaw.com/Faculty%20of%20Law/comm
/The%20Police%20Role%20in%20Wrongful%20
Convictions.pdf

McKenna, P., & Murray, C. (2007). *Rethinking police governance, culture and management.* Retrieved from http://www
.publicsafety.gc.ca/rcmp-grc/_fl/eng/rthnk-plc-eng.pdf

McTaggart v. Ontario, [2000] O.J. No. 4766 (QL).

Midland Police Service. (n.d.). *Community-Based Strategic
Plan Report—2010 to 2012* [Handout]. Retrieved from
http://www.police.midland.on.ca/files/Strategic%20
Plan%20Handout%20(web).pdf

Miller, J. (2002). *Civilian oversight of policing: Lessons from
the literature.* Retrieved from http://www.vera.org
/download?file=93/Civilian%2Boversight.pdf

Ministry of Community Safety and Correctional Services
(MCSCS). (2009, December 7). *Review of conducted
energy weapon use in Ontario: Report of the Policing
Standards Advisory Committee.* Retrieved from http://www
.mcscs.jus.gov.on.ca/stellent/groups/public/@mcscs/@
www/@com/documents/webasset/ec081155.pdf

Ministry of Community Safety and Correctional Services
(MCSCS). (2010). Policing: Use of force guideline.
Retrieved from http://www.mcscs.jus.gov.on.ca/english
/police_serv/ConductedEnergyWeapons/Guidelines
/CEW_guidelines.html

Ministry of Community Safety and Correctional Services
(MCSCS). (2011a). Constable selection information
package: Minimum requirements and competencies.
Retrieved from http://www.mcscs.jus.gov.on.ca/english
/police_serv/const_select_sys/const_select_info
/info_what_it_takes/info_what_it_takes.html

Ministry of Community Safety and Correctional Services
(MCSCS). (2011b). Constable selection information
package: Physical Readiness Evaluation for Police—PREP.
Retrieved from http://www.mcscs.jus.gov.on.ca/english
/police_serv/const_select_sys/const_select_info/prep
/performance/PREP_performance.html

Ministry of Community Safety and Correctional Services
(MCSCS). (2011c). Constable selection information
package: The selection process. Retrieved from http://www
.mcscs.jus.gov.on.ca/english/police_serv/const_select_sys
/const_select_info/info_selection/info_selection/info
_selection.html

Ministry of Community Safety and Correctional Services
(MCSCS). (2011d). Constable Selection System:
Becoming a police constable. Retrieved from http://www
.mcscs.jus.gov.on.ca/english/police_serv/const_select_sys
/become_police_const/become_police_const.html

Ministry of Community Safety and Correctional Services
(MCSCS). (2011e). Constable Selection System:

Self-assess—medical requirements for candidates.
Retrieved from http://www.mcscs.jus.gov.on.ca/english
/police_serv/const_select_sys/Self-Assess-
MedicalRequirementsforCandidates/Self_Assess.html

Ministry of Community Safety and Correctional Services
(MCSCS). (2011f). Ontario Police College calendar. Retrieved
from http://www.opconline.ca/calendar/Calendar.pdf

Ministry of Community Safety and Correctional Services.
(2012). Major Case Management. Retrieved from
http://www.mcscs.jus.gov.on.ca/english/police_serv
/MajorCaseManagement/mcm.html

Ministry of Municipal Affairs and Housing. (1996). *Report of the
Who Does What Panel: The exchange of provincial and
municipal responsibilities in Ontario.* Toronto, ON: Author.

Ministry of Public Safety and Solicitor General, British
Columbia. (March, 2003). *Municipal police board gov-
ernance in British Columbia.* New Westminster, BC:
Police Academy, Justice Institute of British Columbia.
Retrieved from http://www.pssg.gov.bc.ca/policeservices
/shareddocs/policeboards-governancereport.pdf

Ministry of the Solicitor General. (2000, February). *Policing
standards manual (2000).* Toronto, ON: Author.
Retrieved from http://www.ontla.on.ca/library
/repository/ser/10256510//200107.pdf

Ministry of the Solicitor General and Correctional Services
(MSGCS). (1999a, January). *Guide to questions and
answers on the adequacy standards regulation.* Toronto,
ON: Queen's Printer. Ministry of the Solicitor General
and Correctional Services (MSGCS). (1999b, January).
*Implementation supports for the adequacy standards
regulation.* Toronto, ON: Queen's Printer.

Ministry of the Solicitor General and Correctional Services
(MSGCS). (1999c, January). *An overview of the ade-
quacy standards regulation* [PowerPoint slides]. Toronto,
ON: Queen's Printer.

Ministry of the Solicitor General and Correctional Services
(MSGCS). (1999d, January 11). Policing Adequacy and
Effectiveness Standards Regulation under the *Police
Services Act.* [All Chiefs and OPP Commissioner memo-
randum]. Policing Services Division, MSGCS.

Ministry of the Solicitor General and Correctional Services
(MSGCS). (1999e, January). *Self-assessment tool for
the adequacy standards regulation.* Toronto, ON:
Queen's Printer.

Murphy, C., & McKenna, P. (2007). *Rethinking police governance, culture and management.* Retrieved from
http://www.publicsafety.gc.ca/rcmp-grc/_fl/eng
/rthnk-plc-eng.pdf

Nelles v. Colbourg Police Service. (2007, May 3). OCCPS
07–04. Retrieved from http://www.ocpc.ca/files
/M2002007790590086I11CP07P759F6.pdf

New Westminster Police Service. (2011). Sir Robert Peel's nine principles. Retrieved from http://nwpolice.org /inside-new-westminster-police-department/history/

Nicholson v. Haldimand-Norfolk Regional Board of Commissioners of Police, [1979] 1 S.C.R. 311. Retrieved from http://scc.lexum.org/en/1978 /1979scr1-311/1979scr1-311.pdf

Nishnawbe-Aski Police Service. (2011). Hiring information. Retrieved from http://www.naps.ca/index .php?option=com_content&view=article&id=81&Itemid=69

Office of the Independent Police Review Director (OIPRD). (2009). *Rules of procedure.* Retrieved from https://www .oiprd.on.ca/CMS/oiprd/media/image-Main/PDF /OIPRDRules_of_Procedure-july-14-_v5_-09.pdf

Office of the Independent Police Review Director (OIPRD). (2010). *Statement of operations: October 19, 2009– March 31, 2010 annual report.* Retrieved from https://www.oiprd.on.ca/CMS/oiprd/media/image-Main /PDF/2009-10-STATEMENT-OF-OPERATIONS-March-29.pdf

Office of the Independent Police Review Director (OIPRD). (2011a). Investigations. Retrieved from https://www. oiprd.on.ca/CMS/Investigations.aspx

Office of the Independent Police Review Director (OIPRD). (2011b). *Making connections: 2010–11 annual report.* Retrieved from https://www.oiprd.on.ca/CMS/oiprd/media /image-Main/PDF/6022_OIPRD_AR2011_EN_Final.pdf

Office of the Independent Police Review Director (OIPRD). (2011c). Sample draft completed OIPRD complaint form. Retrieved from https://www.oiprd.on.ca/CMS/oiprd /media/image-Main/PDF/Sample-Complaint-Form.pdf

Office of the Independent Police Review Director (OIPRD). (2011d). *Talk to us* [Brochure]. Retrieved from https://www .oiprd.on.ca/CMS/oiprd/media/image-Main/PDF /OIPRD_PublicComplaintsSystem_Eng.pdf

Office of the Independent Police Review Director (OIPRD). (2011e). *Talk to us: Dealing with your complaint by local resolution* [Brochure]. Retrieved from https://www .oiprd.on.ca/CMS/oiprd/media/image-Main/PDF /OIPRD-DealingWithComplaint_Eng.pdf

Office of the Independent Police Review Director (OIPRD). (2011f). *Talk to us: How to request a review* [Brochure]. Retrieved from https://www.oiprd.on.ca/CMS/oiprd /media/image-Main/PDF/OIPRD-RequestAReview_Eng.pdf

Office of the Independent Police Review Director (OIPRD). (2011g). *Talk to us: Step-by-step—how to make a complaint against the police* [Brochure]. Retrieved from http://www.oiprd.on.ca/CMS/oiprd/media/image-Main /PDF/OIPRD-MakeAComplaint_Eng.pdf

Office of the Independent Police Review Director (OIPRD). (2011h). What we do. Retrieved from https://www .oiprd.on.ca/CMS/About/What-we-do-(1).aspx

Office of the Independent Police Review Director (OIPRD). (2012). *Policing the right to protest: G20 systemic review report.* Retrieved from https://www.oiprd.on.ca/CMS /getattachment/Publications/Reports/G20_Report_Eng .pdf.aspx

Oliver v. South Simcoe Police Service. (2010, February 10). Decision of retired Superintendent Neil Tweedy [Unreported].

Oliver, C. R. (March, 2008). Tools for working through ethical dilemmas. *Let's Talk, 32*(2). Retrieved from http://www.csc-scc.gc.ca/text/pblct/lt-en/2008 /32-2/8-eng.shtml

Ontario Civilian Commission on Police Services. (1997a, October 27). *In the matter of an application by the Town of Goderich for consent to the abolition of the Goderich Police Service.* OCCPS 97–04. Retrieved from http://www .ocpc.ca/files/074Q200334025013HW116D011G34UF.pdf

Ontario Civilian Commission on Police Services (OCCPS). (1997b, December 19). *In the matter of an application by the Town of Goderich for consent to the abolition of the Goderich Police Service.* OCCPS 97–046. Retrieved from http://www.ocpc.ca/files /MD0N2003V802A4137211D515QQ232P.pdf

Ontario Civilian Commission on Police Services v. Wallaceburg Police Services Board, [1997] O.J. No. 1413.

Ontario Civilian Police Commission (OCPC). (2011a). Role of the commission. Retrieved from http://www.ocpc.ca /stellent/groups/public/@abcs/@www/@ocpc /documents/abstract/ec157377.pdf

Ontario Civilian Police Commission (OCPC). (2011b). *2010 annual report.* Retrieved from http://www.ocpc.ca /stellent/groups/public/@abcs/@www/@ocpc /documents/abstract/ec095639.pdf

Ontario Civilian Police Commission (OCPC). 2012. Mission statement. Retrieved from http://www.ocpc.ca/english /index.asp

Ontario Human Rights Code, R.S.O. 1990, Ch. H.19. Retrieved from http://www.e-laws.gov.on.ca/html /statutes/english/elaws_statutes_90h19_e.htm

Ombudsman Ontario. (2008). Oversight of police: *Oversight Unseen.* Retrieved from http://www.ombudsman.on.ca /Investigations/SORT-Investigations/Completed /Oversight-of-police—em-Oversight-Unseen—em-.aspx

Ombudsman Ontario. (2011). SORT investigations. Retrieved from http://www.ombudsman.on.ca/Investigations /SORT-Investigations.aspx

Ombudsman Ontario. (2012). Ombudsman to investigate OPP handling of stress injuries [News release]. Retrieved from http://www.ombudsman.on.ca /Newsroom /Press-Release/2011/Ombudsman-to-investigate-OPP -handling-of-stress-in.aspx

Ontario Provincial Police (OPP). (2009a). Application process. Retrieved from http://www.opp.ca/ecms/index.php?id=95

Ontario Provincial Police (OPP). (2009b). What we do: Municipal policing. Retrieved from http://www.opp.ca/ecms/index.php?id=13

Ontario Provincial Police (OPP). (2010). *Annual report 2010.* Retrieved from http://www.opp.ca/ecms/files/250258838.6.pdf

Ontario Provincial Police (OPP). (2011). *Strategic plan 2011–2013.* Retrieved from http://www.opp.ca/ecms/files/259349814.2.pdf

Ontario Provincial Police Human Resources Bureau. (2006, July 21). The impact of stress on officers and the OPP response. Retrieved from http://www.attorneygeneral.jus.gov.on.ca/inquiries/ipperwash/policy_part/projects/pdf/Tab9_TheImpactofStressonOfficersandtheOPPResponse.pdf

Ontario (Provincial Police) v. Favretto, 2004 CanLII 34173 (O.N. C.A.). Retrieved from http://www.canlii.org/en/on/onca/doc/2004/2004canlii34173/2004canlii34173.pdf

Ontario Regulation 3/99, *Adequacy and Effectiveness of Police Services.* Retrieved from http://www.e-laws.gov.on.ca/html/regs/english/elaws_regs_990003_e.htm

Ontario Regulation 36/02, *Courses of Training for Members of Police Forces.* Retrieved from http://www.e-laws.gov.on.ca/html/regs/english/elaws_regs_100267_e.htm

Ontario Regulation 263/09, *Public Complaints—Local Complaints.* Retrieved from http://www.e-laws.gov.on.ca/html/regs/english/elaws_regs_090263_e.htm

Ontario Regulation 266/10, *Suspect Apprehension Pursuits.* Retrieved from http://www.e-laws.gov.on.ca/html/regs/english/elaws_regs_100266_e.htm

Ontario Regulation 267/10, *Conduct and Duties of Police Officers Respecting Investigations by the Special Investigations Unit.* Retrieved on from http://www.e-laws.gov.on.ca/html/regs/english/elaws_regs_100267_e.htm

Ontario Regulation 268/10, *General (Code of Conduct).* Retrieved from http://www.e-laws.gov.on.ca/html/regs/english/elaws_regs_100268_e.htm

Ontario Regulation 354/04, *Major Case Management.* Retrieved from http://www.e-laws.gov.on.ca/html/regs/english/elaws_regs_040354_e.htm

Ontario Regulation 420/97, *Costs of Ontario Provincial Police Services to Municipalities under Section 5.1 of the Act.* Toronto, Canada: Queen's Printer. Retrieved from http://www.e-laws.gov.on.ca/html/regs/english/elaws_regs_100267_e.htm

Ontario Regulation 421/97, *Members of Police Service Boards—Code of Conduct.* Retrieved from

http://www.e-laws.gov.on.ca/html/regs/english/elaws_regs_970421_e.htm

Ontario Regulation 550/96, *Violent Crime Linkage Analysis System Reports.* Retrieved from http://www.e-laws.gov.on.ca/html/regs/english/elaws_regs_960550_e.htm

Oppal, W. T. (1994a). *Closing the gap: Policing and the community—The recommendations.* Victoria, BC: Policing in British Columbia Commission of Inquiry. Retrieved from http://www.cacole.ca/resources/publications/CloGap94-eng.pdf

Oppal, W. T. (1994b). *Closing the gap: Policing and the community—The report* (Vol. 1). Victoria, BC: Policing in British Columbia Commission of Inquiry.

Orr v. York Region Police. (2001, March 26). OCCPS 01–02. Retrieved from http://www.ocpc.ca/english/DecisionInformation/Disciplinary/disciplinary.asp?tpl=search_disciplinary_detail.asp&tid=916320031X02NN052H136P24175576

Ottawa Police Service. (2010). Voluntary Alternative Dispute Resolution Program (VADRP). Retrieved from http://ottawapolice.ca/en/ServingOttawa/SectionsAndUnits/ProfessionalStandardsSection/VADRP.aspx

Ottawa Police Service. (2012). Voluntary Alternative Dispute Resolution Program (VADRP). Retrieved from http://ottawapolice.ca/en/ServingOttawa/SectionsAndUnits/ProfessionalStandardsSection/VADRP.aspx

Ottawa Police Services Board. (2011, December). *Policy manual.* Retrieved from http://ottawapoliceboard.ca/opsb-cspo/images/stories/2011_December_Policy_Manual_EN.pdf

Ottawa-Carleton Regional Police Services Board v. Ontario Civilian Commission on Police Services, [2000] O.J. No. 2099 (QL) (Div. Ct.).

Ottawa-Carleton Regional Police Services Board v. Ontario Civilian Commission on Police Services, [2001] O.J. No. 5498 (QL) (Div. Ct.).

Packer and Toronto Police Service. (1990). OCPC 90–01. Retrieved from http://www.ocpc.ca/files/1K1920045C047T21L514V735IX20YW.pdf

Palmer v. The Queen, [1980] 1 S.C.R. 759. Retrieved from http://scc.lexum.org/en/1979/1980scr1-759/1980scr1-759.pdf

Perry and York Regional Police Service (1972), 1 O.P.R. 89 (OCCPS). Retrieved from http://www.ocpc.ca/english/DecisionInformation/Disciplinary/index.asp [insert]

Peterborough Police Service. (2012). Police services board policies and bylaws. Retrieved from http://www.peterboroughpolice.com/Police_Services_Board/Policies___By-Laws.htm

Plumptre, T. (2007). *Strengthening governance at the RCMP: A report to the Task Force on Governance and Culture.* Ottawa, ON: Institute on Governance. Retrieved from http://www.publicsafety.gc.ca/rcmp-grc/_fl/eng/strgth-ggov-eng.pdf

Police Services Act (PSA), R.S.O. 1990, c. P.15. Retrieved from http://www.e-laws.gov.on.ca/html/statutes/english/elaws_statutes_90p15_e.htm

Pollock, J. (2012). *Ethical dilemmas and decisions in criminal justice* (7th ed.). Belmont, CA: Wadsworth.

Precious and Hamilton Police Service. (2002, May 10). OCCPS 02–08. Retrieved from http://www.ocpc.ca/files/G6432003O402T0104U13WC39JF339D.pdf

Proctor v. Sarnia Board of Commissioners of Police, [1980] 2 S.C.R. 727.

Purbrick and the OPP. (2011, May 25). OCPC 11–08. Retrieved from http://www.ocpc.ca/files/8M7D2012110 23814B51548599Z32PY.pdf

R. v. Allen (1979), 46 C.C.C. 253 (Ont. H.C.J.).

R. v. Beaudry (2007), 1 S.C.R. 190, 2007 SCC 5.

R. v. Campbell, [1999] 1 S.C.R. 565.

R. v. Conway, [2010] 1 S.C.R. 765. Retrieved from http://scc.lexum.org/en/2010/2010scc22/2010scc22.pdf

R. v. McNeil, 2009 S.C.C. 3, [2009] 1 S.C.R. 66. Retrieved from http://scc.lexum.org/en/2009/2009scc3/2009scc3.pdf

R. v. Metropolitan Police Comr., Ex parte Blackburn, [1968] 1 All E.R. 763 (C.A.).

R. v. Peel Regional Police Service, Chief of Police, 2000 CanLII 22808 (O.N. S.C.). Retrieved from http://www.canlii.org/en/on/onsc/doc/2000/2000canlii22808/2000ca nlii22808.pdf

R. v. Stevenson and McLean, [1980] 57 C.C.C. (2d) 526, 19 C.R. (3d) 74 (Ont. C. A.).

R. v. Wigglesworth, [1987] 2 S.C.R. 541. Retrieved from http://scc.lexum.org/en/1987/1987scr2-541/1987scr2-541.pdf

Ray and Cole [public complainant] and OPP. (2007, December 18). OCCPS 07–18. Retrieved from http://www.ocpc.ca/files/8P0D200712123919A61149599C18OB.pdf

Reilly and Brockville Police Service. (1997, May 12). OCCPS 97–01. Retrieved from http://www.ocpc.ca/files/1H7U20 034A066Q06J41176522U0187.pdf

Roach, K. (2007). Four models of police–government relationships. In M. E. Beare & T. Murray (Eds.), *Police and government relations: Who's calling the shots?* (pp. 16–95). Toronto, ON: University of Toronto Press.

Roach, K. (2011). *Police independence, the military police and Bill C-41.* Retrieved from http://www.mpcc-cppm.gc.ca/alt_format/1100/1102-eng.pdf

Rose v. Sault Ste Marie Police Service. (2010, July 9). Decision of retired Superintendent Joe Wolfe [Unreported].

Royal Canadian Mounted Police (RCMP). (2007a, July 9). The RCMP's history. Retrieved from http://www.rcmp-grc.gc.ca/hist/index-eng.htm

Royal Canadian Mounted Police (RCMP). (2007b, August 23). RCMP 2007 Environmental Scan—Forward. Retrieved from http://www.rcmp-grc.gc.ca/es-ae/2007/foreword-avant-propos-eng.htm

Royal Canadian Mounted Police (RCMP). (2009). Recruiting, Physical Abilities Requirement Evaluation (PARE): Guidelines. Retrieved from http://www.rcmp-grc.gc.ca/recruiting-recrutement/documents/pare-tape/pare-tape-requirement-exigences-eng.pdf

Royal Canadian Mounted Police (RCMP). (2010, April). *National Recruiting Program Audit, Final Report.* Retrieved from Government of Canada Publications: http://publications.gc.ca/site/eng/389343/publication.html

Royal Canadian Mounted Police (RCMP). (2011a). Basic requirements. Retrieved from http://www.rcmp-grc.gc.ca/recruiting-recrutement/rec/requirements-exigences-eng.htm

Royal Canadian Mounted Police (RCMP). (2011b). Initial Rank List (IRL). Retrieved from http://www.rcmp-grc.gc.ca/recruiting-recrutement/rec/irl-plc-eng.htm

Royal Canadian Mounted Police (RCMP). (2011c). PARE—Physical Abilities Requirement Evaluation. Retrieved from http://www.grc-rcmp.gc.ca/recruiting-recrutement/htm-form/pare-tape-requirement-exigences-eng.htm#tphp

Royal Canadian Mounted Police (RCMP) (2011d). RCMP Police Aptitude Battery (RPAB). Retrieved from http://www.rcmp-grc.gc.ca/recruiting-recrutement/rec/rpab-btatpg-eng.htm

Royal Canadian Mounted Police (RCMP). (2011e). Suitability/reliability interview and polygraph examination. Retrieved from http://www.rcmp-grc.gc.ca/recruiting-recrutement/rec/poly-eng.htm

Royal Canadian Mounted Police (RCMP). (2012a). Cadet selection process. Retrieved from http://www.rcmp-grc.gc.ca/recruiting-recrutement/rec/process-processus-eng.htm

Royal Canadian Mounted Police (RCMP). (2012b). Canadian Police Information Centre (CPIC). Retrieved from www.rcmp-grc.gc.ca/nps-snp/cpic-cipc-eng.pdf

Royal Canadian Mounted Police (RCMP). (2012c). Current operations. Retrieved from http://www.rcmp-grc.gc.ca/po-mp/missions-curr-cour-eng.htm#ministry

Royal Canadian Mounted Police (RCMP). (2012d). RCMP careers. Retrieved from http://www.rcmp-grc.gc.ca/recruiting-recrutement/index-eng.htm

Royal Canadian Mounted Police Act, R.S.C., 1985, c. R-10. Retrieved from http://laws-lois.justice.gc.ca/PDF/R-10.pdf

Royal Canadian Mounted Police External Review Committee. (1991). *Discussion Paper 8: Sanctioning police misconduct—General principles.* Ottawa, ON: Minister of Supply and Services Canada. Retrieved from http://www.erc-cee .gc.ca/publications/discussion/dp8/dp8-eng.aspx

Royal Canadian Mounted Police Regulations, 1988 (SOR/88-361). Retrieved from http://laws-lois.justice.gc.ca/eng /regulations/SOR-88-361/index.html

Sheehan, D., & Van Hasselt, V. (2003). Identifying law enforcement stress reactions early. *FBI Law Enforcement Bulletin, 72*(9), 12–17.

Shepell·fgi. (2012). About us. Retrieved from http://www .shepellfgi.com/EN-CA/AboutUs/index.asp

Skolnick, J. (1987). *Justice without trial: Law enforcement in a democratic society.* New York, NY: McGraw-Hill.

Sossin, L. (2007). The oversight of executive police relations in Canada: The Constitution, the courts, administrative processes and democratic governance. In M. E. Beare & T. Murray (Eds.), *Police and government relations: Who's calling the shots?* (pp. 96–146). Toronto, ON: University of Toronto Press.

Special Investigations Unit (SIU). (2011a). Director's welcome message. Retrieved from http://www.siu.on.ca/en/index.php

Special Investigations Unit (SIU). (2011b). *SIU 2009–2010 Annual report: SIU forging forward.* Retrieved from http://www.siu.on.ca/pdfs/siu_annual_2009-2010.pdf

Statistics Canada. (2010). *Police resources in Canada.* Catalogue no. 85-225-X. Ottawa, ON: Minister of Industry. Retrieved from http://dsp-psd.pwgsc.gc.ca /Collection-R/Statcan/85-225-XIE/85-225-XIE.html

Steil, L., Watson, K., & Barker, L. (1983). *Effective listening.*

Reading, MA: Addison-Wesley.

Supreme Court of Canada. (2005, April 29). *Bulletin of proceedings.* Retrieved from http://scc.lexum.org/en/ bulletin/2005/05-04-29-bul.wpd/05-04-29-bul.wpd.pdf

Sutton, N. (2005). *Community policing: Exploring issues of contemporary policing.* Toronto, ON: Edmond Montgomery.

Synyshyn, S. (2007). *Civilian oversight of police in Canada: Governance, accountability and transparency.* Winnipeg, MB: Manitoba Association for Rights and Liberties. Retrieved from http://www.marl.mb.ca/sites /default/files/CIVOVER%20Executive%20Summary%20 06-06-2008_0.pdf

Thibault, E., Lynch, L., & McBride, R. (1985). *Proactive police management.* Englewood Cliffs, NJ: Prentice Hall.

Thomas, N. (2007). Discussion paper on police/government relations (presented to the Ipperwash Inquiry, June 2006). In M. E. Beare & T. Murray (Eds.), *Police and government relations: Who's calling the shots?* (pp. 401–425). Toronto, ON: University of Toronto Press.

Tinsley, P. A. (2009). *The Canadian experience in oversight.* Retrieved from http://www.mpcc-cppm .gc.ca/1000/1000/1001-eng.aspx

Toch, H. (2002). *Stress in policing.* Rockville, MD: National Criminal Justice Reference Service. Retrieved from https://www.ncjrs.gov/pdffiles1/nij/grants/198030.pdf

Toronto Police Service. (2008). 2008 Environmental Scan. Retrieved from www.torontopolice.on.ca/publications /files/reports/2008envscan.pdf

Toronto Police Service. (2011). Community consultative process. Retrieved from http://www.torontopolice.on.ca /communitymobilization/ccc.php

Toronto Police Services Board. (2010). *Terms of reference for the independent civilian review (G20).* Retrieved from http://www.g20review.ca/docs/terms_of_reference.pdf

Toronto Police Services Board. (2011). Police board to meet on Thursday [News release]. Retrieved from http://www.tpsb.ca/News_Releases/task,view/id,161/

Treasury Board of Canada Secretariat. (2003). Values and ethics code for the public service. Retrieved from http://www .tbs-sct.gc.ca/pubs_pol/hrpubs/tb_851/vec-cve-eng.pdf

Trimm v. Durham Regional Police, [1987] 2 S.C.R. 582. Retrieved from http://scc.lexum.org/en/1987 /1987scr2-582/1987scr2-582.pdf

Trumbley and Pugh and Fleming (1986), 55 O.R. (2) 570 (QL).

Van Maanen, J. (1981). Observations on the making of a police man. In R. Culbertson & M. Tezak (Eds.), *Order under law* (pp. 111–126). Prospect Heights, IL: Waveland Press.

Venables and York Regional Police Service. (2008, October 3). OCCPS 08–08. Retrieved from http://www.ocpc.ca /files/8D1620082V104M06C21555100651Q5.pdf

Wallaceburg Police Services Board v. Ontario Civilian Commission on Police Services [1997] O.J. No. 1413. (QL) (Div. Ct.).

Watson v. Peel Police Service, 2007 ONCA 41 (CanLII). Retrieved from http://www.canlii.org/en/on/onca /doc/2007/2007onca41/2007onca41.pdf

Whitelaw, B., & Parent, R. (2010). *Community-based strategic policing in Canada* (3rd ed.). Toronto, ON: Nelson.

Whitton, P. (2011). *Ethical survival* [PowerPoint presentation]. Orillia, ON: Professional Standards Bureau, Ontario Provincial Police.

Williams v. Ontario Provincial Police. (1995, December 4). OCCPS 95–09. Retrieved from http://www.ocpc.ca/files /Y1Z72003HX06MN061H145P48C70576.pdf

Winnipeg Police Service. (2011). What is community policing? Retrieved from http://www.winnipeg.ca /police/AboutTheService/community_policing.stm

York Regional Police. (2009). Quality service standards. Retrieved from http://www.yrp.ca/qss.aspx

Index